THE BIGGEST BOAT

BOAT

i could afford

LEE HUGHES

SHERIDAN HOUSE

SEAFARER BOOKS

*This book is dedicated to all the people without whose
help I could not have completed this adventure:
My mother
Stan and Madeleine Murdock
Frank Dye
Brian McCleery
Geoff Orr*

*and of course the redhead who started it all:
Adrienne Faherty*

Copyright © 2004 by Lee Hughes

This edition published 2004 in the United States of America by
Sheridan House Inc.
145 Palisade Street
Dobbs Ferry, NY 10522
www.sheridanhouse.com

And in the UK by
Seafarer Books
102 Redwald Road
Rendlesham
Woodbridge
Suffolk IP12 2TE

Library of Congress Cataloging-in-Publication Data
Hughes, Lee.
    The biggest boat I could afford / by Lee Hughes.
        p. cm.
    ISBN 1-57409-192-1 (pbk. : alk. paper)
    1. Boats and boating–Atlantic Coast (U.S.) 2. Hughes,
    Lee–Travel–Atlantic Coast (U.S.) I Title.
GV776.A84H84 2004
797.1'09163–dc22

                                        2004001286

A CIP catalog record for this book is available from
the British Library, London.

US ISBN 1-57409-192-1
UK ISBN 0-9542750-4-7

Cover design by Katy Yiakmis
Photos by Lee Hughes
Printed in Australia

Contents

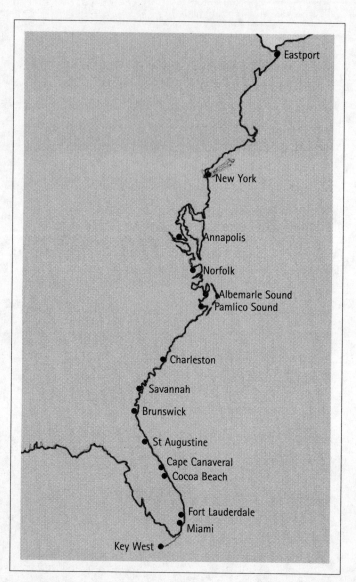

The Wanderer's *track.*

The first of all my fears

IT WAS ALL the redhead's fault. If it wasn't for her I'd never have left my armchair and risked life and fortune on the ocean in a lengthy attempt to overcome a lifelong fear. Though to be completely truthful, perhaps it wasn't all Adrienne's fault that I ended up casting myself onto the waters. No, I think it was partly down to me and the silly pleasure I take in occasionally teasing my gal. She deserves better from me and one day I'll stop doing it, but back then we were at my house in Auckland about eight months before my job was due to end. It was a mid-summer Sunday and we'd just finished brunch in the garden. It was the highlight of my month to have Adrienne up to stay for the weekend and then to cook a breakfast together and eat it under the shade of the elm tree while reading the Sunday paper. The whole day stretched out in front of us like a lazy cat – breakfast, a little light shopping and strolling in the trendier parts of town, an afternoon ice cream, an early dinner and maybe a TV movie in bed later on.

A perfect day for both of us made even more delicious by the fact that we only got about one or two of these each month. That's what happens when you live 800 miles apart and can only afford to see each other when your respective jobs happen to take you to the same cities on business. But we'd made the best of this situation for the previous two years and enjoyed a relationship free from bickering or boredom. Though we wondered if it was a case of absence making the heart grow fonder, we were becoming keen to test the proposition by moving in together. The only question was when and where this would happen. I pretended to hold out hopes that Ady might join me in Auckland though I knew full well that it would be me who moved to Christchurch. But I enjoyed putting up light resistance to this idea. Just on general principle I felt it was wise not to agree too quickly with everything she suggested.

I finished the sports section and reached for the situations vacant. Adrienne noticed this and took it as her cue to raise a subject I'd been avoiding.

'So what are you going to do when your job finishes?' she asked nonchalantly. I wasn't fooled by the tone or the text of this enquiry. I knew just what freight that train of thought was transporting but I played it straight anyway.

'Not really sure,' I replied, and then provocatively added, 'but I've been thinking about that dinghy thingy.' A big fat lie as it turned out, but I felt it wasn't wise to bolt towards the inevitable conclusion to this conversation.

'You mean sailing up the coast of the US. In a dinghy. By yourself. For a year?' I felt this summary was a little violent in its brevity, but it was pretty accurate.

'Mmm, and maybe I could visit Stan and do some cowboying for a while, too.' I was enjoying this. I knew full well that the end of my job in Auckland was the obvious signal for me to emigrate to the barren wastelands of the South Island and move in with Adrienne. I'd surely be able to find some kind of job down there.

'Cowboying *and* sailing. Well that ought to be fun for you,' she added ominously. I struggled to detect if there was a full stop in that sentence, as in 'ought to be fun. *For you.*' I decided there wasn't and since I wasn't even halfway serious about this idea but I was enjoying needling her a little bit, I pressed on.

'But you could come and visit me in Wyoming on the ranch. And on the boat too if you wanted,' I said generously.

'That, babe, will be the bloody day.' A little of the red light from her hair started to flicker in her eyes. Ooh, this was fun.

'No really, you'd love Wyoming and if I went there straight after my job finishes, I'd be in time for the fall drift in September. You could join me a few weeks later and we'd have a ball. It's a really grouse ranch and Stan and Mad are just the nicest people in the world.'

This was all true and I had long ago decided that I wanted to return to their ranch for a month or two of vacation. I figured I could do this in August and return to New Zealand in December for the summer and then look for a job and probably move in with Adrienne. The boat trip was only mentioned because . . . well . . . because it had been in the back of my mind for ages and it just sort of . . . slipped out. I wasn't serious about it at all. Not at this time anyway.

I had been seriously considering sailing a small boat over a long distance for a number of years but I had never set aside time to do it, I just thought I'd do it 'someday'. This loose lack of planning for my future in the broadest terms is a characteristic of mine that is at odds with my far more scrupulous planning of each day and each small project. To adopt an economic analogy, I do look after the pennies, but I hope that the pounds will look after themselves.

Adrienne is the other way around. She likes to carve out the big plans well in advance and then wrestle with the little details as they pop up. That makes us a good team. She settles on plans and plunges into them and I follow her up and make them work.

Adrienne said nothing from behind her half of the paper so I ploughed on.

'And after the ranch, I could start sailing in Florida in January, and later on, say maybe by May, I could sail the boat up the Potomac and meet you in Washington DC. We could do the tourist thing and I could take you sailing on the river. You'd love that, wouldn't you?' I said with a Big Teasing Smile. The paper rustled and she looked over the top at me.

'I don't think so. It would be unsafe,' she said definitely. The atmospheric pressure dropped and the air seemed a little cooler. She seemed not to have noticed that I was joking and suddenly I was a little niggled by her apparent refusal to automatically accept everything I knew about boating as the gospel truth.

'Nonsense. Safe as houses,' I stated with equal firmness. A small cloud seemed to have covered the sun and the garden seemed rather less warm.

'*Really*?' she said — and in a tone that sent the temperature plunging again.

'Yes, *really*. You know I would never ask you to do anything dangerous and if you just tried it, you'd see how safe these boats are. The whole thing's a doddle.' I wasn't ploughing on now — I was ploughing myself under.

'A *doddle*?' She tilted her head to the side and raised her eyebrows. Too late for me to back out now. If I didn't press on she'd know I was, in fact, very much afraid of sailing a small boat. Anywhere. Let alone up the entire east coast of the US.

'With a capital Dod,' I replied.

'I see,' she said.

Silence.

'Well, you have to do what you have to do,' she said, 'but all I want to know is if you're going to do it now or not' — clearly hoping for the 'or not' response.

But it was too late. She said it and there it was. A great big dare.

Only one answer to that, obviously.

'Oh, I'm going to do it all right. Been looking forward to it for ages,' I said with as much conviction as I could muster. Which was just enough to convince her that I was in earnest — though it wasn't near enough to convince me. A giant chill wriggled all the way up my back and I wondered if Adrienne felt it too. She was ahead of me again.

'Of course,' she added brightly, 'if you survive, you can always write a book. And *this* time I'll be able to check it for accuracy first,' she said. And therein lies another tale . . . .

~~~

IT IS BECAUSE I am so un-practised at having a proper girlfriend that I was actually scared by entirely the wrong thing. I was only afraid of the sailing. Any halfway sensitive new age guy (SNAG, pronounced 'wanker') would have been afraid that this might spell the end of a very meaningful relationship, but not me. With a total disregard for anything that Adrienne might be feeling and the possible effects on our relationship, I merely focused on my own concerns. These were three in number:

- How would I avoid drowning?
- How would I pay for this adventure?
- How would I avoid additional drowning?

I focused on numbers one and three mostly because I have long had a powerful fear of the sea. Every sensible sailor has this, but my fears were bordering on irrational and they were deeply rooted indeed.

My family, like most New Zealanders, lived near the beach and the shore was a favourite and cheap way of entertaining the kids. Dozens of times each summer, we'd load up for a day at the beach and pile into my father's cavernous 1948 Ford V8. On arrival at the beach, after an endless 15-minute drive from our house, the doors would be flung open and we would sprint straight down to the water and dive into it, shrieking at the chill. But unlike my three brothers and my sister, all of whom would immediately swim straight out into the deep water, I was slow to follow. I couldn't swim, though I had a good reason for this. It was because I was afraid. Oh, I paddled in the shallows and fossicked for crabs and poked at anemones in the rock pools at the base of the cliffs, but I never ventured into water over my head unless I had an inner tube to hang on to. I still have no idea where this fear originated. I recall nothing traumatic as a child about the sea – I never nearly drowned and I wasn't attacked by a shark or even stung by jellyfish. I was just scared of the sea for no particular reason.

Despite this, I liked a day at the beach as much as the rest of the family did. I loved to dig in the sand, play catch with tennis balls thrown in shallow water and eat the glorious multi-course picnic lunches that my mother made. In the late evening, after perhaps 10 hours on the beach and with a healthy dose of sunburn (and sunburn *was* a sign of health in those days because you didn't want to look like those poor Health Camp kids, all pale and spindly), we would all line up and walk slowly along the section of beach we had occupied searching for 'treasures'. These particular treasures were aluminium ring pulls from beer cans. For a long time I thought they were some kind of finger ring that had been accidentally lost in great numbers. I'd never seen a beer can up close and I wasn't all that smart either but at least I did my bit to help keep the beach as clean as my mother thought it ought to be. Finding treasures was jolly good fun.

Another part of a typical day at the beach wasn't so hot. Eastern Beach, in Auckland's inner Hauraki Gulf, was our favourite and its white sand stretched for a mile or so. At each end it finished in cliffs. For all the rest of the family (excluding my mother who preferred to sit out anything more overtly physical than a crossword), it was neat fun to climb up or down one of the cliffs along a steep, narrow clay path between the rock pools at the bottom and the golf course and gardens at the top. For me it was an utterly terrifying thing that I was guaranteed to confront 20 or 30 times a year. When halfway up the cliff, at a point where you actually had to cling to the crumbling clay and slide sideways along the path past a bulge in the cliff face, you had no choice but to look down and check where you were putting your feet. The reward for this was the horrible sight of surging waves at what seemed like a thousand or so feet below. This neatly combined my fear of the sea with my other bowel-clenching fear — that of heights. I feared the sea — but I was absolutely shit-scared of heights.

There was no avoiding this, though. If everyone was heading up to the golf course to explore the flax bushes or to walk in the gardens of Musick Point, then there was no choice but to follow. Apart from being left behind in isolation and boredom, there was the fear of being found out to be a chicken. So I hated it, but I went. The only consolation was that once you were up the top, you were a long way from the sea and therefore safe from that. And once you were down, you were a long way from any heights and therefore safe from them too. But in between . . . a brightly lit nightmare: cold feet, sweaty palms, nervous anticipation — I mined a lifetime's supply of fear from this one rich vein.

And I even managed to add a little refinement to one of these two giant fears. Once, when I was about eight years old, I raised a subject with my mother that I had recently read about.

'How far would a tidal wave go up the beach?' I asked, expecting that such a wave might angrily swirl up to the far side of the road. Her answer pretty well staggered me.

'I think it would go over the cliffs,' she said simply.

JIMINY FUCKING CRICKET!

I was horrified, and for some reason that horror never left me. If that was true, then if you were close enough to *see* the sea, as far as I was concerned, it could reach out and *kill* you any time it wanted to – even if you were hundreds of feet above it. The nightmare had a new dimension, but there were more to come.

Being something of a physical coward, I adopted a few of the habits of a sissy and one of them was to read voraciously. Over the following years, this reading led me to uncover more and more terrifying tales of disaster at sea – not just mind-blowing, town-levelling tidal waves, but hurricanes, rogue waves, shipwrecks, sharks, killer whales, icebergs, octopuses, jellyfish, kelp, whirlpools, lobsters, swordfish, moray eels, marine volcanoes, nuclear submarines that get caught in fishing trawls and drag the boat down, deep-sea divers whose surface supply of air is hand-pumped down a pipe that is ripe for

'Sissy' author (dressed for a school play I hope).

cutting by a giant clam, sucker fish, electric eels and stingrays. I had a morbid fascination with these stories even though they reinforced a phobia that was now strong enough to support the lifestyles of several shrinks. But I was a junior Kiwi bloke and Kiwi blokes don't believe in counselling or even giving voice to fears, so instead, like everyone else, I choked that phobia down and got on with being a kid.

A curious side-effect of these two dominant fears was that other things that bothered many people had less power to scare me. I think I was so filled up with these two fears that I never had very much room for worries about spiders or public speaking or being accidentally found naked at school assembly.

Luckily there was also another factor involved here. My bigger brother Graeme got me to swim. He was nine years older than me, stood over six feet tall with muscles to match and he didn't like the fact that I was seven and still couldn't swim, so one day he just ordered me to learn to swim before he got back from his summer job working on our uncle's farm. No one had thought to do that before and it didn't occur to me that I could disobey him, so by the time he came back, I could do something better than a dog paddle, though not exactly an Australian crawl. It didn't help that I swam with my head above the water − all the better to spot tidal waves, icebergs, sharks, etc. But at least I could swim in water deeper than me.

Graeme's education of me continued on land. He was a real whizz at cricket and at hockey, which he only took up because he wore glasses and couldn't play rugby. We would play endless games of these in our backyard in summer and winter. Playing against Graeme, I pretty quickly got used to playing a much harder game than anyone else my age. I was too small and slow and uncoordinated to play rugby and too lacking in ambidexterity for soccer, but despite my sissiness I was good at hockey. The years of brutal whacks on the shins with the stick, bat or ball, the hard missile flying at your face with all the power of teenage shoulders behind it, the illegal body blocks and the psychological intimidation all gave me a powerful advantage when I played against my own age group. I was no sporting star but at least I wasn't a total drip and when I was in high school I had a tiny bit of athletic credibility when I captained the senior hockey team for a few years.

Subconsciously I absorbed a lesson from all this that helped me years later. I learned that it was possible to overcome some fears by confronting them − and that once you had overcome them − they were gone for good. This realisation didn't come quickly to me, though, and all through my childhood I saw myself quite accurately as a weedy scaredy-cat. That's not a promising combination when you've set your heart on joining the army and winning a VC.

I had read omnivorously as a child since I was four. By the time I was ten and had access to pocket money I was reading carnivorously – as many *Sabre* and *Commando* war comics as possible, plus every other type of military fiction and non-fiction. By the time I was ready to leave high school, I was convinced that martial glory awaited me and at 16 I applied to become an army officer. The army said I should come back in a year's time, which I did. Six months later I enlisted as an officer cadet and a year after that I was commissioned as a second lieutenant in the artillery. The highest hurdle for me that year as a cadet was literally that – climbing up and over the 12-foot wall on the confidence course. I almost froze every time and only got through it thanks to my fractionally greater fear of public humiliation. Climbing up the ropes to the roof of the gym was just as bad, but at least the death grip I maintained on the rope was helpful.

After training as a gunner, my first posting to an artillery regiment landed me in command of a troop of field gunners of whom about half were trained as parachutists. This regiment had the task of providing a troop of three 105-mm howitzers and a small command post party that could be air-dropped if necessary, plus a party of forward observers who could call in fire for the infantry. The equipment was dropped on pallets – the gunners had to parachute in. Still petrified of heights I had absolutely no intention of having anything to do with any of this and that was how things remained until the Battery Sergeant Major volunteered me and other new arrivals to the unit for routine parachute training.

Instant petrification, but I had no way of refusing. For several weeks, anticipatory fear gnawed away at me, but then at the last minute I was reprieved when the course was cancelled due to a lack of serviceable aircraft. To occupy the blank space in the training calendar, the BSM instead devised several types of adventure training and allocated an officer to each activity.

I was scheduled to do scuba diving. More sweaty fear, more sea-going misery and I had my basic scuba-diving ticket. Three weeks later I was re-rostered for parachuting.

By the end of that year I was both lightly qualified and heavily scared as a diver and parachutist. And though I continued to do occasional diving and fairly regular jumping, that was basically how I remained for the next decade. I expect that I'd still be in that state if it hadn't been for a lucky chance and a healthy dose of greed.

~~~

BY 1993 I was living in Britain after a year-long holiday in the US. I was working part-time as a bartender and I wanted another job. In a work centre in Oxford I saw an ad for bungy-jumping crew. This was a new craze in those days in Britain and every macho wideboy, every Essex Man and many party girls wanted to do it. The bungy company wanted ground staff as well as jumpmasters and they were paying up to £50 for a day's work. That was three times what bartending paid. I was there in a flash and applied for a ground-crew job — though that paid the least of all the crew positions.

Basically, the company would hire a mobile crane — between 150 and 300 feet tall — slap up posters all over a town and on the appointed day would go to a pub carpark or fairground and set up a jump site. Ground staff met the jumpers, cautioned them, took their money, weighed them, removed all loose items from their pockets, strapped them into a harness almost identical to a parachutist's and then teased them with tales of disaster until they were wound up tighter than the clockwork that drives Arnold Schwarzenegger. In full view of the public it was too late to flee so the customers were loaded into a small steel cage and a rubber rope was attached to their ankles.

The crane lifted the cage to a safe height, and on the way up the jumpmaster and his assistant checked all the connections and either soothed the jumper or wound them up tighter, depending on what they thought the customer deserved. Two hundred feet up in the air, the lurching cage was secured to the boom of the crane so that it provided a stable platform, the wire door was opened and, after a good look waaaay down at the crowd, the white-faced customer was invited to step off the edge.

For the few seconds of terror that followed they paid £35. Cost to the company for laying all this on was about £2 per customer —

assuming you got at least 25 customers per day to cover the base costs of crane and crew. Profit for a single day's jumping could hit £3000, which was approximately NZ$10,000. All over Britain, entrepreneurs could see that, while it lasted, this craze was like minting money.

Naturally, I could see that a very few days of this work would equal a great many hours spent pouring beer. The money had the potential to be so good that the lust for it overcame even my numbing fear of heights. All I had to do was learn how to operate a whole site and then I could set up my own company and operate it – preferably from the ground. But first I had to get off that ground and learn how to dispatch jumpers and so I began to volunteer for work as an assistant and then as a jumpmaster. Short of reliable staff, this was welcomed by the owners and soon I was working all over Britain, spending my weekends two or three hundred feet up in the air, standing on steel mesh, hanging underneath a crane while radiating false confidence to blanched punters. To soothe myself I developed a rule of always holding on to the cage with one white-knuckled hand, of always tying my own safety line to the cage, of always having it independently checked by another qualified crew member and of always checking the connection of the cage to the crane at least three times before starting and finally, of always going to the toilet before getting in the cage. Beyond that I simply ignored the possibility that the crane operator might one day become distracted and forget to stop lifting the cage upwards. That had happened in Europe and the whole cage was pulled up over the top of the crane boom and fell to the ground, killing a couple of crew and fatally surprising the crane driver when it struck his cab. We crew made sure we always told new crane drivers about this story right at the start of the day. We kept the lesson simple – 'pay attention mate or we'll plummet down from the sky and obliterate you'. And each Sunday evening I pocketed my pay and wondered whether I had the nerve to show up next weekend for another 10-hour dose of raw fear.

A few weeks after starting to work aloft I was approached by two lads who saw the same potential for easy money and who wanted to recruit some trained staff to work for them and to run a crew or two of their own in the Midlands. In quick order, I quit my job, moved to Birmingham with the partners and we set up a rival operation.

Being a former paratrooper I already understood the value of using proven drills for jumping from aircraft. All I had to do was apply the same process to this job and I felt I could manage a site. Because the sport was so new in Britain there were few established systems and the health and safety (HSE) inspectors were sceptical of safety standards. In quick order I applied my military training to the process and managed to create a whole franchise training system that covered everything involved in commercial bungy operations. The whole thing was documented in a fat procedures manual that I wrote and which carried the name of the international association that we formed to endorse it and which was accepted by the UK's HSE inspectors. In fact, the system was so complete and so good to operate that pretty quickly we found it more profitable to engage primarily in training other entrepreneurs than to go out and sell jumps to actual customers. Within a few months I was travelling all over Britain teaching new operators how to do it safely. And the money rolled in like a tide.

That was pleasing, but there was another entirely unexpected side-effect. It's hard to recall the exact moment that it happened, but one day, about six months after I started, I noticed that I was no longer holding on to the cage when I was up in the air. In fact, I was utterly nonchalant about spending eight or more hours a day hanging in the air by a one-inch cable. As an instructor and site manager I was so busy looking out for my staff, the customers and the public that I just didn't have time to be scared any more. I hadn't exactly confronted my fear of heights, but I had danced around it until it got tired and left. It seemed that I had accidentally completely conquered the greatest of my two primal fears. And that was worth more to me than all the money we made that year.

I had so thoroughly conquered my fear of flying that later that year I invented a mobile bodyflying machine, patented it and formed a partnership to build and operate it after the bungy craze inevitably died down. Bodyflying is akin to skydiving, except that instead of plunging to the ground the flyer is held aloft by a current of wind directed upwards from a fan beneath him. As long as you maintain a symmetrical stable position that exposes plenty of surface area to the windstream, you can float and manoeuvre – rising, falling, tumbling, swooping and diving, flying in the seated position or outstretched like a starfish – even standing on a boogie board and surfing the air.

That whole project ended up costing the partners, the banks and the government several hundred thousand pounds but everyone got their money back and the machine is still operated all over Britain by my friend and former partner Mark Robson.

Snowboarding on air.

Soon after the trial flights had proved the engineering was sound, I pulled out of the partnership due to a disagreement with one of my partners, but I enjoyed it immensely and still hold the record for the stupidest test flight ever.

Just after we took delivery of the engine, we had once again come to the end of our line of credit at the bank and needed more money. That meant we had to impress the bank manager and the only thing he wanted to know was whether this lunatic contraption that had so far consumed about £100,000 of NatWest's money actually worked. We had just hooked up the brand-new 900-HP Isotta Fraschini marine diesel engine to the 96-inch purpose-built fan that morning.

We had payments to make and needed the money from him immediately. So to demonstrate that it worked – and we had no idea if it actually would – I (the designer and chief engineer and thereby the *de facto* test pilot by a vote of two partners to one) whacked on a crash helmet and a bungy harness. While the bank manager watched from a vantage point atop the access ladder, two friends who were helping us build it grabbed the webbing straps to hold me down, Mark turned on the fan and I jumped into the roaring airstream. Directly underneath me was a metal grill to stop me falling down into the air duct, and to the side of that were iron girders that would later support the cushioned flying platform and the safety cage. Below the girders was 10 feet of ordinary air and then some very ordinary concrete. To my side and above me was nothing at all. We hadn't yet constructed the temporary dome cage that would keep the flyer in bounds, nor had we received the inflatable ring that would cushion flyers inside the cage from the inevitable crash landings. (These things cost money that would have to come from the bank.)

Well, it worked of course — quite a bit better than we expected. I shot up into the 100-mph airstream and was held down by the two assistants. After giving some cheerful and confident thumbs-up signs to the banker, I became emboldened by the success and signalled the anchors to let go. For a moment I flew stably at an altitude of about 15 feet above the girders, but it didn't take long before I became a little

I am about to do something stupid.

bit unsymmetrical, which is like being a little bit pregnant. Shortly afterwards, gravity and the girders afflicted me as hard as they could. I was damn lucky not to plunge right through the gaps onto the concrete 25 feet below but even so I was winded. Luckily, my partners saw what had happened and engaged the bank manager in conversation while the assistants dragged me down off the machine and laid me out on the concrete out of sight behind some packing cases. They wisely kept the machine running to drown out my groans. Ten minutes after the delighted banker had left, they hauled me to my feet and I inspected the damage. Deep, deep bruising and some cracked ribs but no major bones broken. And we had the money. Purrrfect!

It was this lesson that I wanted to apply to my second great fear – the sea. Perhaps by sheer persistence and repetition and prolonged contact with it I could wear away my fear of the water until one day I might look around me and actually enjoy being afloat. And that's what this adventure was really all about – conquering a small boy's fear. It had nothing at all to do with seeing the sights, learning to sail, loving the sea or the outdoor life. It was all about just being tired of being scared. It was the last stage of my adolescence and I felt that – at the age of 40 – it was time I got a grip.

The second of all my fears

NATURALLY, ADRIENNE KNEW none of this. And I didn't know whether she'd tolerate my absence for all that time. It didn't seem likely though, since the longest I'd ever managed to keep a girlfriend before her was six months — and that was a long time ago. That's my record — never married, longest relationship: one semester. Pitiful really. Anyway, some women might simply accept a decision of this sort from their boyfriend without question, but Adrienne isn't that type. She is rather more assertive. I didn't really know *how* assertive until three years ago.

At that time, I had recently published a book called *Shooting From The Lip* — a collection of tall but basically true tales of my army life. Before the book was printed, the publishers, and my agent, enquired whether there was any chance we might be sued by anyone mentioned in it, since it contained a few embarrassing tales. I hastily assured them that no one named in it could afford to sue me because I had in reserve even more damning tales about them that I would release if they dared litigate. And if they hadn't been named, they'd have to confess to their identities in order to sue me and none of them would be fool enough to do that. This was sufficient and the book was published. It was quite a success and everything passed off smoothly until one day a letter was forwarded to me by the publisher. I read it and discovered that I was indeed about to be sued.

In the book, I told a story of how I had met a woman 17 years before on a blind date when I was an innocent young army officer of twenty-two. This date was an older and more worldly divorcée who was acquainted with a close friend of mine. He arranged for her to meet me at a regimental dinner in the officers' mess. The evening went astoundingly well. So well that my date accompanied me that night back to my eighths (like quarters but smaller). Indeed, we went out together for the rest of the year. The affair petered out after six months (see record above) and the inevitable separation occurred painlessly for both of us when I was posted to another army camp. Those were the facts and I had a diary to prove them and I made good use of it when I recounted the tale in my book. However, that's not quite the way the lady recalled it.

She was alerted to the existence of the story a few months after it was published. A friend of hers noticed it in a bookstore, glanced at a photograph of her taken all those years ago and hurried off to tell the lady that she was immortalised in print. My ex-girlfriend seized a copy immediately, devoured the passages relating to her and rather than being immortalised she was in fact scandalised.

Author and future litigant on a blind date in 1983.

Three things offended her mightily. Firstly, the part where I said she had led me off to my room on the night of our first date. Secondly, the part where I stated that the lady was 'eight or nine years older than me'. And thirdly, the fact that her teenage nieces had read all this and were teasing their aunt about being a red-hot, man-trapping cradle-robber Who Went All The Way on the first date. Or as they put it, 'Oooh, Auntie Adrienne – you big slut!'

That really put the fat in the fire. I didn't know quite how badly until I got the letter from my publisher. In it the woman thanked me for my description of her as 'beautiful, funny and smart' but nevertheless she still threatened legal action for slander on the grounds that she

DID NOT, HAD NEVER and WOULD NEVER consider sleeping with any man on the first date. She wasn't that sort of girl. Plus, she wasn't eight or nine years older — she was much younger than that, though she declined to state how much. Accordingly, she felt that she was due damages and an apology and unless these were forthcoming immediately, she would sue. It was signed in a confident cradle-robbing hand.

To cut a long story short (and to avoid setting off another lawsuit), let me just say that we met and immediately conducted intensive and prolonged negotiations. I am also happy to state for the record that Miss Faherty is far younger than I reported. She may even be younger than me and based on physical appearance seems to be growing younger every year.

The morning after our negotiations were concluded, the lawyers were stood down and we began meeting in her city or mine or sometimes in between, and usually courtesy of our employers. We still aren't certain whether we should celebrate our 20th anniversary or our third but either way, she's still the relationship record holder.

And not a woman to be taken lightly. I mean most of them don't think of suing you till it's all falling apart, but this one sues you right at the beginning of the relationship to make sure she's got your attention.

Did I mention she was a redhead?

~~~

BOATS ARE SOMETHING I'm new to. It's terrible to admit it, but though I'm a Kiwi bloke, I not only didn't play rugby as a kid — I didn't learn to sail a dinghy either. For anyone outside these shores reading this, that sort of thing is like being an American who has never eaten a Big Mac or a Pom who thinks England is part of Europe. Scarcely believable, a bit unpatriotic and even slightly sinister. Blame my family for this one, though — we never had a sailboat of any kind. Of course, almost anyone gets on a boat occasionally, but I was about 16 when I first got on any type of sailing vessel. My older brother Malcolm had just bought his first and only yacht — a 28-foot sloop that he lived on for the next 24 years. And in all of those years, I spent a total of perhaps 50 or 60 hours on it under sail. Very early on I was scared by it. There was a lot of creaking and flapping and practically every part of it looked to be under enormous strain. The angle that it heeled over at as it surged through greeny-grey waves alarmed me. Malcolm explained the laws of physics that prevent a keeler like that from capsizing and I was pretty relieved to hear that it couldn't ever turn turtle.

'Well, not exactly *ever*,' he went on. 'It could turn over if it got hit by a rogue wave,' and with that my new-found confidence evaporated. At best I could tell the bloody thing was on borrowed time already. My reading over the years had informed me that the mighty Southern Ocean was in fact the breeding ground of most of the planet's giant, killer, rogue waves. And New Zealand was in that ocean. So bugger sailing, I thought – I'll leave it to the navy.

In the 1980s the navy did, in fact, take me to sea. All the way to Australia in a frigate. The trip across was pleasantly boring as a 3000-tonne warship is a stable platform even in the Tasman Sea and Pacific Ocean. But on the trip home, we followed a tropical storm and pitched up and down so badly that for three days I ate nothing other than a single chocolate biscuit which bounced straight back up.

After that I didn't get behind a sail until a decade later when I met a statuesque East German girl who hinted that nothing put her in the mood faster than the sound of water rushing beneath the keel. I was into that idea like a rat up a drainpipe and made immediate plans to rent a small sailboat for a fortnight's holiday at Christmas. I'd done a Coastguard Boatmaster course at work and had learned about navigation and the principles of operating small boats, but only in the classroom. It was useful, but even so, I was extremely cautious when I took over the hire boat. It was 24 feet long with a small cabin and a centreboard and some water ballast. It had only two sails and we were prohibited from taking it outside the mouth of the Bay of Islands. The sailing was handicapped by a serious lack of wind, but with the assistance of my more experienced sailing partner, we stayed off the rocks. Or at least the boat did. The relationship was scuttled by me

After the explosion – before the refurbishment.

after just a week when I felt that she was a little too clingy. After she left in disgust, I took the boat out once by myself for a two-hour sail and that was my sole time alone on a sailboat. Ever.

In fact, that was the end of my 'marinating' until four years later when I helped sail Malcolm's yacht about 160 kilometres from the Bay of Islands back to Auckland for a refit shortly after his accidental death. A gasoline explosion had damaged the boat and badly burned my brother. He fought back for four months in an intensive care ward, but with 80 percent burns it was never probable that he would survive. Amazingly he came within an ace of recovering twice, but in the end an infection took hold that couldn't be beaten and events finally ran their course. It was awfully hard on my mother – especially when we came to settle Malcolm's estate. After the funeral, the family decided to keep the yacht and repair her. It prompted so many memories of Malcolm that none of us wanted to sell it.

To begin with we had stripped it of all amenities and interior fittings until below decks it was nothing more than a wooden hull with two appliances in it – a hand pump and a 10-HP diesel engine – both freshly installed by me for that trip. I had tested each installation once and knew that they had worked then, but I also knew that this was the first time I'd ever done any kind of repair or maintenance work on a boat and I had to hope that I'd fitted them well enough to keep working. I did know one thing – that the engine couldn't be hand-cranked and that the brand-new starter battery was not yet connected to a recharging circuit, so each time I pressed the starter button I was draining the life out of it. So far I'd started the engine three times. I had no sure idea how many more times I could expect it to start.

This trip could have easily killed us all. The crew was myself, my sister Cathie and my friend Al. No one seemed to be the skipper and Al, the most capable sailor, assumed that Cathie or I was in charge. The weather turned steadily worse soon after we left the shelter of the bay, and almost immediately, Al and Cathie were seasick. Oddly, it didn't affect me until many hours later. By last light the clouds had arrived and in steady rain, moderate fog and rising winds we were fully reefed and were pumping her out for about 15 minutes in every hour. (Part of the refit to be undertaken in Auckland was to replace a bulkhead that had been unwisely removed many years earlier. Without the bulkhead, the mahogany plank hull flexed too much and now it leaked ominously.) By midnight we were embayed on a lee shore. I'd read enough to know that this was how 99.9 percent of avoidable shipwrecks begin. To be embayed means to be stuck inside a bay with the wind direction sufficiently opposed to you that you cannot tack out of the bay. You can only anchor or else tack back and forth until you are blown onto the rocks. That knowledge didn't help at all. Unable to beat out of the bay, we were getting pushed closer and closer to the shore. Peering into the night, I pointed at a wavy white strip.

'What's that, Al?' I asked.

'Don't know – sandhills maybe?' There were sandhills far back on the shore according to the chart. I studied the dim white line a little harder.

'Umm, Al, I don't think that's sandhills. I think that's SURF!'

It was, and we were probably just yards from touching the keel on the bottom – and then we'd see how well she capsized, wouldn't we? This was clearly the time to start the engine. I dived below to hit the temporary starter button and Cathie controlled the gear lever (middle position for neutral) and throttle lever (at the back for idle) from the cockpit controls as I had explained to her the day before.

Once, twice, three times . . . 10 times, 20 times. Just spluttering from the engine as the battery got weaker and weaker and we got closer to the surf. Any second now we'd touch and then in an instant we'd be on our side and swimming for shore while the boat my brother had lived on and loved was slowly beaten to death by the full force of the storm combined with our own incompetence.

Finally, in desperation, when I estimated that I had maybe one attempt left, I put my head up to see if Cathie was ready to give it some extra throttle instead of setting it at idle. There was the gear lever (back) and the throttle (middle) so – wait a minute! Noooooooooo. In panic I reversed the positions of the two levers and

After the refurbishment.

punched the starter button. Instantly, the little diesel coughed into life. Saved!

I throttled it up until it warmed, then I slammed it into gear, gunned the engine and pointed the bow directly towards the wind, Chile and safety. We didn't turn it off until we limped into the next safe harbour 14 hours later. All night long we motored and pumped and chundered and made about two miles an hour into a sea that was long ago vacated by anyone with any sense. Eventually we stumbled into a harbour where Al had family who drove us back to Auckland. A week later, with the aid of Cathie's boyfriend, Jeff, who is a boatbuilder and a real sailor, we collected the boat, screwed one more start out of the battery and then motored her the remaining 40 miles to a marina on flat calm seas, accompanied by dolphins outlined like neon signs by the phosphoresence in the water.

I spent the next three months refitting the yacht inside and out with Cathie and Jeff's help. I built three new bunks, a galley, a chart table, a head and put in new floorboards. I installed a complete wiring loom and interior lights and 12-volt power points. I painted the interior and re-routed the bilge pump. Jeff installed a replacement bulkhead and Cathie repainted the exterior. We bought new sail covers and re-upholstered the seats. It cost over $20,000, and not long after we finished it, we sold the boat. None of us seemed keen to experience another trip like the one we'd just had and by then the boat was transformed and memories of Malcolm were fixed with us in other ways. I still see it at anchor nearby and it looks tidy and well used.

And that is all my boating experience. A fraction more than nothing at all, but a good deal less than I would have liked. Based on this sketchy knowledge I would never have planned such a venture if it hadn't been for the books.

Chapter
3

Hooked on books

THERE WERE SEVERAL things to think about when I began idly roughing out the shape of this adventure a couple of years before that conversation with Adrienne. They all come under the general heading though of 'Books'.

Firstly, in 1995 I had written *Straight From The Horse's Ass*, which was a success in New Zealand. Soon afterwards, the publishers and my agent began to ask when I would produce another book like that. The result in 1999 was *Shooting From The Lip*, which dealt with my nine years in the New Zealand army and the disasters I inflicted on myself and my fellow officers. It too was a success since it had a ready-made market in the 5000 or so soldiers that passed through the army in the 1980s and who knew the people and places involved in my yarns.

It was an ego booster at a time when middle age was lowering my opinion of myself. I took a good look in the mirror and started to think of that wonderful time after I finished riding my horse to Mexico when I was lean and mean and wore a gun and twirled a rope and was oh so pleased with myself. The answer was pretty clear. I could lose weight, get fit, become famous, earn some money, write a book and banish slothful middle age for another few years if I just had Another Long Adventure. Of course if you're poor like I was, then the central qualifier in that phrase necessarily gives rise to another – Cheap. *Another Long* **Cheap** *Adventure* then. But what kind?

I'D DONE THE backpacking thing in my army days and had had more than enough of dragging my house around on my back like a turtle. I'd done the leisurely car-driving tourist thing all over North America and there wasn't much vigorous adventure there. It's the same with trains. I'd done the horse-riding thing already and I was unable to afford the dog sled thing at all. I'd be buggered if I'd try to bike anywhere. So that left sailing, camels, balloons and microlight aircraft. Since my fear of heights was already conquered, and since they were bound to be expensive too, I scratched all the flying options. Camels are a pain. But sailing? Hmmm. A small boat might be cheap to buy. You could cruise forever on pennies and go nearly anywhere in the world. Anywhere they spoke English by preference, and that meant England, Australia or America.

The second point was the easiest to solve. The climate in the UK is 'variable' – a Latin word meaning in this context 'crap' – so exit the UK as a destination. Australia is home to the world's largest supply of box jellyfish, whose sting is more fearful than a Tabasco enema. So let's just avoid that. But there are over 300 million literate North Americans and they are the friendliest and most generous people in the world and they have brilliant hospitals, dentists and coastguards and I thought I might need all three.

I'm serious about the hospitals and coastguard and stuff. The US is civilised compared to, say, the coast of Africa or Asia or even some parts of Europe. There are no pirates in US waters, the GPS coverage is superb, you can get accurate weather forecasts on the radio, there are libraries ashore with free emailing facilities, they have pharmacies, groceries, free clean water at every tap, plentiful gas stations and chandleries, second-hand bookshops and chart sellers. They have ATMs everywhere and uncorrupt policemen. In short, everything you need is available along the entire coast and never more than 100 miles away. And you can leave your boat untended and unlocked practically anywhere and it won't get stolen. Plus you don't have to go through customs every second week – it's a big coast.

Further research revealed that the US east coast is the warmest. The Gulf Stream warms it, whereas the Humboldt Current actually chills the west coast. And the Atlantic coast is the most sheltered one with thousands of bays and harbours. Plus, for a goodly portion of it, the Atlantic Intra-Coastal Waterway (ICW) provides shelter from the Atlantic Ocean. I'd seen parts of the ICW on an earlier holiday and remembered it as a series of wide rivers and narrow lakes joined by stretches of canals big enough to take large barges or small cruise ships.

The main part of the ICW runs from Norfolk, Virginia, at the bottom of the Chesapeake Bay all the way south to Miami, Florida – a distance of 1095 miles. From there, you are sheltered first by the outer reefs and then by the inner islands of the Florida Keys that extend all the way to Key West – just 90 miles north of Cuba.

Furthermore, if you headed north from Norfolk, Virginia, you could sail up the 200-mile-long Chesapeake Bay and into a canal at the head that joins the Delaware River. Then you could go down that bay to Cape May, New Jersey, but just before you burst out onto the Atlantic Ocean, a short stretch of 120 miles of the New Jersey ICW begins again and takes you behind barrier islands right up to New York Harbour. Only after that are you forced to sail entirely on the ocean if you want to go north to Canada. There were lots of small boats in New England so clearly it was yachting territory, but although I'd heard of small boats in Canada, I'd also read Farley Mowat's two terrific books about going out on Canadian waters. The first was called *The Boat Who Wouldn't Float* and the title tells you plenty. The second was called *The Gray Seas Under*, a collection of true Canadian seafaring stories and it will scare you shitless.

So, cold, rocky, beautiful, lonely Eastport, Maine, was the northern end of the road for me and the other might as well be at the southern start of the US coast – warm, busy, sandy, inviting Key West, Florida. I guessed that 20 miles a day was the speed I could average in the long term, allowing for rest days and bad weather. The distance between Key West and Maine is 2350 statute miles. With a bit of to-ing and fro-ing I figured on sailing 2500 miles or 4000 kilometres. At 20 miles per day that would take 125 days or more and that was plenty. It certainly ought to be enough to conquer my fear.

Now I just had to find a boat that was suitable for the trip. It would have to be small and cheap, but quite seaworthy. Initially I had in mind something like a titanium barrel with a mast. Something that sailed about as well upside down as right side up, because I had a feeling I might need that kind of performance.

On and off for the next two years I studied all sorts of boats. I bought copies of *Classic Boats* and *Wooden Boat* magazines and read all about famous American and English small-boat designs. I looked at plans for DIY Herreshoff boats, at cat boats, luggers, mini-keelers and skiffs. I considered building my own in the US. I read everything I could find on the subject. And I talked about the idea occasionally to Adrienne. But that was all I did. Until a certain Sunday morning when I shot my mouth off just a bit too far.

So now I had to get serious and settle on a type of boat. I couldn't do anything else in the way of planning the trip until that was decided. The budget dictated all other options and its chief component was the cost of the boat. And once again Adrienne was the key. She was unconvinced that this whole idea was safe, but I was busy telling her that it was a cinch because I was only planning to sail up the coast — not across the Atlantic Ocean like that madman who did it in a hurricane in a . . . ? In what-the-hell kind of a boat was it? Hadn't I read a book years ago by a guy who'd sailed a teeny-weeny boat to Iceland or Greenland from somewhere in Britain? What was that book? Maybe another trip to the library was in order.

And there it was. The book I remembered reading years ago. *Ocean Crossing Wayfarer* by Frank Dye. I re-read it that weekend and realised again what fantastic eccentrics England produces. They turn them out like clockwork and Frank is typical. In 1962 he'd bought a plywood Wayfarer dinghy — an open boat just 16 feet long, named *Wanderer*. It was sold as a coastal cruising dinghy, built for a couple to spend a weekend pottering around the river mouths of England. It looked like something you would buy specifically for the purpose of showing your 10-year-old how to sail, but you could put a tent up on the boom and sleep in it. Definitely a boat for sheltered waters, and yet, accompanied by a friend, these two fools had set out to sail from Scotland to Iceland.

They made it in after a couple of weeks. Oh, they got caught in a force 8 storm and got rolled over three times by waves and broke their mast. But they righted the boat each time, bailed her out, jury-rigged a mast, took a deep breath and kept sailing. Two years later Frank sailed the same boat from Scotland to Norway across the awful North Sea. Both stories were in the book I read along with a detailed description of the incredible little boat he had used. It was a Wayfarer. And clearly a Wayfarer was a Tough Little Boat. That was the type of boat for me. A little boat that could be handled by one person. A little boat that could handle situations I would never plan to get into. A little boat that could probably sail itself better without me on board. A little boat that would be cheap.

Back to the library to see what happened to Frank. If he did this sort of mad thing twice then clearly he was unteachable and would have continued to do it until he was lost at sea. In that event, someone must have written an obituary. I searched the database in several city libraries for 'Dye, Frank' and came up with the most astounding information. He was still alive, in good health and still sailing a Wayfarer. In fact, he'd published a book in 1999 about a trip that he'd made, mostly accompanied by his wife Margaret, all the way from Florida, up the US east coast, across to Canada, around Nova Scotia and up the St Lawrence River to the Canadian Great Lakes.

He'd called it *Sailing to the Edge of Fear*, which I thought was a trifle overdramatic until I read his explanation of what he meant by it:

> *The water is always changing, fascinating, sometimes incredibly beautiful, and it drowns those who are careless or contemptuous of its dangers. People talk about 'a respect' for the sea but respect is based on fear. When fascination outweighs fear, I sail on. When the balance changes it is time to stop.*

That was exactly how I intended to approach the thing – when I got too scared, I'd stop sailing and, little by little, I'd push back the scary limit until I was no more than normally afraid of the sea. Just like Frank, who had clearly pushed it back so far that it was just a dot on the horizon. For me it was still the size of an IMAX movie screen.

Each year Frank would come back out from England to sail some more in North America. From 1995 onwards he'd quartered the dinghy in Ontario, Canada, and used it to sail on the rivers and canals of that province. Obviously, after 40 years of sailing this type of boat, he was pretty satisfied with it. That was good enough for me. I wanted a Wayfarer just like Frank's.

Aside from the outstanding seakeeping qualities of such a boat, I also had a feeling that it met another critical criteria: at 16 feet long it was very probably the biggest boat I could afford.

~~~

I KNEW FROM my work refurbishing Malcolm's boat how expensive a yacht can be. My mother, sister and I had poured over $20,000 into the project and luckily got almost all of it back when the boat was sold, but I'd seen once and heard many times how the prices for everything on a boat skyrocket as its length and tonnage increase. Here's an example. Malcolm's yacht *Sheba* was 28 feet long and weighed about 20,000 pounds. An anchor for a boat that size costs about $300. A small dinghy of say 15 feet weighs only 500 pounds and an anchor costs about $30. There's a saving already, but let's keep looking. The anchor chain for the larger boat is $4 a metre versus $0.65 a metre for a dinghy. And a large boat needs more chain to hold the extra weight. The anchor rope needs to be heavier too – and longer. And the cleat that the rope is attached to must be stronger and more firmly anchored to the boat with heavier and more expensive fastenings. You might then even need an electric anchor winch to haul the thing in. In short, the whole anchoring system for Malcolm's yacht (including second anchor, etc.) will cost darn near $1000 new without a winch or self-draining storage compartment. A dinghy system will cost less than $100.

That applies to everything on a boat. As you add each metre in hull length, you roughly double the cost. By the time you've built a luxury yacht of over 70 metres, it's costing someone over $1 million *per metre*.

So, back home to look at the bank balance. This did not take long. I estimated that I could live indefinitely on a small boat in US coastal waters on a budget of NZ$40 a day, which should pay for all food, gasoline, entertainment, film, souvenirs, repairs, marina fees, taxi fares, etc. If I sailed for the whole six months of spring and summer weather that would eat up $7200. Say another $3000 for air fares to the US and bus fares to the east coast and that left about $9000 for the boat and equipment.

Frankly I didn't think it was enough, but maybe I could borrow some more money and then pay it back by selling the boat at the end and by writing a book about the trip. I might get an advance for a book and I could probably recover 50 percent of the cost of the boat.

Now what did a Wayfarer cost? A search of the Internet revealed two Wayfarer associations in North America. American boats were available for between $3000 and $10,000. Most good-looking second-hand ones with plenty of gear like sails, trailer, motor, etc. were between $4000 and $6000. That looked good. Now I made a more detailed but still rough budget, which gave me a projected cash surplus of NZ$1140.

So far so good. The money might just be enough, assuming I could get to the US and find a boat – preferably in Florida where I planned to begin the trip. That was a no-brainer. I wanted to sail north with the advancing summer weather from a warm Florida winter towards a warm Maine summer. The next question was when to start and that was pretty easy too. My job finished in August, and that was the start of the most enjoyable time for cowboying in Wyoming – the fall drift – when cattle are brought down out of the mountain pasture to the ranches in the valley for the winter. That process ends with the start of winter feeding by December. So if I cowboyed for a season, I'd be free from early December onwards. Allowing a week or two to get hold of a boat and get it to Florida and put it in the water, I might be ready to set sail in January. And January in Florida is very pleasant. As the seasons advanced, so I would sail north, until I found myself in Maine in late July – at which time my visitor's visa would run out and I could return home to find work and pay off my credit card.

That was all the planning done. Now I just had to call Stan and wangle an invitation to stay on his ranch for a few weeks, find a suitable boat in the US, apply for a 12-month US visitor's visa, pack my house up and go on holiday for a year. Easy-peasy, now that I had A Plan.

Fate: It should carry a health warning

ONCE I WOULD have begun my search for a boat with a trip to the library and then some long-distance phoning, but now it's easier to search the Internet. On the two North American websites, prices ranged from US$1500 for a boat in need of TLC to $10,000 for a mint-condition boat on a trailer with all mod cons. (Mod cons is a bit of an excessive description for a boat as sparse as a Wayfarer — unless you consider oars and bailers as 'mod cons'.)

My budget limited me to about US$3000 but there weren't any available in Florida at that price. I'd already tried looking for an example in New Zealand but the manufacture of Wayfarers is controlled to the extent that it seemed that only boatbuilders licensed by the designer could make one. The option of buying plans and building one at home did not exist. Since DIY was out, I contacted the North American websites and asked for help in finding a boat over there. Both sites replied to me with useful advice that I followed up, but I still didn't find what I wanted. I did, however, come across tons of information about Wayfarers generally — the different types, their history, construction, sailing techniques, famous cruises and so on.

I read everything I could find on all the sites and after a few weeks I had refined my search for a Wayfarer down to two types. I wanted a fibreglass boat instead of a plywood one (less maintenance and less weight) and I wanted either a Mark 1A or a Mark 3. These differed in a few details – chiefly in their storage and flotation chambers. They seemed to be better suited for cruising than the other types, which I thought were better for racing. The more I read, the more determined I was to obtain my preferred mark and also to fit it with a number of devices that would improve the safety and the ease of handling for a solo sailor. I wanted to add buoyancy to the boom and mast so they would float if I capsized. I wanted roller reefing for the jib or genoa, slab reefing for the main, a larger anchor and a spare as well. I wanted rollers to haul her up on a beach, oars in case the wind failed, a motor in case *I* failed, a boom tent for shelter, camping gear, flares, a bilge pump, spare parts, repair kits – dozens of things, in fact, that tended not to come with bare boats like those advertised on the websites.

At the same time, I started reading and re-reading all sorts of books about small-boat adventures including Frank Dye's *Sailing to the Edge of Fear,* Margaret Dye's *Dinghy Cruising – The Enjoyment of Wandering Afloat* and her book on interpreting weather signs, plus numerous others dealing with dinghy handling, long-distance cruising and sailing in general. In short, I did a *lot* of reading but no sailing. You may wonder at the aptness of this preparation programme, but I didn't. I simply assumed that since 10-year-olds could sail little dinghies, then so could I. I mean, how hard could it be? Those kids are little! Puny arms like matchsticks to pull on the ropes. No body weight to act as moveable ballast. I was a medium-sized bloke, so it ought to be a breeze for me. And I wasn't planning to cross the Atlantic – I was only going to sail from bay to bay, up a well-charted, well-populated coast, on days when the weather was fine and bright. At no point did I plan to be more than a few miles from land, so it wasn't as if I'd have to master techniques like astral navigation, heaving to in a hurricane or lying to a sea anchor (oooh anchor, you look lovely in that light). In other words, there was no point at which I envisaged that things would become more complicated or perilous than they are for the average nipper. And that was fine by me since I wasn't planning to follow Joshua Slocum or Francis Drake. I only planned to slowly overcome my dread fear of being afloat in a boat and have a lovely summer holiday at the same time. Modest aims in keeping with my modest common sense and sailing ability.

By now, though, three months had passed while I fiddled about refining my plans. I had arranged with Stan to go and play at cow-boying in Wyoming on his ranch in August. I had managed to save some funds for the trip and I had updated my passport and applied for a visa. But there was no boat in sight yet. My beloved had refrained from saying anything on the subject, but I was well aware that having already shot off my gob, I now had to either make good or back down and begin life immediately as a co-habitee – and a whipped one at that.

At this point, Fate, which had not lifted a finger to help me before this, wheeled up a barrowful of good luck. One Sunday in March I was browsing the webpages of the Canadian Wayfarer website when a new ad appeared in the For Sale section. Well, Holy Cow! Frank Dye was selling *Wanderer*. The very same boat in which he had sailed from Florida to the Great Lakes. A fibreglass Mark 1A Wayfarer. With every modification and piece of equipment that I had on my list. And it was already stored in a barn near Ottawa so it was practically on the east coast already.

The price was roughly US$2500 – just within my budget. And there was no other boat even remotely as good as this on offer anywhere in the world and hadn't been for the last three months. This was such a perfect proposition. I thought about it hard for perhaps 45 seconds and then emailed an offer to Mr Dye and crossed my fingers. A day later I had his answer.

He'd already sold it.

Bugger, bugger and damn!

I thought it would be polite to thank him for his quick reply so I wrote back expressing my regrets that it wasn't available and then sulked over the news that I would either have to keep looking or give up the idea altogether.

Frabjous joy. A day later another email from Mr Dye told me that the new owner was having trouble arranging to move *Wanderer* from Ontario to the US midwest. Frank said he'd keep me informed as there was a possibility that the deal might fall through. At which point I decided to let Fate determine whether or not I'd go ahead with this adventure. If the deal went ahead, I'd forget the sailing idea, move in with my girl in Christchurch, cease having adventures, quit writing books and die a dry death years from now. But, if the deal fell through . . .

A day later it did. Frank said that the boat was mine if I wanted it. I said I did. We agreed on a price and I emailed the money to him in Britain. At that point, although no bill of sale was provided, *Wanderer* was mine. I now owned a boat I had never seen, of a type I had never sailed, bought from a man I had never met. He had my money in Britain, I was in New Zealand and my boat was in a barn somewhere in Canada, so I couldn't even see it for another nine months.

I emailed this wonderful news to Adrienne. News that confirmed I had bought a pig in a poke and soon intended to sail said pig on the Atlantic for the better part of a year. Her response to this was a lot better than you might think. At no time from then until now did she ever suggest that I not do it, nor did she complain that it would mean leaving her behind for 12 months. In fact, she did pretty much the opposite. Some weeks later when I was refiguring my holiday budget, and I mentioned that there was a slight fiscal gap, she just nodded and a few days later on my birthday she gave me an extra envelope. In it was $1000 – the amount of my budget shortfall.

I had no fear that Frank's boat would prove to be unsatisfactory. Frank is a retired English gentleman adventurer with an international reputation in sailing circles. He is recognised on the street (or canal) in several countries, one of his boats is in the British National Maritime Museum, and besides – he is a sailor.

There are almost no people alive more vulnerable to theft than sailors, and as a result, sailors tend to be the most honest community of people on the planet, so I was certain that I'd made a good deal. In fact, the only thing that troubled me a little was that I might have bought a boat that was too well known. I worried that it might be like buying Elvis's pink '56 Cadillac – what would Frank's fans do to me if I sank his famous boat? There was a picture of him on the website next to the ad for *Wanderer* and he looked like a proper square-rigged gent to me.

Satisfied that I'd got exactly the boat I wanted, I settled down to gloat over pictures of my purchase. The best ones were drawings of Wayfarers obtained from the websites. I studied them closely because I needed to know what all the bits were so that I could relate them to the instructions in the various 'how to' books I was also reading.

A glance at the drawing on pages 80–81 will reveal that the raw boat lacks a few of the amenities more common to larger vessels. That was an advantage since I didn't have to master new terms like 'galley, head, berth, cabin, fo'c'sle, poop deck, mizzen mast or forepeak'. I didn't even have much use for old ones like 'roof, bed, table, tap, sink or electricity'. But I did get plenty of use out of 'bucket', 'sleeping bag', 'wet-weather gear' and 'leaky tent'. What it lacked, it lacked in abundance.

Fortunately I had plenty of experience at camping so I was used to being deprived of the comforts of home. I was quite at ease in a tent – especially one so roomy as a boom tent 12 feet long and four feet high. And there was plenty of room in the storage lockers for two self-inflating sleeping mats and two sleeping bags for extra warmth and comfort. Plus tons of spare clothes, a pressure lantern, a pressure stove, gallons and gallons of water, ample canned and fresh food, even books to read. Best of all, I didn't have to tote any of this around in a backpack. Nor did I have to cram it into saddlebags and load it onto a tired horse. I regarded this as camping luxury compared to my own experiences in the army. On the other hand, I had vastly improved my chances of drowning over those of hikers.

By now it was clear that the trip could go ahead and so I announced to my employer and my friends that I was off to sail a dinghy a few thousand miles come August. Mostly they took this news with a bemused tolerance and only a slight curiosity. I don't know whether this was because they thought it was a routine sort of adventure that hardly offered any thrills or because they thought it was impossible and that I'd never get it off the ground. For me it didn't matter, since I was totally confident that I could do this thing and I was used to scepticism from the public.

One curious thing happened this time, though – everyone who thought they knew anything about sailing assumed I planned to catch a ride on the Gulf Stream. That tropical stream flows within the Atlantic Ocean from the Caribbean, up the US coast to Canada and then across the Atlantic to warm the western shores of the British Isles. It moves at about five knots most of the time and boats make correspondingly faster passages if they hitch a ride. But it does have a drawback.

The part of the Gulf Stream that I would have had to sail in lies chiefly within an area of sea known as the Bermuda Triangle and these two facts are not unrelated. One of the possible explanations for the loss of so many boats in this area is that when the northerly current (which flows from the south to the north) is opposed by a northerly wind (blowing from north to south), it throws up waves of unusual height. These waves can kill a small boat and even some rather large ones have serious trouble. Wind against current (or tide) always does this, but the effect in the Gulf Stream is more pronounced because the winds are stronger out at sea and the current is more powerful too. The marine weather forecast that I listened to every day gave a good indication of the size of the problem. Typically the forecast for inshore waters (out to 20 nautical miles) would say, 'Winds northerly, 10–15 knots, waves 2–3 feet' and for the Gulf Stream at the same time it would say, 'Winds 15–20 knots, waves 9–13 feet'. Now these aren't the nice, smooth, long, high Atlantic rollers either. They are nasty, short-ish, steep waves that are almost as high as my boat was long. Surfing down one would risk broaching, being in the trough of one would rob me of half the wind. I'd be alternately speeding and stalling and bobbing up and down the whole time. Worst of all, there was nowhere to run to if bad weather came up. If I was sailing with a crew member, I'd be able to stay out overnight if I had to – even heaved to – but sailing single-handed deprived me of that option. Much larger boats than mine would wait for days or even weeks in Florida for a non-northerly wind before tackling the crossing of the Gulf Stream on their way to Bermuda or the Bahamas for the winter.

And the Gulf Stream isn't all that close to the coast either. At Fort

Lauderdale and Cape Hatteras it comes in to within a couple of miles of shore but for the rest of the time it's at least half a day's sail out from the coast (say 20 miles) and often as far as three days' sail away. Before I even got to it I'd have to turn back to make it to an anchorage near land before dark. So the Gulf Stream was of no use to me and after a while I got a little tired of people telling me I should be using it to whisk myself to Canada. The way I saw it, it would only whisk me to a drowning.

Announcing the plan publicly though, served to bind me to it. If I backed down now I risked public humiliation and that was worse than the prospect of eight months at sea in a bathtub. Plus, the more people that knew I was doing it – the larger the rescue party!

One of the people who enquired and encouraged without racing to judgement was my sister-in-law Sue. She's a lovely lady who found out what I planned and then said that she had a friend in the US who I should look up if I was out there. I was instantly sceptical since plenty of people offer help: 'You're going to the US? – Oh, I have a friend there you could stay with – she's in Detroit. Or is it Denver? Is that near Florida? We went to kindy together – you could stay with her. Now what's her married name?'

I'd got used to that sort of thing so I was mightily surprised when Sue emailed me a few days later and said she'd contacted her friend and told him I was coming to do some sailing and that he'd invited me to stay at his place.

'Where is that exactly?' I asked Sue. 'And what does he do there?'

'He lives in Fort Lauderdale – that's in Florida, isn't it? And you're going to Florida, aren't you? Geoff's a . . . a . . . what's the word – you know, he supplies boats. *Chandler*, that's it – he's a chandler,' she said.

Son of a bitch! A chandler in Fort Lauderdale. Wooohooo! An advance base camp! Purrrfect!

~~~

THE LAST COUPLE of months before departure were spent earning a living, handing over my job to a replacement as well as planning the trip and preparing to pack up my house. Reluctantly I surrendered the lease and sold off all those things I wouldn't need when I got back – furniture, whiteware, car etc.

Adrienne had invited me to come and live with her in Christchurch after the trip and though I had some doubts about living down there, it was so convenient to have someone to take care of my mail while I was away and to meet me when I got home that I wasn't about to say no to that. Having what polar explorers would call a manned base camp was a new experience for me. On previous adventures like this, I'd always packed it in with my girlfriends at about the same time as I got on the plane. This one was a bit different, though. After two years I was starting to form the impression that she might be a keeper. For a start, I owed her a grand. That was the first time I'd ever been obligated to a woman. Looking back, I wonder if that was a cunning tactical move on her part.

Sailing the prairies

NOW I WANT to be clear about this – I didn't deliberately choose to begin a sailing vacation in the middle of winter from a starting point high in the Rocky Mountains – that's just how it happened. I'd first met Stan and Madeleine and their son Scott years ago when I spent part of a winter on their ranch waiting for the spring grass to arrive, and this seemed like a perfect chance to revisit them and their hospitality. I left New Zealand at the beginning of August and Scott met me off the plane and drove me to the ranch. Stan and Mad were the same as ever and it didn't take me long to slip right back into the cowboy routine. Getting up early for a big cooked breakfast and lots of strong coffee, then saddling a horse or firing up a tractor or a pickup truck to go and tackle whatever needed the attention of an amateur cowpoke.

Roping.

The next eight weeks just flew by – I took it easy and had a roaring good time while driving all the haymaking equipment and stacking

Fencing.

hay and tightening fences and fixing trucks and generally doing guy things. Adrienne came to visit for 10 days in October, as arranged. I didn't want her to miss seeing this important part of the ranching year so the morning after she arrived, when she was still bleary with jet lag, I woke her at 5.00 am after five hours' sleep, prised her eyes open, got her dressed and into the barn and showed her how to saddle a horse.

An hour later she was helping us sort and move cattle on horseback. I was pretty surprised at how well she rode since she had no prior experience. Six hours later we had the horses back in the barn and I asked her how she managed to do so well.

'I took some lessons at home because I wanted to keep up,' she said.

And that's another thing I like about this gal – she's willing to give stuff a try. Sneakily, I seized on this fact and used it to persuade her to try all sorts of new, exciting, cowboy things with me like driving big trucks and tractors, fixing pole corrals and five-strand barbed-wire fences, pounding posts, stacking hay bales in the barn, chasing stray cattle across creeks and swamps in a snow storm, slopping through ankle-deep cowshit pushing cattle through the yards for pregnancy testing and other fun things.

But we also found time to take the four-wheeler motorbike or a pair

Bison in Yellowstone.

of horses to ride around Stan's 6000-acre ranch. We saw beavers, coyote, porcupine, antelope, mule deer, skunks, foxes, moose and all kinds of bird life, not to mention cattle, cows and beef. We walked and rode across hayfields and up into the sage-scented hill pastures. Sometimes we'd stand in the yard and look up at more stars than darkness. We had beers and shots at the bars in town and met old friends of mine at the social centre of the universe – the Wrangler Café. We ate French Dip and sourdough hamburgers, short stacks of flapjacks with maple syrup and gobbled down pecan pie with Dr Pepper chasers. We drove to Yellowstone Park and saw bison and elk, geysers, mudpools, rolling snowy fields, frozen waterfalls and pine trees that sparkled with frost. And then, much too soon for either of us, it was over and the neighbours were gathered in Madeleine's big living room to say goodbye and to give Adrienne a hug and shake her tiny hands in their big capable cowboy mitts and say 'Come back soon' and 'We loved having you' and things that make it even harder to leave because suddenly you feel like you could live there amongst such fine people for ever. And the next morning I put her on the plane and waved goodbye and even before the propellers turned over I wondered what the hell I'd do without her for the next eight months.

I'll admit I was mighty let down after Adrienne left. For two months I'd been excitedly planning her arrival on the ranch and all the fun things we'd do when she got there. But that was all over and all I had to look forward to now was the strange and fearful business of sailing.

I consoled myself with the thought that if she spent plenty on her credit card, she could accumulate enough air miles to visit me again – maybe next May when I planned to be somewhere on the east coast around Washington DC. But that was still a long time off, and in between I had to get to Canada, examine the pig-and-poke combination that was waiting for me in a barn near Ottawa and then somehow get it all into the water in Florida so that I could teach myself to sail it.

I planned to leave the ranch on 7 December and catch a Greyhound bus to Ottawa. Riding a doggie isn't my idea of great travel but at $89 versus $540 for a flight I felt that two days sitting up and dozing in a seat was worth it. I said goodbye to Stan and Mad, and then Scott drove me 100 miles to the bus station in Rock Springs. I had examined my budget and though I had spent a bit more than I'd planned while in Pinedale, I still thought I had enough to complete the journey, as long as I didn't get hit with any major disasters. Above all, I wanted to move as fast as I could from Pinedale to Ottawa to Florida and onto the boat. I knew that I'd burn money five or ten times as fast on land as on water and so I needed to gather up my dinghy and get it launched as soon as I could. Luckily, while on the ranch in Pinedale I'd had two emails that were typical of the type of help I'd get throughout the whole trip.

The first came from Brian McCleery, Frank Dye's friend in Canada, who had been keeping an eye on *Wanderer* when Frank was in Britain. He said he'd been out to check on her at the barn where she was stored next to his, near the little town of Kars, outside Ottawa. He offered to meet me when I got off the bus and said he would take me to see the boat and that I could stay at his house while I figured out how to ship it to Florida. 'We're not fancy here,' he added helpfully in the email – in case I was the kind of person who only stayed in first-class hotels when I wasn't living on an open dinghy.

The second email came from Geoff Orr – the chandler in Fort

Lauderdale who was a friend of my sister-in-law Sue. I'd written and asked if it was OK to use his address as a destination for the delivery of the boat if I had to get it shipped to Florida. He'd written back and said that was no problem and in fact I could come and stay at his place if I wanted. It backed onto a canal on the New River in Fort Lauderdale and he said there was a dock at the bottom of his garden where his own yacht was tied up, with room there for mine too.

This was truly outstanding news. The three things I had feared would be difficult and expensive to do were to collect the boat from a barn in the middle of a Canadian winter and prepare to transport it 2000 miles by unknown means, then to find a way to ship it to Florida, and finally to unload it somewhere near Miami and rig it for sailing. Now, with two emails from two strangers it seemed as though two-thirds of the things that bothered me the most were largely solved. I had a reception party at the end of both legs of the next 4000 miles of travel and places to stay as well. Purrrfect!

The 48-hour Greyhound ride was a trial – tiring, noisy and slow. Aside from that, the ride was uneventful and even got in a little early.

Brian was waiting for me in the bus station and although I should have recognised him from his photograph in the ad for *Wanderer*, I finally phoned his mobile number and caught him answering it as he walked past the phone booth. Brian is an expat Irishman and is mostly retired, along with Doris, his Canadian wife. Of course, he was a Wayfarer owner as well and he'd met Frank Dye some years before when Frank was sailing on the Rideau Canal system that passes near to Brian's house. He knew all about *Wanderer* and had taken care to keep her covered and safe with all her gear stowed for her new owner.

As we walked to the car I reflected on how lucky I was to have Brian's help. Firstly, without it I'd have had to hire a car in Ottawa, buy a road map, call Claude Le Page, the farmer who was storing my boat in his barn, and ask for directions and then drive to the farm, where if I wanted to move the boat, I'd have no extra hands to help me. Then I'd have to look for a motel to stay in for a day or two while I got her sorted out, and then I'd have to borrow or buy whatever tools, materials and tackle I needed to get her ready for transportation. Then

I'd have to rely on Claude's help to fabricate a shipping cradle or to manhandle it onto a trailer. (As I later discovered, Claude had a crook back and that wouldn't have been possible.) And I might have to buy a trailer and a car or truck to tow it, which would mean shopping for these and then dealing with paperwork for the car purchase (licensing, insurance, importation to the US, etc.). All this can add up to a surprising amount of expense.

But Brian took away all these worries. He knew where to go, he knew Claude, he had a garage to work in, he had tools and he knew what kind of cradle to build. He knew where to shop for wood, trailers, cars — everything, in fact, that I didn't know, he did. And he placed himself at my disposal completely for as long as I needed. He even re-arranged his job at an agricultural laboratory to accommodate my schedule. He said I could use his phone, his email connection, his garage and tools and of course, if I needed to get around, he had a van that wasn't being used and I could borrow that! But right now we had to go see the boat and make sure I was happy with it and then get home to his place quickly because Doris wanted to meet me and she was cooking us tea.

I couldn't wait to see what I'd bought so he drove me straight to Claude's barn, about 10 miles from Brian's home. Claude was pretty much retired from dairy farming and now leased his fields for crops, but he used one of his barns to store cars and boats for townies. Brian said he had gone there earlier in the week and moved *Wanderer* on a dolly from the back to the front where I could clamber in and see all the gear that came with her.

We pulled up to the farm and I met Claude. He was a big, hearty guy, dressed just like the cowboys in Wyoming — in quilted coveralls, insulated jacket and woollen Elmer Fudd cap. It was a typical Canadian winter day — a little below freezing, with a bitter cold wind and a clear sky. Claude said 'ello in a strong French accent and then stood back and gazed at me like I was some unusual sort of wildlife.

'So you are going to sail thees boat to Florrydah, heh?'

'Umm no, I'm going to take her down there and then sail back up to Maine.'

'Ahh. That's bettaire. Too cold 'ere for sailing now. Too cold for any damn ting. I'm going to 'Awaii next month. Like Florrydah — nice and warm. Well, 'ere is your boat.'

He slid back the barn door and there indeed she was — my *boat. My* boat. MY BOAT. If you've never owned a boat before, then even a small one like this tends to get thought of in capitals. She looked exactly like I had expected, except bigger. In fact, she seemed very large

And there she was at last.

indeed. Nothing like a P-class dinghy that I'd mentally sized her as. She was easily twice the length and at two metres wide, she was roomy too. The first thought that struck me was how open and wide the cockpit was and therefore how much room there was for water to pour in and sink her. In fact, if she ever turned . . .

'. . . 'ave sailed a lot before, heh?' Claude was talking to me.

'Umm, no actually, I've never really sailed at all,' I replied.

'But you 'ave sailed ozzer boats before now, heh? Not this one, but ozzer ones? Yes?' He stated it rather than asked it.

'Nope. Never really sailed any boats at all.'

'Oh?'

His eyes flicked quickly towards Brian for confirmation of the fact that I was indeed a lunatic. Brian nodded slowly and a little sadly it seemed to me. I formed the impression that they both liked me but were distressed that I planned to kill myself this way.

A thought struck Claude and he said brightly, 'But you will 'ave someone to 'elp you, non?'

'Non,' I said. 'I will sail by myself.'

'Oh,' said Claude. He really looked unhappy now and I felt I should cheer him up.

'But I've read a lot of books and little kids sail these things so I'm sure it will be fine.'

'Books, heh?' said Claude dubiously.

'Books,' echoed Brian.

'Books,' I said cheerily. And that was the end of the discussion about my sailing skills.

~~~

FRANK HAD LEFT behind all the gear mentioned in the advertisement but obviously quite a few other items as well. These were all stowed in *Wanderer*, which Brian had covered with a tarp to protect her from bird droppings. A mouse had taken up residence in one of the canvas bags and had shredded a newspaper for nest material but aside from that, she was clean and tidy. I had no idea if anything was missing but Brian immediately started to show me the rigging and tried to explain how it was all assembled and how it differed from his or other Wayfarers.

'The roller block fits on here with a gudgeon pin, or you can splice it to the chine, and then run it back to the jam sheets. That way you can furl the topping lift without heaving to and it leaves you a free hand to gybe the pintles. They're self-bailing you see, but Frank never used them because he didn't have a motor. He's old school.'

Ignoring all the techno-babble I seized on the one fact I understood.

'I shall fit a motor,' I said. 'I'm not an experienced sailor and I think it wise to have one.'

'Wise, yes indeed,' agreed Brian.

'Mmm, vairry wise,' said Claude who was as baffled as I was by the description of *Wanderer*'s modifications.

'Now you fit the boom crutch here and secure it with a rolling over-hand binnacle hitch but be careful to always . . .'

Brian helpfully continued with his explanations as I crawled in and under and around her looking at everything with a keen but ignorant eye. I had already decided that it would only make sense to me once I tried to unravel the mysteries of the ropes and rigging myself at a far slower pace. I had some pictures of Wayfarers, some descriptions of such things as reefing systems and I was sure I could devise something that would use all the parts Frank had left. Right now it all looked like a wigwam for a goose's bridle, but I'd seen enough for one day. *Wanderer*'s hull was sound, *Wanderer* was obviously abundantly equipped and *Wanderer* was freezing bloody cold! There was nothing I could usefully do in that frigid barn except load her up, get her to somewhere that would melt the pool of ice that had collected in the bilge and then set about putting together all the parts of the puzzle. Florida was the place for that.

'Well, if you've seen enough we can go and get some tea and get you settled in at home. I expect you'll want to email the ranch to let them know you've arrived. Tomorrow we can come back and collect all the stuff Frank left and you can go through it at my house. We can store it on the porch and work inside in the warm,' said Brian.

'And then I can look at ways of getting it to Florida,' I said.

'Florrydah,' said Claude wistfully and he looked at the acres of snow around him with fresh disgust. 'Yes, you will do well in Florrydah,' and he clapped a friendly arm around my shoulders and steered me out of the barn and into the icy wind.

~~~

BY THE END of the next day, with Brian's help, quite a lot had been accomplished. I'd met Doris, had dinner in their big kitchen, gone to see their grandson play ice hockey, checked my email and let Adrienne and Stan know where I was, been back to the barn, collected all the moveable stores from *Wanderer* and stacked them on Brian's porch, arranged with Claude that I would remove the boat in three days' time and begun to explore ways of getting *Wanderer* to Florida.

That night I phoned Frank Dye in the UK and spoke to him for the first time. I needed a bill of sale for *Wanderer* in case the US Customs challenged my ownership of the boat. Frank sounded exactly as I'd expected and was only too pleased to email and fax a bill of sale to me immediately.

I also arranged to hire a U-Haul truck big enough to fit the boat inside. It would be much less hassle then buying a car and trailer to tow the boat to Florida and I would be assured of mechanical reliability for the trip. Plus the market in Florida for used Canadian cars is weak on account of rust. The truck I chose would cost me $975 for the one-way rental plus about $350 for gasoline. I called back to check a couple of details and they quoted me a lower price. That was nice, and I confirmed it was big enough to take the 24-foot mast inside as well and so all I needed to do was whip up the cradle to hold the boat.

I discussed the making of it with Brian and we settled on a simpler plan of his design that only required some four-by-twos and screws. We measured it up against the boat and I drew the plan with a mixture of measurements in inches and millimetres because neither Brian nor I are fully converted to the American way of doing things. The USA can be a backwards place. The next day, in Brian's van, we collected the timber and I cut it up and screwed it together in his garage and tacked some carpet on it to protect the hull paint. The total cost was about $30, and thanks to the odd mixture of measurements it almost fitted the hull. Three days later, when I put the boat on it I had to add a couple of blocks to make it fit, but that was easy enough.

I also contacted US Customs to check about bringing *Wanderer* into the States, and US Immigration about reapplying for an extension to my six-months visitor's visa. I had already asked for an extension to take me up to a total stay of one year, but when I left the US to come to Ottawa, I had accidentally invalidated it. I would have to reapply (cost $140) and hope that the Americans let me back in on Friday when I rolled up to the border in my U-Haul. If they didn't then I would be in a pretty pickle. I got hold of the US Coastguard to see what rules I had to comply with, and because *Wanderer* was so small and had no motor, they said there were no federal regulations applicable to me at all and probably no state ones either. I called U-Haul back to finalise the booking and pick-up time and they reduced the price again. Now it was only $775 plus gas. I had a little spare time so Brian and I took a trip into town and at a bookstore in Ottawa I stumbled on a copy of Frank Dye's *Sailing to the Edge of Fear*. I thought it would help explain what I was doing to strangers and add to the credibility of my plans if

I could point to the cover and say 'see that boat, that's mine now and I'm going to do half of what he did and take twice as long to do it'.

On Thursday, after making a small adjustment to the cradle (damn those metric measurements) we loaded the U-Haul truck with *Wanderer* and she was surprisingly easy to slide on her rollers up the ramp and into the truck.

I stacked all her stores around her and tied the mast, jib and boom to the side of the truck. The whole lot barely took up 20 percent of the space in the back. It seemed silly to be sailing such a long way with so little gear but I figured I could make it.

The variety of Frank's gear was interesting. While sorting through it over the previous couple of days I had discovered:

- every useful thing listed on the advertisement,
- a few items of doubtful value like crippled binoculars, an ancient sun umbrella, some elderly provisions and a couple of bottles of unknown liquids,
- a medical supply bag that would do good service for a battalion in combat,
- evidence that he had a serious issue with mosquitoes (three

Building the shipping cradle in Brian's garage.

kinds of repellent spray and lotion, two kinds of bite-soothing stick, several packets of smoky mosquito coil, a mosquito net and a mosquito-proof hat-cum-veil),

- torches and transistor radios that required every size of battery between AAA and D cell size – but no two the same,
- a few books loaded with stories of seafaring tragedy,
- a highly serviceable set of good-quality foul-weather gear, including seaboots that fitted me very nicely indeed, and
- spare parts of every kind supported by the usual hideous sailor's collection of decrepit hand tools.

Of course I had only a passing idea how Frank managed to unite all these elements and create a fully rigged and equipped sailing vessel, but I had a feeling that most of the things would only work if fitted one way (i.e. correctly) and that ought to make the job easier. For the time being, though, that was a long way off. First I had to drive to Florida and that was no trouble at all for a cowboy-soldier like me with years of truck-driving experience in the snows of Wyoming and Waiouru.

No, actually the first thing I had to do was get Claude to fetch a tractor and haul the U-Haul out of the snow where I had parked it and where it now was spinning its wheels on a bed of icy slush. Then I'd drive to Florida where there was no damn snow and I'd get on a boat with no damn wheels and then I wouldn't be embarrassed this way by delinquent machinery.

Are we there yet?

BRIGHT AND EARLY the next morning Doris fed me breakfast enough for a coal miner instead of someone who was about to sit on his air-conditioned ass for three days. I thanked her and Brian again for all their hospitality. Then, armed with my map and some instructions from Brian about how to find America (down the road, turn left and across the bridge to the men in hats with guns), I climbed up into the cab, gave them a wave, gunned the engine and broke for the border. I was rather worried that I might experience problems getting back into the US and I wanted an answer as soon as possible. Post-9/11 there were plenty of stories of people who had been denied entry for all sorts of curious reasons. One local Canadian who had regularly bought cheaper gas in the US was detained by immigration officers when he crossed the border after hours without the requisite stamp and ended up spending a month in jail while they established his bona fides. My situation was a bit different, but I'd already had four months in the US and I wondered whether they thought I might have left the US to go to Canada purely to circumvent their regulations. I had taken the precaution of explaining to the US consulate in New Zealand six months earlier that I wanted to spend a year in the US and I had a record of all the correspondence and supporting documents. It showed that I was quite open and honest about my plans and that I wasn't trying to illegally emigrate to the States.

Brian and Doris, the first taste of the kindness of strangers.

At the crossing point at Ogdensburg, NY, I parked the truck and walked into the border post to sort it all out. On the wall was a poster of wanted men, with Osama bin Laden at the top. I doubt he'd try to enter the US, but it still felt unusual seeing a wanted poster like that. In due course Officer W. T. Leary asked me what I was planning and I explained that I was here to sail a boat from Florida to Maine.

'Where's your boat now?' he asked.

'Right there in the back of my truck.'

He looked at me with raised eyebrows and then he called a friend over and they both went and looked at the boat and returned to say things like 'that's a mighty small boat' and 'is there any more coming or is that all there is?' I smiled and took the joshing as it was meant. Mr Leary confided that he was an ex-navy man and I admitted I was unfortunate enough to be an ex-army man and he said that explained a lot and perhaps I'd been drafted so it might not be all my fault. He said he knew some other ex-army men and he thought they were OK. Considering.

Right away I liked Officer Leary and I could tell he liked my little boat. I showed him all my paperwork – the application, the extension, the invalidation, the intention to reapply for another extension if he allowed me back in temporarily and so on. I had all my documents neatly in a folder – original application, passport, original visa, proof of funds, letter from my publisher expressing interest in a book about the trip, letters from folks who had promised help in the US if I needed it, bill of sale for the boat, etc. My aim was to cover all likely questions with a piece of paper and thereby ensure that he could make a decision on the spot and later be able to justify it to his boss if needed. It is an approach I have used before and this time it worked a treat, too. Armed with plausible answers and supporting documents he called the immigration bigwigs and worked all his magic and came back to me and said, 'Well, it's obvious you wanted to stay for a year at the time you entered the US and you made that clear and you have all the answers here and so I'll just go ahead and give you a visa for eight months. Beats me why they didn't do that right off the bat at LA – you can stay till 7 August and that's plenty long enough on a boat that big.' I wanted to jump up in the air and scream 'Yahoooooooo!' but I just said, 'Thank you very much – this is just what I needed.'

'You know, I had a boat like that too,' he said as he walked me to the door.

'Yeah?' I said, taking the bait.

'Uh huh, in a bottle,' he said and smiled as he waved me away.

'Good luck, Kiwi,' yelled his friend and for a moment I didn't want to leave their company. They weren't like any other border guards I'd ever seen before, but they were helluva good at making you feel welcome in the US of A.

Doris and Brian had insisted I call them as soon as I was through the border so I did that and then gassed up the truck and headed onto I81 for the long haul south. It was cold and overcast with thick snow on the trees and houses, but that sort of winterscape is quite attractive to someone raised in Auckland's balmy climate and I didn't mind it. I was looking forward to the drive south. The U-Haul was easy to drive – heated cab, comfy seat, automatic transmission and power steering, and no special licence was needed either.

When darkness came around 5.30 pm I'd made it to Pennsylvania and I decided to stop in Harrisburg for the night. There's something very pleasant about being temporarily adrift. Here I was with only minimal responsibilities, adequate funds and nothing very hard to do for a couple of days. At the end of that a whole bear pit of work and worry and fear and expense was waiting for me, but right now I was in limbo. I couldn't deal with any of the problems yet and so all I had to do was keep driving and looking at the scenery and listening to the radio until I got to Florida. It was a kind of holiday within a holiday and I knew even then that I wouldn't be this relaxed again for a long time to come.

The next day I saddled up and under grey skies I piloted myself another 700 miles south, through Pennsylvania, Maryland, Virginia and North Carolina to Brunswick, South Carolina, and another cheap motel. From there I called Geoff Orr in Fort Lauderdale and got directions to his house on the river. He sounded delighted to hear from me, but I couldn't figure out why. The last day's drive was pleasant enough, though the cold weather continued all the way through Georgia. By early afternoon I was crossing into Florida for the last leg down the coast. About then, the sun came out, the palm trees appeared and suddenly I was hot. I started discarding my gloves, hat and coat, and by the time I was looking for the exit to Fort Lauderdale I was in shorts and T-shirt. The warm tropical air poured into the cab, and once again I had that 'first day of the holidays' feeling.

At 4.30 pm on a quiet Sunday afternoon I eased down the little lane between the overhanging tropical trees to Geoff's house. Like many boating communities, all the land near the water was heavily used and parking the truck was a problem. Normally it's because there isn't much flat land in a port, but in Florida there isn't anything but flat land – the highest point is Space Mountain at Disney World. Despite this abundance there was hardly any room to manoeuvre. Fort Lauderdale is a very rich city and land is expensive and intensively occupied. Geoff had told me that there was a boatyard a couple of hundred yards away that I might use so I drove down to see it and turn the truck around. I stopped back in front of his house and went to knock on his door. After a bit of searching and yelling a figure turned up with a big smile on his face and his hand outstretched. I later discovered that this was his natural state.

'Hi, I'm Lee,' I said.

'Yeah, yeah, great to see you mate, how was your trip? You found the place all right? Shit, you can't park there – my neighbours'll go nuts, but no worries. Sort that out later, eh? Where's your gear? Let's get that inside – you can sleep on my boat or crash in the lounge. Sue said you were going to sail to Canada – it's a bit early in the season for that – better stay here for a while. Don't want you sailing into a snowstorm, eh?'

'I only plan to stay here for . . .'

'This your boat, eh? She's a cracker – I reckon you got a nice one there.'

Carrying one of my bags, he led me through the bungalow and into the back garden, past the swimming pool toward a garden gate.

'This is Sandy – my girl.' He broke off and I was able to drop my bags and shake hands with a willowy American woman stretched out on a sun lounger. She had a big smile too and loads to say.

'Oh wow, Geoff said you were sailing a little boat from Canada or something – that's so neat. You've sailed a lot before, I guess. Here, give me that bag – and you're a cowboy too? That's amazing. How did you learn to be a cowboy – I mean you're a Kiwi – do they have cowboys there?'

'Well, actually I . . .'

'This is your bedroom – unless you'd rather not sleep on a boat,' Geoff said and led me through a garden gate to a 45-foot sloop that was tied up to his dock. It floated in a 20-yard-wide canal that joined the upper reaches of the New River – the same sort of arrangement that existed for the 15 miles of river between here and the start of Port Everglades – which was the official name of Fort Lauderdale's harbour. Thousands and thousands of boats slumbered in the canals off the New River and every canal between there and Miami, and you could tell by looking at them that they were too clean and perfect to have ever been used for much more than an annual weekend cruise by an absentee owner. But this one had the robust, smart and tidy look of a boat with a lot of miles under her keel. The master berth was a comfortable double bunk – approximately the size of my entire cockpit. I would have no trouble sleeping on it at all. If I did, then there wasn't any hope I'd be able to sleep on *Wanderer*.

'I know what you should do,' said Geoff. 'Go park your truck down in the boatyard – I know the guy there and that'll be all right for tonight – and then come back and we'll have some dinner. You hungry? Course you are. How about salmon – you like fish? With peas and corn. Yeah, that's the ticket, mate. You look a bit starved.'

'That'd be grea . . .'

'Hey, Sandy – show Lee the spare bathroom so he can have a shower if he wants. Make yourself at home, mate; help yourself to anything in the fridge – fancy a beer? I'd go a beer, Sandy – you want a drink? – maybe we'll open a wine, eh?'

Another bloke appeared – early thirties, big smile, suntan, golfing clothes.

'Lee, this is Dave – he's staying here, too, in the spare bedroom – that's why you're on the boat. He's a Pom, but he's all right. Aren't you, Dave – eh, you old bugger.' By now Geoff was mining for food

Geoff and Sandy, a bloody good bloke and his most excellent partner.

in the freezer cabinet and scattering ice on the kitchen floor. Sandy was pulling wine bottles out of a cupboard and Dave was offering me a smoke.

'Hey, Lee – Geoff said you was sailing a bloooody dingg-ey. Alone, eh? Mad basstards, you Kiwis. All of you. Do my 'ead in that would.'

'Oh, it's not that ba . . .'

Another English guy in his mid-thirties wandered into the kitchen.

'How do, Andy – this is Lee – he's another blooody Kiwi – beats me why the Yanks let 'em in. State of this fookin colony . . .'

'All right, Lee? – I'm in the flat

above,' Andy said as he shook hands. ''Ow'dja golf go, Dave? Break a hundred – or break a club?' he asked and they set to dissecting the round. Geoff was singing as he started cooking and Sandy was talking on the phone and turning up the stereo to drown out Geoff.

Clearly, keeping a conversation going wouldn't be something I had to work too hard at in this house. Talking was a competitive sport here.

That night I retired to my bunk on the yacht somewhat dazed by the speed and force of my welcome. As well as Geoff and Sandy I'd met Dave and Andy – both marine engineers on luxury yachts – along with John, a Canadian marine cabinetmaker, and Erin, his Australian wife. Mr Orr, it seemed, had quite a collection of itinerant friends and now he had added another.

The next day was typical of Florida at this time of year – perfect. Warm, sunny and flavoured with tropical garden scents. I put on shorts again and joined Dave for an early cup of coffee and a cigarette on the back porch. It was quiet and cool under the palm trees. We chatted for a bit and he said that since he was on holiday waiting for his girlfriend to arrive for Christmas, as soon as I had the boat unloaded he'd give me a hand to antifoul it. I'd planned to check out the cost of doing this at the local boatyard, since I didn't want to make a mess in Geoff's

yard or outstay my welcome. Dave warned me that Somerfield's Yard charged a lot and said that preparing the boat in the yard might be a whole lot easier and he assured me that Geoff wouldn't mind.

A few minutes later Geoff came roaring into the kitchen, banged a cup of coffee down and dashed out the door, yelling over his shoulder that he was late, he would call me here this afternoon to see what I needed and that I should tell Somerfield's that I was a mate of his and should ask for a discount. Then he was gone to the

Dave and his indelible smile.

sound of a slamming door. I soon learned that this was Geoff's normal method of departure for work – fast and late.

By noon I had talked with Somerfield's and done my sums. By the time I had paid their charges for unloading, daily yard rates, materials (which I had to buy through them at their prices) and then launching *Wanderer*, it would cost me about $450 for three days. That was outrageous, so after conferring with Dave I brought the truck back and we unloaded her in Geoff's front yard.

After unloading all my gear and stacking it on Geoff's empty trailer I spent the rest of the afternoon trying to rig *Wanderer*. Fitting the mast was easy. It slipped into the tabernacle and the pivot pin that secured it was simple enough to fit. The two shrouds also pinned onto the chainplates smoothly – though I was still appalled at how flimsy all the fittings were. It looked as if you could snap them by hand. Even Dave looked at them with raised eyebrows. Rigging the genoa stay was the next chore. In principle it was simple but the ropes left by Frank for this purpose had strange loops and splices in them that complicated things immensely.

I knew how things should work – the genoa stay had the roller

Wanderer *in Geoff's yard ready for rigging.*

furling mechanism mounted on it already and this was a permanent fixture. When you pulled on the rope leading from the reel at the bottom, the sail would furl itself by being wrapped around the genoa stay. This was a huge convenience for a solo sailor as it meant that I could raise or furl the genoa in less than two seconds just by pulling on either the genoa sheet or the furling line. And because I could partially furl the sail to give myself just the right amount of sail for any wind condition I didn't need a storm jib for bad weather.

But first I had to get the genoa stay secured. Normally it would be shackled permanently to the bow because this stay also supported the mast and prevented it from leaning backwards. Since the mast could pivot on its mounting pin in the tabernacle, it needed a tight genoa stay to keep it upright and to maintain the tension on the lateral shrouds. But for *Wanderer* I also needed to be able to lower and raise the whole mainmast occasionally so that I could slide under low bridges on the ICW. That meant that the genoa had to be tightly secured while sailing, but must be easily released too. Obviously I couldn't mess about with shackles and pins up on the bow. I needed to be able to stand at the tiller and raise or lower the mast from there.

The answer was a pulley, which was fitted at the bow already. I tied a rope to the deck cleat next to the mast and took it forward to the pulley on the bow. I threaded it around that and up to the shackle on the bottom of the genoa stay. Then back down round the other side of the pulley and back to the deck cleat where I secured it. I had about four metres of rope left, which I coiled. Now, to drop the mast all I had to do was to step forward to the mast, ease the main halyard and lower the mainsail a couple of feet, then slide the boom off its gooseneck and lay it in the bottom of the boat. Then I uncoiled the four metres of genoa stay rope, took it off the deck cleat, and as I stepped back to the tiller, I paid out the rope slowly and down came the mast with the mainsail still attached. Easy-peasy. The whole thing took about three minutes to raise or lower. With the mast down I could glide under a four-foot-high bridge.

Bright and early the next day, Dave and I flipped *Wanderer* over after I had de-rigged her mast. As she weighed only a few hundred pounds empty, she was quite easy to handle even by myself and later I flipped her back upright after the paint dried. To begin with, though, Dave sanded her down while I nipped down the road in my U-Haul truck (which I still had out for another three days) and bought paint and rollers and brushes. We then reapplied blue antifoul to her bottom. I took a look at the rudder blade too and I didn't like the way a sort of wavy hairline crack had fractured the varnish just below where it was inserted into the rudder mount. It looked weak to me and maybe a little rotten as well. I had read everything about Wayfarers on the Whiffle website (the Canadian Wayfarer Owners' Association). One article recommended applying fibreglass to the rudder and the centreboard to strengthen them. The rudders do have some stress applied and with a long tiller acting as a lever, the helmsman doesn't always appreciate how much force can be applied to the blade when steering. The centreboard is stood on by one or two crewmen when righting the boat after a capsize and as some folks stand on the tip, which is four feet from the hull aperture, it has to handle up to 300 pounds' weight at a fair distance from the fulcrum. Consequently, they sometimes snap off. Fibreglassing them would take some time and I was conscious of the number of people already occupying Geoff's house, so I scratched that idea for the time being.

Three days had passed now and I still hadn't sorted out the rigging problem. I finally sent an email to Frank asking for advice on how to set it up. I hadn't re-rigged the mast yet because I still hadn't got *Wanderer* in the water. She was upright and the paint was dry but Geoff's backyard didn't offer a suitable launching ramp and so I was looking about for a nearby free slipway. Even though *Wanderer* was so small, just tossing the boat off the bank was not a good idea because the water was too low in the river and she would either be damaged or would spear in nose first and fill up with water. Somerfield's Yard had no slipway – just a travel-lift boat crane that would cost $100 or so to use – even for such a little boat. Bugger that – so I thought I'd truck the boat to a ramp and then row it back to Geoff's dock and finish rigging it and install the motor there.

In the end, Dave took us to a boatyard he knew and persuaded them to let us slide her into the water from a causeway just outside the boatyard. We eased her down the ramp on rollers up to the water's edge, manoeuvred her past some big rocks and slipped her into the water. She floated high as she had no stores and no rigging. I fitted the oars and scrambled in while Dave hastily closed up the truck and got it out of the way. For the first time in a couple of years, *Wanderer* was back in the water and I was now in command of my own boat. Some sort of ceremony seemed to be in order but the wind was pushing me into some overhanging trees with sharp rocks in the water below, so instead the launching was accompanied only by some authentic naval swearing before I settled down to row her the two miles back to Geoff's place.

She slid through the water more easily than many wooden tenders half her size and I had no trouble moving her along. The wind died away, the sun blazed down and I steadily worked the oars from a comfortable seat amidships on the centre thwart. In about an hour, after passing under a couple of bridges and easing past half a dozen giant luxury motor yachts, I was nosing up to the dock at Geoff's place – the first trip was completed and my tally of sinkings and capsizes was an unblemished nil. So far so good!

~~~

THAT AFTERNOON, GEOFF arrived to take me shopping. He had local knowledge and I put it to good use. By teatime I had spent several hundred dollars and had more food and gear than I thought I could ever pack into the boat. Luckily most of the food was due to be consumed by us over the next few nights since I planned to cook my favourite (i.e. only) four dishes for the household. Geoff wouldn't hear of me paying board or rent or anything like that and their beer fridge was full so this was the only way I could think of contributing to the cost of my stay. Even so, it was miles cheaper and more convenient than staying in a motel. Geoff promised to look for a second-hand three to five-HP outboard motor for me and I searched the For Sale columns of papers and magazines as well. I'd settled on this tiny size of engine on the advice of Frank, and others I had contacted through the Whiffle site. Smaller motors offered less power for cruising and hence much slower speeds as well as less power in an emergency like bad weather or a strong opposing current, but they were also cheaper to buy, easier to mount and simpler to service. And the weight of a small engine wouldn't upset the balance of the boat or strain the hull when it hung off the back of the transom. So I opted for a teeny-weeny kicker to the considerable dismay of Geoff and everyone else. But they weren't Wayfarer sailors and I was following my self-imposed rule about taking advice from those who know.

I had no idea how to mount the motor and wasn't sure whether to approach the problem by finding a motor mount that would work for the motor and then fitting it to the boat so that it cleared the transom and the rudder and didn't foul the mainsheet, or by finding a shape that fitted the boat and then making it work with the motor. In the end I opted to buy the cheapest mount and try it out on the reasonable grounds that it was the cheapest mount and I was a cheap bastard at heart. If it worked, then good. If not, I'd have to look at a more expensive option. But first I needed a motor. Amazingly, given the thousands and thousands of boats in Fort Lauderale I really struggled to find a supplier of small engines. Eventually I settled on a slightly used and modestly discounted Mercury 3.3 HP from a West Marine chandlery shop. My plans to cook were stymied by Dave announcing that he was taking us out for a curry.

I spent all the next day fitting the motor mount. I tackled it much more carefully than usual since I didn't want to put any more holes in the hull than necessary. I followed the old rule of 'measure twice – cut once' and even after marking the positions for the mounting holes I deliberately went away and came back after a cup of coffee to look at the positioning of the mount for a second time before drilling. I was glad I did. Because the boat was in the water, I was standing on a short ladder that rested on the bottom of the canal. The boat was tied stern-on to the dock and I had removed the rudder so that it wouldn't get banged on the dock. While I was holding the engine mount in place with one hand, balancing on the ladder as it sunk unevenly into the mud and trying to pencil-mark the drill holes with the other hand, I managed to forget about the rudder. Now I noticed that when I turned too sharply starboard, it would bang on the mount. Bugger. I scrubbed away the pencil marks and began again. Basically the problem was that there were very few places to mount the engine. It had to be offset to avoid the rudder in the centre, but the transom was low and the hull curved under the sides so that there was little room to move it up or down, left or right. The whole time I was balancing on the ladder and pushing the mount against the stern to test it in various places, Newton's third law caused the boat to slide away from me and this caused me to overbalance and fall in the water. If I tightened the mooring ropes to stop the boat moving away, there wasn't room for me to get in behind the boat and do the work. Somehow I managed to mark various possible places for the four mounting bolts on the transom. Then I would check these by measuring their position on the outside from a single reference point. Then I would get into the boat, lie on the stern lockers and peer upside down into the stern locker and try to apply those measurements to the inside of the transom. Once I was fairly sure I had them re-created accurately on the inside, I could see if it was possible to get a spanner on the nuts to tighten them up. Mostly it wasn't possible. But if it was, then I had to check if they were mounted through the thicker part of the transom wall. If not, then they would only be secured to fibreglass three millimetres (an eighth of an inch) thick and that was no good. It didn't help that on the whole transom there was only one reference point (a single bolt) that was identifiable both inside and outside of the transom. It was very tempting to just drill one convenient central hole and use it as a reference point, but that would mean having to plug it later and I didn't think that was professional.

After four hours of fiddling, moving, measuring, marking and oc-casionally diving for my pencil, I gingerly took up Geoff's drill and made the four holes I needed. I carefully spread silicone on the bolts, nuts and washers, then tightened them up. The result looked good. It was level, low down (so the water intake for the motor would be far enough underwater) and three of four bolts were fastened securely to the thicker parts of the transom. The rudder swung freely in both directions and it seemed to me that I'd done a good job. All I needed to do later on was to cut a piece of half-inch plywood to fit as a backing plate to the one bolt that went through a thin part of the transom, but that could wait. For now, I wanted to fit the engine and go for a spin. I attached the outboard, carefully followed all the instructions for starting it and gave it a pull. Nothing. Not even a cough.

Two hours, three phone calls and some bad language later I was back at West Marine arguing for a refund or a replacement. Bearing in mind the discount I'd got the used engine at originally, I wasn't too upset when they finally agreed to give me a brand-new one, still in its box, for just an extra $30. I took it home, popped it on the back, choked it, gave it a pull and with a healthy kick it buzzed into life. *Wanderer* was under power now for the first time in her life.

I didn't have time to take her for a spin, though, as I was late for dinner. That night Dave and I joined John and Erin for a meal at a steakhouse. At least Dave let me pay for his meal to thank him for the use of his car over the previous three days. We finished the night drinking with Geoff, Sandy, Dave, John, Erin, Andy and their many other friends. I wasn't allowed to buy a single beer. 'Keep your money for the trip,' they all said. I didn't know what to say, but I resolved to cook a fabulous meal the next night, which would be my last in Fort Lauderdale. I wanted to set off bright and early on Sunday morning as I'd only ever planned to stay four days at Geoff's, and here it was nearly a week and I still hadn't rigged the boat or loaded stores. Tomorrow would be busy.

Rigging the mast on Saturday was easy enough and although I hadn't received an answer yet from Frank about how he secured the genoa stay, I just rigged it how I wanted it and knew it would work. Then a new problem emerged. Once I had the genoa stay up, I threaded the mainsail into the mast groove and raised it. That worked fine so I began rigging the reefing lines. Try as I might, I couldn't see how Frank had set them up. I knew how they could work and should work, but when I threaded the ropes through the existing leads and cleats I could tell from the wear patterns on the fittings that the ropes were running backwards to the way Frank had set them. Geoff couldn't figure it out either and so eventually I just said 'the hell with it', and switched the fittings around and rigged the simplest lines I could. I tested them and they worked and that was how they stayed for the rest of the trip.

Loading *Wanderer* up with stores was an exercise in confusion. Unlike camping, I had no clear idea which stores I would use regularly and which would seldom be touched, so stowing the pile of food, clothing, sleeping gear, cooking equipment, boat stores, tools, spares, flares, navigation equipment and toiletries was a chore. I got it all in with few crannies spare but I knew I would spend plenty of time reorganising it later on. I freely confess to being an unnaturally tidy person – especially for a bloke. If things are in a mess, I'm unhappy. I want things to have places and to be in them at all times – not because I'm a control freak, but because I hate wasting time looking for things. My army training has taught me to expect the worst and to be ready for it. That means having instant access to whatever equipment you possess and might need to handle the emergency. On a boat that is in constant danger of being swamped or capsized it doesn't help to have a lot of gear loosely lying around either. Since I anticipated that this trip would consist mostly of a series of wrecks and emergencies it seemed to me that stowing things correctly would be a big safety feature. It is not, repeat NOT because I am an anal-retentive, obsessive-compulsive, control freak as Adrienne has been known to mutter. I'm just tidy and well prepared and the world would be a better place if there were more people like me.

Got that?

Rigging and stowing and some last-minute shopping with Dave were all I had time for that day as Geoff and Sandy and the household crew were off to a pre-Christmas barbecue at a South African friend's home and I was invited too. My big meal for the house wouldn't get cooked after all. Instead, I met another collection of Geoff's friends, and once again found that my money didn't work and I couldn't buy them a beer.

I spent the whole time talking about the trip to strangers who seemed terribly interested in it. Looking back I can see how odd the adventure must have seemed. At the time, the plan seemed full of common sense and practicality. It sprang from a series of deductions on my part that gave the whole adventure a strong internal logic. I was afraid of the sea and felt that prolonged exposure to it would help overcome that fear. At the same time I would learn to sail. To reduce overall costs I reduced the size of the boat. That in turn restricted my cruising options to coastal waters and eliminated the need for crew – hence I would sail alone. From the inside looking out, it was all very simple and sensible.

But from the outside looking in, it was all very simple and crazy. Clearly I was some sort of disaster in the making and who could resist looking at that? I must have had all the fascination of a sputtering fuse on its way to a barrel of gunpowder.

Nearly sailing

SUNDAY 22 DECEMBER. Up at 4.00 am to pack my gear and tidy up the litter I'd made while working on the boat. Dave and I nipped out in his car to buy fresh bread and I brewed strong coffee for my thermos flask and concentrated on stowing my food and perishables and my dried laundry aboard *Wanderer.* I kept out a tiny bottle of champagne sent to me by Adrienne in my Christmas parcel so that I could launch the trip in the correct style. All the guys who had helped me get *Wanderer* ready hopped in the boat and we sprayed the tiny bottle around while Sandy took our picture. Geoff gave me a 'Yacht Chandlers' company baseball cap to wear and I put it on top of my own cap for the photos. I decided I would save it for best-wear occasions as it now had sentimental value to me. Sandy gave me a big bag of designer chocolates to help ward off scurvy and slimness. Dave gave me a punch in the stomach and Andy said I was a twat. I had no idea they were so emotional. Then, while I stayed aboard *Wanderer,* they climbed onto Geoff's yacht.

The plan was that Geoff and crew aboard his yacht *Braveheart* would motor ahead of me down the river to Port Everglades while I puttered along behind. They'd go through all the bridges and get them open for me so I didn't have to worry about that − I could just get used to driving *Wanderer* under power, which was still something I hadn't yet done. My testing of the engine after I bought it hadn't included time to cast off and practise handling it − I'd just run it in place for a few

Champagne farewell – Andy, Lee, Geoff, Dave.

minutes. How hard could it be to control 16 feet of boat and 3.3 HP?

By lunchtime we were ready to cast off and they moved slowly down the canal and around the corner onto the river while I untied *Wanderer* and followed them. At this point, a few neighbours had gathered in their backyards – attracted by the noise and laughter from the canal – and so there were plenty of witnesses on both banks to watch my departure. They saw me pop the outboard confidently into gear, then rev it up heartily, turn the tiller and immediately blast straight across the narrow canal and smack smartly into the other concrete wall. Amazed by the acceleration, and surprised by the lack of turning despite having the tiller hard over, I took a moment to recover and in that time I bounced off the bank, accidentally managed to turn the bow downstream, scraped along the bulkhead, ricocheted off a dock piling and narrowly missed another moored boat before turning the wrong way at the corner and heading up another canal.

A few seconds later the spectators saw me come whizzing back, keeping well to the side of the channel for safety, but forgetting that my mast was above me, as I tore some smaller branches from an overhanging tree with the shrouds. I lurched back into the middle of the canal as a gentle shower of leaves descended into the turbid water behind me. Trying to put the best face on it, I turned calmly back to the gaping neighbours and waved serenely with one hand as I tried to throttle the engine up with the other. Instead, I grabbed the choke and by moving this I managed to flood the engine and stall it. Momentum carried me out of sight of the neighbours and all they heard a moment later was the sound of me sawing away with the starter cord as I re-fired in a cloud of smoke. It wasn't my grandest moment, but I had taken the first step of the journey and they say that's the hardest one.

Braveheart idled around the bend of the river waiting for me and soon I tucked in behind her and began the eight-mile journey down to the port where I would turn south on the ICW towards Miami and Key West, while they turned east onto the Atlantic to go sailing for the afternoon. I organised myself a little better and concentrated on steering a safe course. This wasn't all that easy as *Wanderer* certainly didn't answer the helm willingly. She seemed to turn very slowly and this was unwelcome because there was a lot of traffic on the river as big and little boats set out for Sunday cruises.

The New River also has many bascule bridges on it – these are the kind that open in the middle to allow spectacular car chases to be filmed in which the hero leaps his car across the chasm. There are hundreds of these bridges on the ICW and about half of them will open on request for any size boat that wants to pass through them. Others open only at specific times, mainly coinciding with commuter rush hour, and boats must queue up and wait to pass through. Fort Lauder-dale has lots of traffic so we had to wait for several bridges to open, but this simply meant slowing down to an idle and drifting up to the bridge, or occasionally having to motor in small circles for a while. These bridges were fairly low – less than 20 feet above the water – and I took 23 and a half feet to the top of the mast and *Braveheart* needed over 50 feet.

At this point I should make something clear to readers about the metric system and the terminology used in this book. I am bi-scalar and can happily think in both metric and imperial measurements but the rest of the world prefers metric measurements. The rest of the world except for three countries, that is – Liberia (that famous home of cutting-edge technology), Myanmar (the cradle of free thinking) and . . . the USA. It may astound American readers to discover that the other 200-plus countries of the world can agree on something, but they have, and the thing they've agreed on is the metric system. In fact, it's the only thing they've agreed on. Anyway, the US is allegedly bi-scalar too, but they still cling to quaint measurements like pounds, feet, poles, acres, fahrenheits, hundredweights, short tons and quintains (a type of small migratory bird used to measure the width of canvas, in case you were wondering).

But since our story takes place in the USA, I shall adopt the habits of the natives, and from now on my progress will be measured in miles and feet and hogsheads and so on. Regular statute miles, too – not those silly nautical miles. On that subject, quite a lot of that jargon exists in nautical circles and so perhaps I should now explain a few terms that will be widely employed in this book:

Anchor   honestly, if you don't know what this is you have no business reading this book.

Berth   a place to sleep. On *Wanderer*, a patch of floor on the port side furnished at night with two self-inflating sleeping mats and a sleeping bag.

Bilge   the area underneath the floorboards used to keep beer cool.

Boom   1. the horizontal pole that extends from the bottom of the mast and to which the bottom of the mainsail is attached. 2. a light wind-change indicator that works by tapping the sailor smartly on the temple to show that the breeze has backed or veered a little. 3. a gybe-reporting device that works by smacking the sailor hard upside the head to tell him that he has just gybed. 4. the ridge pole for the boom tent.

Boom tent the canvas shelter erected each night over the boom and fastened to a line running around the hull.

Boom vang a rope that hauls the boom downwards in order to ensure that the mainsail stays tight and aerodynamically efficient. Also known as a kicking strap because it stops the boom from kicking up.

Bow/stem pointy end – the front of the boat.

Bow locker(s) watertight storage cupboards located forward of the mast and not normally accessed during the day when sailing alone.

Broach a large step towards a wreck roughly akin to a four-wheel sideways drift in loose gravel just before the car hits the ditch causing a capsize. Occurs when sliding too fast down a wave.

Capsize the overturning of a small boat in the water caused by a head-on collision between said craft and the laws of probability. Usually caused by inattention in gusty winds or overzealous trimming of the sails while racing.

Centreboard the pivoting and retractable keel-like device that pokes down through the bottom of the boat and helps keep the craft upright and on course. Acts to provide stability like the fin on the back of a cruising shark (and incidentally, like a shark's fin, when also seen above the waves is a sign that things are going horribly wrong for the person in the water next to it).

Centrecase the narrow box-like structure that rises inside the cockpit from the slot in the bottom of the boat through which the centreboard pokes down. Because the centrecase is higher than the water level outside the boat (which is controlled by laws of nature and isn't just a lucky fluke), it stops water from pouring in through the slot in the bottom and sinking the boat. Also a convenient place to drop small valuable items that you wish to be permanently rid of.

Cleats a fitting used to secure a line by tying it to or by wedging it inside same.

Cockpit the inexplicably **undecked portion** of the hull (in a Wayfarer comprising about 80 percent of the craft), conveniently left open so as to provide a suitable aperture for the slow disposal of up to a ton of seawater by a sailor armed with a five-gallon bucket. Also a portal by which a ton of seawater can enter in an instant.

Compass a device to blame when lost.

Furling a tidy way of **putting away a foresail** by wrapping it around its stay, thereby achieving the same effect as reefing, but more completely.

Flaking a less tidy but unavoidable way of **putting away a mainsail** by gathering it and laying it along the boom in large pleats, creating a zigzag pattern. It is then secured with small ropes or bungies.

Galley the **kitchen of the boat.** On *Wanderer* located as needed on the floor just forward of the stern locker and comprising the pressure stove, a billy, a spoon and not much else.

Genoa the **smaller sail** on the boat that hangs from the genoa stay in front of the mast. Just like a jib but a bit bigger.

Genoa stay the **wire** that runs from the mast down to the bow from which the genoa hangs, and which also supports the roller furling mechanism. It also stops the mast falling backwards. An important wire.

Gooseneck a flexible **fitting that attaches the boom** to the mast. It allows the boom to swivel left and right as well as up and down and, unless the boom vang is tightened, also allows it to slide off the fitting and fall into the bottom of the boat when the sail is lowered.

GPS 1. a **magical box** used by sailors, pilots, hikers, nuclear missiles, etc., to find their position on the face of the earth. 2. an enormous **boon** to society that has saved countless lives and prevented much wasted effort, provided free to an ungrateful world by Uncle Sam at a cost to the US taxpayer of many billions of dollars.

Halyard   the **rope** that runs up the mast, **used to haul the mainsail up** to the top of the mast. In this case it could also be used as a topping lift to hold up the boom when the sail is not engaged.

Head   on fancy boats a **five-gallon container of expensive chemicals used for toileting.** Formerly a simple flush toilet that discharged overboard but that now, due to environmental legislation,

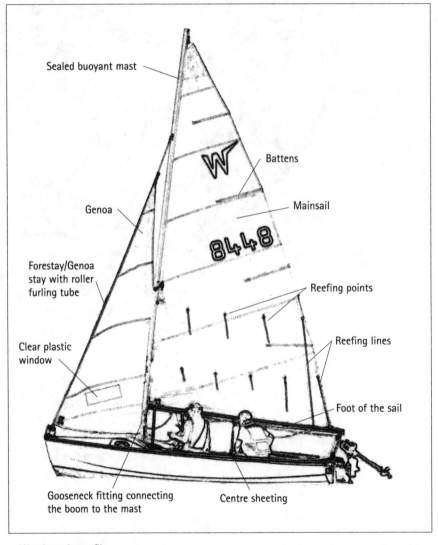

Wanderer in profile.

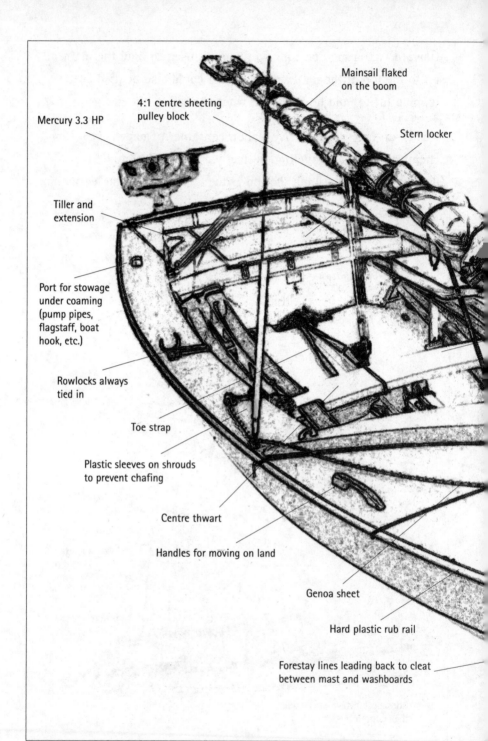

Mainsail flaked on the boom

4:1 centre sheeting pulley block

Mercury 3.3 HP

Stern locker

Tiller and extension

Port for stowage under coaming (pump pipes, flagstaff, boat hook, etc.)

Rowlocks always tied in

Toe strap

Plastic sleeves on shrouds to prevent chafing

Centre thwart

Handles for moving on land

Genoa sheet

Hard plastic rub rail

Forestay lines leading back to cleat between mast and washboards

Wanderer's deck layout.

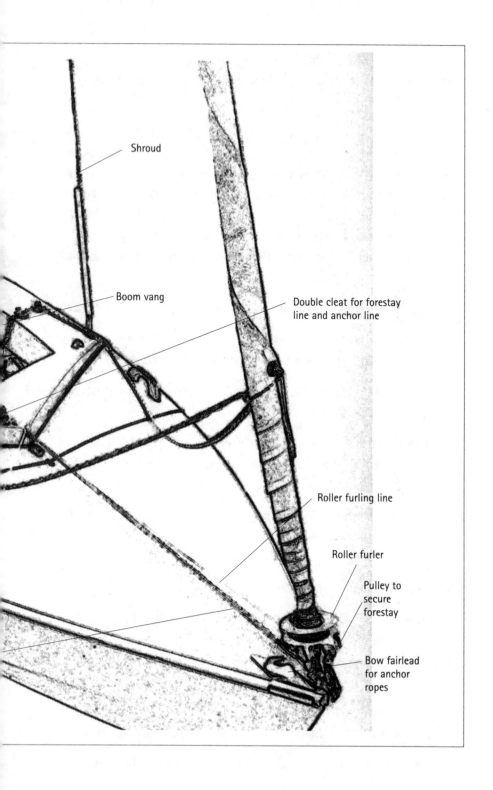

Shroud

Boom vang

Double cleat for forestay
line and anchor line

Roller furling line

Roller furler

Pulley to
secure
forestay

Bow fairlead
for anchor
ropes

must discharge to a holding tank for later disposal on land. Replaced on *Wanderer* with an unfixed three-gallon **Tupperware container** clandestinely flushed overboard.

Hull   the **bathtub**-shaped assembly of $^1/_8$ inch-thick fibreglass that serves the opposite purpose to a bath. By repelling the entire ocean and keeping it at all times a mere pencil-leadth away from the sailor, it gives the mariner: **a.** a degree of **seaworthiness** that is hard to believe; **b. somewhere to paint** a witty name ie. *$ea Note, Meandher, O'Debt*; **c.** an **identifiable cost centre** for tax purposes. Without this the sailor would just be randomly buying chandlery to no plan and would also have nowhere to store it.

Mainsail   the **biggest sail** on the boat that hangs behind the mast.

Mainstays/shrouds   the **two side wires** that run from the mast down to the side decks and which keep the mast upright.

Mast   the big **upright pole** in the centre of the boat that exists to hang the mainsail off.

Outboard motor   a **propulsion device** frequently used but always under-reported by sailors. On *Wanderer* speeds ranged from *too fast* in an anchorage, to *barely enough* in a heavy sea or strong current.

Port/starboard   left and **right** side of the boat respectively when looking from the stern to the bow.

Reefing   a way of **reducing the amount of sail** exposed to the wind by gathering some of it in and securing it to the boom or genoa stay.

Reefing points   shoelace-like **strings on the mainsail** used to tie a lower portion of it to the boom after the sail has been partially lowered because of strong winds.

Roller furler   a **reefing and furling device** by which the genoa can be made to wrap itself around the genoa stay in the manner of a roller window blind simply by pulling on a rope connected to a reel.

Rudder   the **steering blade** that hangs down behind the transom.

Sheets fancy name for any **rope used to trim a sail,** i.e. mainsheet, genoa sheet.

Stern **blunt end** – the back of the boat.

Stern locker the watertight **boot or trunk** at the back of the boat, handily located and easily accessible at all times.

Tabernacle the fixed **base housing** for the mast which allows the mast to pivot from horizontal to vertical around an axle pin driven through the tabernacle.

Thwarts rigid and unyielding surfaces (hence 'thwarted') upon which an inexperienced sailor can sit and worry, also known as **seats.**

Tiller 1. the **long handle** that is used to turn the rudder from side to side. 2. **something to foul the reefing lines** when flaking the sail thereby temporarily eliminating all forms of steering control and precipitating a **wreck.**

Transom the **back wall** of the boat where you would attach the number plate and tow bar if it were a car.

Trimming **adjusting the sails** to make them work better by pulling them in tighter or letting them out.

Washboards on the deck just forward of the mast, the washboards stand upright allegedly to deflect water that comes over the bow, over the sides so that it doesn't pour back into the cockpit.

Wreck nautical milestones charting the progress of novice sailors: 'I had a wreck there, and there, and twice over there and now I think we have one here.'

And that's about all the gibberish needed to understand the layout and equipment of *Wanderer*.

I was still puttering along behind *Braveheart* as we made our way down to the port. Occasionally I waved to Sandy or Geoff, but mainly I tried to follow my progress on the small chartbook of the ICW, which I would use to navigate the 35 miles or so south to Miami. It gave a lot of information about the river and canals and the ICW, but the detail it provided did not include larger views of the surrounding areas and it was a little claustrophobic. After an hour or so we came to the entrance to the turning basin. This is where big ships manoeuvre before docking, and every large port has one. They tend to be large, open, windy areas with plenty of chop thrown up by vessels, but this one was calm and smooth. Just beyond it to the east was the channel leading onto the Atlantic Ocean. To the south of it was the ICW where I was headed. While Geoff and company waited for the big bascule bridge near the northern entrance to open and let them into the basin, I drew up beside them and said my goodbyes. I could easily pass under the bridge without waiting 30 minutes for its next scheduled opening. Sandy blew me a kiss and the others waved and took photos as I bimbled past them. The last I heard was 'good luck' as I slowly drew under the bridge and into the turning basin. I should have felt more emotional at saying goodbye to such marvellously helpful and generous new friends, but in fact I was preoccupied with the business of nauticating.

Fort Lauderdale is home to many big cruise ships that ply the Caribbean and I had to sail right past them in order to get to the quieter ICW channel. A few of them had security patrols that approached in inflatable dinghies and reminded me to keep 200 feet

The first of hundreds of bascule bridges to pass through.

away from the liners, but aside from that they presented no problem. But that didn't stop me worrying about them.

In fact, worrying was my chief occupation for the early days of the trip and if it seems hard to believe that I could worry about anything when in such a simple craft, in warm, calm waters, inside a friendly harbour, then all I can say is that it seems weird to me now, too. It's like learning to drive a car – things that are really safe or simple seem hard and scary at first. But at this early stage I managed to worry about whether I was obeying the rules of the sea (broadly speaking the same as the rules of the road, i.e. keep right) and whether I was navigating correctly through the port towards the ICW or whether I was headed up a forbidden wastewater canal to the intake valve of a nuclear power plant. I worried about the engine suddenly stopping for any reason and leaving me to drift onto rocks or under the bow of an ocean liner. I worried about dropping something valuable overboard like my VHF radio, my GPS or myself. I worried about the fact that I hadn't used the sail yet and the trip was already two hours old.

In the background were the familiar latent worries about rogue waves, whales and katabatic wind gusts (granted they're not exactly common in the flattest state in the union, but tornadoes are a handy substitute for the unhinged mind). When I got tired of worrying about these I worried about running out of gas, about why I hadn't been able to set the rigging up as Frank had it, about whether my money would hold out for the trip and about the size of the wake thrown up by a passing motorboat.

In between these concerns I fretted over the looseness of various parts of the rigging, my inability to tell how much gas I had used, the slow progress I was making, the lack of peace in the Middle East, New Zealand's prospects in the next Rugby World Cup, and the fact that I'd been sailing for three hours now and had only just noticed that the centreboard was retracted.

That explained the crappy steering so far! Without a centreboard down, *Wanderer* didn't turn – she just skidded across the top of the water the way an airplane will skid sideways if it tries to turn without banking first. The centreboard bites into the water and gives the hull traction. I pushed it down and held it in place with the bungy cord provided for that purpose and tried a few slalom turns. Much better. That was one less thing to worry about, but as soon as it dropped from the list, three more sprang up: would I make it to a mooring site before dark, would my pressure lantern and pressure stove work (I hadn't yet tested them), and where the hell was I now?

I put the ICW chartbook on my knees and studied it, looking for clues. There weren't many features to refer to on land and none of them appeared in the book either, so I couldn't take my hand-held compass and do a resection. Nor did the shape of the canal show any identifiable bends or junctions. I was busy trying to assess how far I had come when I looked up and saw I was aimed at the bank. It was a friendly mud bank with no rocks to sink me but even so I steered away and took out my hand-held GPS to see if it was working. It took a moment to warm up and gather its information from the satellites overhead before it produced a position in latitude and longitude. I looked up from this and noticed that I was aimed at the bank again. Even though I was trying to steer a straight course while fiddling with the GPS, it seemed that steering was a full-time occupation all by itself. I corrected my course and set about plotting my position. By the time I had this marked on the chart − bingo, there I was, nosing into the bank again. What was it with this boat? Why couldn't it keep itself out in the channel? Why this fascination with land? Homesick for a barn in Ottawa?

I took her into the middle of the channel and started packing away the GPS into the stern locker where it lived in a Tupperware box. By the time I'd done this, I was nosing into the weeds again. Clearly, a boat wasn't like a car, in that you couldn't steer with your knees and you couldn't rely on the craft to keep a fairly straight course at all. In fact, it swung all over the place if you showed the least inattention. But at least I now knew where I was.

I have to say that in all the months that followed I never really found a way of leaving *Wanderer* to steer herself under power unless I tied the tiller (which seldom worked very well either), and only rarely could I balance her sails so that she would steer straight ahead under these. Although I learned to keep an eye on my course and keep steering while doing things like chartwork, making sandwiches or getting dressed in foul-weather gear, I was handicapped if I tried to do anything that involved moving from my position aft near the tiller.

Mostly, I wanted to leave the tiller for a moment to go forward and get something from the green canvas bags that were fastened under the coaming just aft of the bow lockers. These were handy, dry places to keep things like my camera, transistor radio, chewing tobacco, and so on – a sort of glove compartment. But even if I carefully balanced everything so that *Wanderer* kept a straight course, as soon as I stepped forward two yards, she veered off course. Bugger!

Back to correct her, then wait until she settled and then tentatively ease forward. Evvvver so slowwwly, like she was teasing me, she'd curve off course. Back to correct her, then I'd try again. Same thing – the subtle promise to maintain course while I edged forward, and then while I rummaged in the bag, the sudden turn to port or starboard.

I tried to dash forward and back. I could make it, but not if I lingered at the other end – if I did, she'd turn quite sharply back on herself. The answer was slow in coming but within a few days I had figured it out. For a while I blamed her erratic course-keeping on inopportune water currents and shifting winds, but actually it was a shifting skipper that did it. The wiggly course was due to changes in her trim caused by moving my body weight to a different position. *Wanderer* was so sensitive to shifts like this that eventually I could steer her just by moving my weight from one foot to the other when standing. I could make a gentle course correction of about 5–15 degrees just by shifting my body to one side or the other by as little as the width of my foot. The effect worsened as I moved farther forward, which was why it seemed that *Wanderer* was taunting me by not reacting until I was out of reach of the tiller.

So there it was – lesson one. It was a couple of weeks before I nutted it out, but when I did, it was quite satisfying. For the time being, I did the dash and scrabble if I needed to go forward. Other lessons were starting, too. *Wanderer* was going to put me through an intensive course of instruction in the next two days.

87

Chapter

8

On a one-way
moped to oblivion

I RAN OUT of gas about five minutes later. Two coughs and the wee Mercury stopped. Immediately I noticed that I didn't drift onto rocks or get carried along by the current – I just drifted to a halt and then rocked gently in the afternoon heat. The silence was quite surprising, too. Even though it was only a little engine it made quite a bit of noise and the absence of that racket was a pleasant change. Both sides of the waterway were lined with trees – scrubby dense pines and other vegetation that looked quite rural. I could see birds – herons in the water, pelicans on it and nameless dive-bomber birds above it. There were signs warning of manatees in the water, restricting boats to a 'No Wake' speed. These were the first of thousands of signs in the waterway between north Florida and Key West. Since at full power I threw up only a three-inch wake, and at my normal cruising speed of four to five mph (about 40 percent of power according to my throttle position) I made no wake at all, this wasn't an issue for me.

Motoring in *Wanderer* was exactly like riding a moped on the road. I was slower and smaller than every other craft so I got jostled around by the wind of their progress. But when I had the sails up I felt the virtuous sense of superiority that inflates the chests of cyclists who are doing it the hard way while others use a motor. For now, though, I was crouched behind the handlebars of the moped, so to speak.

In front of and behind me were numbered channel markers whose position was recorded on the charts. Green ones were to be kept on my left and red on my right. The waterway rules said that I should do this all the way south down the ICW to Galveston, Texas. Heading in the other direction – towards the start of the ICW in Norfolk, Virginia, I should do the reverse. These waterway rules were separate and differed from the normal rules of coastal navigation in the USA, which in turn differ from those in the rest of the world. It wasn't hard to remember the right thing to do since the position of the marker in relation to the shore was a dead giveaway. And the waterway at this point was fairly narrow – only about 100 yards wide – so it was easy to see where to steer for the deepest water, right down the middle, veering to the right-hand side to give way to oncoming traffic.

It was awkward perching on the stern locker to hold the re-fuelling tank above the engine but I didn't want to lean on the engine itself for stability as that would add 180 pounds to the weight that the engine mount had to carry and that wouldn't do it or the transom any good. I also decided to take Geoff's advice and carry five gallons of gas instead of two in future.

By now it was three o'clock and I wanted to look for a place to stop for the night so that I had time to try out my lantern and stove before dark. I'd noticed a nook on the ICW that was marked with an anchorage symbol, and according to my reckoning this was only a mile or two ahead – just past another bascule bridge that recorded a height of 22 feet. As I approached it I pulled out my new VHF hand-held marine radio and clipped it to my lifejacket. I was paranoid about dropping it and my expensive GPS overboard and I always clipped them to my jacket so that if I leaned forward and they slipped out of my jacket pocket they wouldn't report their bid for freedom with a small splash that would sound exactly like $400 dissolving on contact with water. At this time, I also obeyed the engine maker's instructions to keep the safety toggle cord attached to my body so that if I accidentally fell overboard, it would pop the kill switch and my engine would stop and

I wouldn't see it and my boat disappearing over the horizon. The problem here was that as soon as I moved forward for any reason the cord tightened, the kill switch worked and the engine stopped. By the end of the next day I'd canned that idea and instead I clipped the toggle cord to the transom so that I could yank it if I needed to stop the engine in a hurry.

I'm familiar with radios from my time in the army but my VHF was a big improvement over my previous ones. It had cost US$260 at the West Marine shop in Fort Lauderdale and that was with Geoff's discount. It worked flawlessly for months. It was so economical with power consumption that I only recharged the battery every three weeks or so and never even used the backup AA cell battery pack at all. I could say nothing bad about that radio – unlike every radio I used in the army, about which I could say nothing good. So it was no trouble to call up the bridge and ask them to open for me. I'd heard other boats do this as I came down the river and I repeated their calls.

'Sheridan Street Bridge, this is little sailboat *Wanderer* approaching from the north. Are you able to open for me in a few minutes, please? Over.'

'This is Sheridan Street Bridge. Yes, Captain. As soon as I see you, I'll open.'

Wow! *Captain*. Me! I hadn't expected to be called Captain, especially since I had such a teeny boat. I soon learned that the size of the boat and the absence of experience of the skipper makes no difference to the bridge tender – everyone is a captain and they'll stop eight lanes of freeway traffic for five minutes just to let me through, exactly as if I was the *Queen Mary*. Oooh, the power!

As I got closer I could see the dipstick attached to the bridge fender that recorded the water height below the lowest point of the bridge. Because it was not quite high tide, it said 24 feet and that would have been enough for me to get through without an opening. Oh well, something to check before going under the next bridge. As soon as I motored under the open span I turned to the east into a tiny anchorage about the size of half a football field. It was a keyhole-shaped bay just to the side of the channel, surrounded by trees and quite private. At the entrance were a few small houses with docks and large motor cruisers tied up to them. One dinghy was tied to a tree on shore, but I had all the mooring space to myself. I decided to buy some more gas first so I motored to the shore, nosed into the sandy bank and tied off to a tree branch. After topping up the gas tank on the engine I walked up to one of the nearby houses and called out to a lady who was sunbathing on the porch. She gave me directions to the closest gas station, and with my red plastic can in hand, I set off to walk there. It was about a mile and a half but soon after I had crossed the bascule bridge over the waterway I saw a little red pickup truck come towards me beeping its horn and flashing its lights. It was the lady who'd given me directions and she said she had needed to go to the store too, so would I like a lift?

'You bet – and thank you very much.'

Her name was Anna, she was from Michigan, on holiday in Florida and she was planning a long cruise by herself in her boat too, but was waiting for a replacement engine part and envied the fact that I was already sailing south. We chatted away while we drove to the gas station where I wanted to also buy another two-gallon gas tank. They didn't have one, but they had something better – two one-gallon tanks. Because they were lighter, they were easier to pour with one hand, and if I dropped one or got water in it, I wouldn't lose so much fuel. And they were easier to stow under the seats where they would be accessible during the day. Anna dropped me by my boat with her good wishes and I pushed off the shore with my paddle.

On this first afternoon I puttered around in circles like a dog looking to lie down, before I found the perfect spot where I would catch the last of the evening sun and the first of the dawn light as well. The water was shallow – about 12 feet – and as it was a dead-end cove there would be no current to fight. I anchored quickly and set about making camp.

Boom crutch in position, ready to anchor.

Getting the bugs out of the system.

The evening was mild and mosquito-free, so after replacing the mantle on the Coleman pressure lamp, I tested it and the pressure stove. Both worked fine and I made a sandwich for dinner and settled down to write my diary. To do this comfortably I had to first make my bed and within two days I had figured out the routine that I would follow until the end of the trip. Putting up the tent was the first step. I took it from its bag beneath the port-side forward seat and laid it across the boom, which was resting in the wooden boom crutch. The crutch was originally a complex affair made of several pieces of wood and designed to work with Frank and Margaret's larger boom tent. I just had their small triangular tent, so I simplified the crutch until it was just two pieces of wood joined towards the top end by a bolt with a wing nut on it to tighten up easily. These pieces of wood formed two sides of a triangle and the boom rested in the joint at the top. The legs of the crutch were spread and slotted into the gutter between the stern locker and the transom. For safety I also tied a loop of string to it and flipped the loop over a cleat on the transom so that if I knocked it over when taking down the tent it wouldn't float away. Once the crutch was

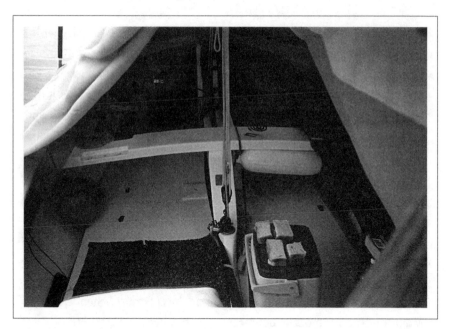

Snug as a bug in a rug.

up and the boom rested on top of it, I could cinch it down tight just by pulling on the mainsheet and cleating it off. It took perhaps 10 seconds to get the crutch out from its place beneath the starboard seat and put it in place with the boom on it. Then I could unroll the tent, drape it over the boom and secure its bottom edges to the line that ran around the hull. The tent had a collar that tied tightly around the mast. If I expected heavy rain I would wrap duct tape around the collar to keep drips from running down the mast, inside the collar and into the boat. The forward edges of the tent were secured well forward of the washboards. The rest of it draped over the side of the boat and was held down by Velcro straps that looped around a thin line that permanently circled the hull. The tent also had some hooks fitted to back up the Velcro and these attached to the hull line too. At the back, the tent door was simply a split down the middle that was closed by a wide Velcro strip. It had a window at each end that consisted of fine mesh to keep out no-see-ums.

No-see-ums are fiendishly aggressive midges that come out at dusk and dawn to feed. These little bastards are a wonder of nature. So small that you can hardly see them, they are nevertheless equipped with a bite that can irritate the hell out of creatures a million times their size. Having sunk their teeth into you and made you jump, knock the end off your cigarette and spill your coffee, they extract about a single molecule of blood before burping and flying heavily off to find a spot to snooze while they digest their stolen goods. Their bite is so far out of proportion to their size and the amount of blood they steal that it's like a single terrorist, armed with a nuclear bomb, holding up the entire city of New York and demanding a nickel ransom before going away. The good news is that they're lazy. They only work for an hour a day, at about the same time as the mozzies. This is most unlike New Zealand's West Coast sandflies and mosquitoes, which operate a coordinated 'Shock and Awe' style around-the-clock assault. The tent was only partially successful in keeping insects out – hence Frank's Maginot line of mozzie defences. I just relied on Bug Off or Deet to cover me for the critical hour or so each night and then I went to bed with the lantern on. Wave after wave of bugs would fly into the hot lantern and drop to the deck, neatly crisped. All in all, it wasn't

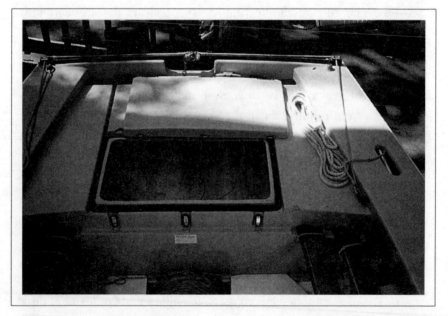

The capacious, watertight stern locker.

too bad and they certainly didn't come out every night. A good breeze always kept them away and many locations didn't seem to support them.

After the tent was up, out came my bed. I began by undoing the single wing nut that held down the long rear seat on the port side. This allowed me to lift it out of its slot and stow it on top of the seat on the starboard side. Then I took the large roller fender from under the seat and put it out of the way on the starboard floor up forward. I took the two oars from under the seat and laid them atop the starboard seat. That left just the one-gallon gas tank on the port side and it was far enough down towards my legs that it didn't bother me. I had then cleared my bed space. The next step was to lay down two of my three self-inflating mattresses and unroll one of my two sleeping bags. Then I took an uncovered foam seat cushion that Brian McCleery had given me and propped it up against the forward edge of the stern locker. With plenty of padding under me and some cushioning behind my back it was as comfortable as a recliner chair. I could sit up and cook, eat, read, write my diary or just look at the scenery, listen to the birds and ponder what the poor folks might be doing right now. If I reached behind me into the stern locker I could pull out food, drinks, VHF radio to listen to the weather forecast or my transistor radio to listen to music or to NPR – the national public radio station network that was the American version of New Zealand's National Programme or the BBC. I had books to read, charts to study and navels to contemplate. If I wanted a beer I could reach down to my knees, pull open the little trap that gave access to the self-bailing fitting in the bilge and feel around for a cool can.

In Florida, the weather was so warm at the start that dinner was mainly fruit, candy and sandwiches. They were easy to prepare, and even though I had no ice or other cooling material aboard, as long as I kept my cheese, sliced ham and bread dry, it stayed fresh for up to five days. After eating, I could smoke, burp, fart and pee over the side with a minimum of concern about what anyone thought. If I was in a crowded anchorage I could use the bucket or bailer in the privacy of the tent. I eventually got so expert that I could take a pee in the bailer without leaving my bed. This, though it may alarm some readers, was perfectly hygienic and put me very close to a bloke's idea of heaven.

When it got dark I would set the lantern on the locker lid behind me, pull the boom tent closed and settle down to read until I was drowsy. Florida in winter takes a little getting used to. For a start, it was as warm as an Auckland summer, but it still got dark soon after 5 pm. This felt strange, since I associate warm days with long summer evenings, but I adapted to the early nights – mainly because I was so tired from all the sailing that I would fall asleep reading a book by 7 pm most days. I had to remember to pull the boom tent closed, though, because some time just before and after dusk, a heavy dew would sneakily arrive. By morning it would have soaked anything left out and before I packed up the tent I would sponge it down and wring out gallons of water. If I was busy cooking or writing my diary or planning the next day's sailing, I often wouldn't notice how wet my sleeping bag was getting until it was too late. Closing the tent too early trapped a lot of heat and made for a sweaty night. The tent was very effective at keeping heat in and draughts out. It was so much warmer at the top of the tent that I could dry clothes or towels up there using the heat of the lantern alone.

I snuggled down to sleep that evening, pretty pleased with myself. Nothing terrible had gone wrong and I was looking forward to hoisting a sail the next day and trying my hand at yachting instead of motoring. There was still plenty to worry about but nothing to do about it right then, so I put it all to one side and concentrated on missing my girlfriend.

~~~

EARLY THE NEXT morning, I began packing away my gear, which took me about an hour. Even months later when I had refined all my drills it still took me at least 45 minutes to calmly stow all my clobber. At this stage I had yet to work out the most convenient places to store my gear and I had an overabundance of equipment – too many pots and pans, too many clothes, too many small items of equipment that would turn out to be unneeded. In fact, one of my clearest memories of the first few days was the constant reorganising and incessant attempts to stow things better. My diary shows that every day for several weeks I spent most of my free time just trying to stow things more conveniently. In the end I got so tired of it that I just got rid of a lot of things, and once that was done, I found I had ample space to organise my lockers into three departments. The stern locker contained six identical large plastic storage boxes with clip-on lids that between them contained my toiletries, a small towel, all my food, mosquito repellent gear, books, navigation gear, cleaning products and laundry detergent. Packed around the boxes I fitted in my spare water, cooking equipment (except for the pressure stove that was ingeniously stowed up forward by Frank underneath part of the deck coaming and held in place with a bungy cord) and a spare wet-weather jacket. On top of the boxes I put my little day-pack that I carried ashore on shopping trips, but which held my ready-use clothes when I was sailing. In the awkward gaps around the sides of the boxes I stored spare boxes of cereal, buns, bread and a roll of paper towels. It also held my 'black box', the rather grand name for an old video camera bag that was well padded and which now held my GPS, VHF, camera, film, radio, spare batteries, Maglite torch and compass. I could access anything in the stern locker by removing at most two items to get to it. It was one of the best features of the boat – the locker was large but completely watertight. The lid could be taken off but was secured with a short cord so that it couldn't be lost overboard. It was held down tightly against a rubber gasket by six latches and it never leaked.

The upper bow locker held all the gear I needed only at night: my two sleeping bags, two good sleeping mats, duffel bag with all my clothing, lantern, diary and souvenir pouch, tobacco and cigar bag and medical kit bag.

The lower bow locker held everything that I needed infrequently. I thought of it as my dirty locker, but I kept it clean. It held hand tools; a box of spare fittings, screws, bolts; two small boxes of repair gear including sticky tape, glues, sealants and a fibreglass repair kit; a box of bungy cords; a spare lifejacket; an inflatable dinghy and foot pump;

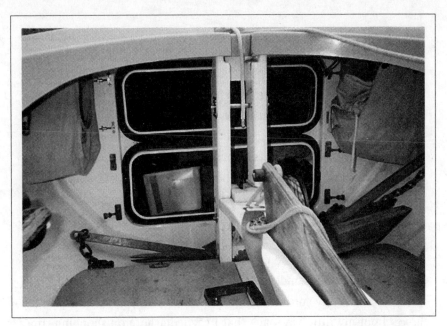

Upper and lower watertight bow lockers.

a gallon can of stove and lantern fuel; a bottle of two-stroke oil; a sea anchor and spare ropes; a box of old safety flares; two boxes of paint-brushes, sandpaper and other painting gear; plus a spare sleeping mat, a couple of pieces of wood from the boom crutch, a collapsible fishing rod and tackle and some cans of paint, varnish and canvas- waterproofing goo. It was a tight fit, but I got it all in. Most weeks, I just opened the lower locker once or twice to get the oil bottle or lantern fuel out. Occasionally I used the tools and box of fittings to replace rivets that popped out of the latches on the stern-locker lid, but in general, this locker stayed shut – ready for an emergency.

Just behind the bow lockers on either side of the boat were two green canvas bags that were attached to hooks screwed into the underside of the deck coaming. These were like glove compartments in that they held things that I often forgot about. One held my chewing tobacco and my camera and transistor, but only if I had them out in fair weather. The other held a couple of handy short ropes to be used as lashings or as replacements for shackles or fittings if anything critical broke in a storm and I couldn't open the dirty locker to get a

Lower bow locker: tools, repair kit, inflatable dinghy, paint, ropes, spares, oil, etc.

replacement. They also held my fire extinguisher (cooking with a naked flame, lighting a newly refuelled lantern and smoking aboard a vessel with gasoline stored in plastic cans seemed to justify the need for an extinguisher), my beach shoes, and a plastic poncho for additional rainproofing if my tent began leaking in the middle of the night.

On the mast tabernacle I attached a diving knife for emergencies. At the base of the mast, the head of the main anchor fitted into a frame set into the floorboards, and when tied in by a short cord this kept it stationary and secure in any weather. This anchor had about 20 feet of heavy chain attached to a long anchor rope that reeled onto a drum mounted on the mast tabernacle. The drum was another of Frank's modifications that made it very simple to let out and recover the anchor neatly and quickly when sailing single-handed. On the starboard side, forward of the seats, I tied in the second, smaller anchor and rope.

Nearby was a two-gallon flagon of water that was stowed forward under the seat next to my boom tent and another that stood in the 'sump' next to the mast. Beside that flagon I laid my sea boots stuffed tidily with my rolled-up wet-weather gear. I also kept a water bottle tucked under the seat. The water bottles and the contents of the green bags were the only things I stood to lose if I capsized. Everything else was held or tied in place and couldn't come out if I tipped over, and virtually all of it could handle a soaking.

Many things were stowed under the seats: two roller fenders, three oars, two plastic tubes used for pumping out, two one-gallon and one two-gallon gas cans, the boom tent, the water flagon, the Whale hand pump, my flare container, the boom crutch, my hand paddle, an extendable boathook, and a small fender.

Lastly, I stowed the paddles for the inflatable dinghy under the deck coaming to the starboard side of the stern locker where they were tightly wedged in. On the opposite side I kept a short boathook, a spare pump tube and a spare sail batten. There was a certain amount of symmetry in the stowage plan that also helped balance the boat. I compensated for the off-centre mounting of the engine by putting heavier things on the port side of the lockers.

As I say, it took a while before I settled on this stowage plan but eventually I got to the point where I never needed to move something out of the way to get another item – it was all arranged so that in the course of the evening as I got things out, I gradually unpacked and exposed the next item needed. It saved a lot of double-handling and I was quite proud of the system, but when I looked at the space my gear took up I marvelled that Frank and Margaret could both fit onto the boat at the same time. If I'd had company littering up the place and upsetting my orderly routine I'd have been reaching for an axe before long.

Tacking in Superbia

BY 9 AM I was ready to sail. There was precious little breeze, but that suited me for my first day at the mercy of the wind. I put on my lifejacket, slotted my boat compass into its groove on the seat and looped its safety line round the thwart. I set out my chart, clipped on my radio and pulled up the anchor. The motor started sweetly on the first pull and I quietly motored into the channel. There was no traffic at all so I drifted to a halt while I prepared to hoist the mainsail. It wasn't a complicated operation: I just took down the boom crutch and stowed it under the seat, unclipped the halyard from the back of the boom, clipped it onto the head of the sail, fed the sail into the track of the mast and pulled it up. I cleated it off, dashed back to steer and watched with absurd satisfaction as I began to move slowly forward. I sat for a moment, revelling in the fact that after months of planning and work I had got myself to this point — sailing my own boat in Florida. That's a long way from driving a desk in Auckland. Feeling bold, I unfurled the jib as well. To do this I simply uncleated the control line and gave a stiff yank on one of the jib sheets. It unrolled and hung limply. There was much less visibility with the jib up and I had to keep peering around to check for other vessels and channel markers but it felt like we were moving faster with it up. I continued to play with the trim and once I had the mainsail going as well as I could, I decided to practise tacking.

Straight away I learned something about tacking – you've got to have a bit of speed up before you start. When you're moving you have steerage – meaning sufficient water is flowing fast enough past the rudder for it to be able to turn the boat. Unless you're moving, the rudder doesn't work. Then you just sit there, waggling the rudder like a dog wagging its tail. But once you begin a tack, you start to spill the wind out of the sails, and you lose speed and thus steerage. So, if you don't have enough momentum to carry you through the turn before the wind fills the sails again from the other side, you can stall in the middle. You come to a stop, facing directly into the wind with the sails flapping loosely. You can't turn, you can't go forward, you can't even manoeuvre the boat to catch more wind and start again. You're stuck. This is called 'being in irons'.

On my first tack, this is what happened. Not knowing what exactly to do, I studied the situation for a bit, then fiddled with the rudder and sails to try to turn side-on to the wind. Nothing worked so I paddled myself around until the wind filled the sails again.

For the next couple of hours I had to tack frequently as the channel wasn't very wide and the wind was light and fluky. I got it down to a simple drill: build up speed, shift the compass and chart to the other side, free the other jib sheet ready to be pulled in and then put the tiller hard over. As soon as the sails flapped, I uncleated the old jib sheet, slid under the boom onto the other seat, yanked in the new jib sheet and straightened my tiller. Hah!

Eventually the wind died even more and I dropped the jib since it was hanging loose and only blocked my view of the scenery. Around noon I began to enter a built-up section of the channel with tall apartments on both sides and numerous bridges. This was suburbia – albeit a very well-heeled part – more like Superbia. Motoring down the New River the day before, I had been pretty distracted but I'd still had time to notice the extraordinary evidence of wealth: enormous houses with huge gardens and luxurious motorboats docked in front of them. On shore I'd seen the abundance of expensive cars and thin, tanned blondes of a certain age. This part of Florida was seriously rich. I'm no stranger to the sights you see in the richest country in the world, but on this day I was gobsmacked. You see, the rich section of this city extended not just a few blocks or across a neighbourhood. Not even for a mile or two along the prime waterside real estate, as it does in, say, Auckland or Sydney. Nor did it just smear itself thinly alongside the ICW for the 35 miles between Fort Lauderdale and Miami. No, this sort of wealth accompanied me almost continuously for about *300 miles*. These houses weren't just comfortable four-bedroom affairs with double garage and indoor-outdoor flow either. I'm talking three-storey, 10 bedrooms, God-knows-how-many bathrooms, pool house, guest house, boat house, car park and multi-multi garage. Plus dock and boat. And all new. From Miami to Saint Augustine, around every turn you risked coming upon a house with the sort of overstated design that marks the nouveau riche. (And I've got nothing against them – I'd like to be riche, nouveau or not.) Most of them had a boat tied up in front that would cost more than any house I've ever lived in. Including the many side canals, I figured I was passing through 3000 linear miles of almost wall-to-wall luxury boats and houses. That's the sort of money that has flooded into Florida in the last 20 years. At perhaps $3 million per property, I estimate that in a month I sailed past about $300–500 billion dollars of visible wealth. Who knows what else they had in their trust funds, foreign bank accounts and safe-deposit boxes too. And since I was on the waterway most of that time and not on the coast itself, I didn't see the really expensive parts. It may be new, a little garish, and it may not be to your taste, but it's humbling to think of a country that can have this much wealth and development and not consider it to be anything remarkable. And in case you're thinking that Florida is just a big mucky sinkhole of ecologically destructive urban blight – you're wrong. It's still a beautiful place with many hundreds of square miles of raw natural beauty, as undeveloped as anything on New Zealand's West Coast. It just has a climate like the south of France.

By early afternoon the wind had dropped away, and as I neared Miami the apartment buildings on either side grew taller and sheltered me from any breeze. Reluctantly I lowered the sails and started the motor. Now I was able to goggle at the city as I came into the harbour.

With my chart on my knees I could ready myself for the passage under the bridges, through the turning basin and past all the cruise liners. My destination for the day was a deserted cove on the far side of the harbour. It was an ideal anchorage for me – too shallow for big boats but still scenic, clean and convenient. But once again, the sheer size and multiplicity of things astounded me. Buildings, bridges, boats – there was a lot of *everything*. And it was all *big*. I hauled out my camera and started snapping. I'm not sure why I was so surprised – possibly it was a hangover from the four months in Pinedale, Wyoming, where things are done on a smaller scale and at a slower pace. I think I'd over-adopted the relaxed rural lifestyle of Pinedale and it had affected my speech.

That first conversation in Geoff's house had given me a glimpse of the problem. I could barely get a word in edgeways. Everyone I met there talked nineteen to the dozen while I limped along behind like some sort of yokel. Now in south Florida, cocaine dust from the '80s is probably in the water like fluoride, but even so, I felt like my conversational equipment was broken. After a while I just shut up and let them do the talking. And the most astounding thing happened. People didn't think any the less of me. Hmmm. There's a lesson there somewhere . . .

I paused to refuel in the middle of the harbour, watched by Coastguard sailors on a patrol vessel. After 9/11 internal security had been significantly beefed up. Airport security was tighter, border controls were stricter, and in ports, marinas and naval bases, the coastguard and police maintained many patrol boats on station all day and night. It wasn't an oppressive sight and none of them ever bothered me, but it was evidence that things had changed since the last time I'd travelled in the US.

Miami across the bay.

Self-portrait at last.

By late afternoon I was idling up into Stadium Cove looking for a spot to drop anchor. First, though, I wanted to take a picture of myself at the start of the journey with *Wanderer*. The shore of the cove was white sand on all sides so I nosed up to the beach with my centreboard and rudder up. I tied off to a tree on shore and then set out to explore. The cove was deserted on this Monday, though it's a popular place for jet-skiers and water-skiers on weekends. It looks out at the entrance on the Miami skyline – it'd be like anchoring at Devonport in Auckland or Kirribili in Sydney – but surrounded by palm trees and white sand and with no houses or people on shore. I took a short stroll around the beach and then set up my camera to take a picture with the timer. I was quite pleased with the result and with the day as a whole. Now all I had to do was anchor out in the cove, set up camp, cook dinner, plan my next day's cruise and then read until I fell asleep. As far as I was concerned, that was how the rest of the trip was supposed to be too. There was just a small fly in the ointment – the sleeping thing was taking a bit of getting used to.

~~~

I'M NATURALLY A fairly light sleeper but I've had plenty of experience sleeping on the ground while in the army and in some very odd positions too. I once fell asleep while standing bent over double with my helmeted head resting on a coil of barbed wire. I fell asleep in a toilet on a Hercules aircraft and I fell asleep behind the wheel of a car as it knocked down small trees on the median strip of a motorway. I've fallen asleep at formal dinners, while leaning on the speaker stand at a Space Waltz concert (a power rock band of long ago), and I slept many hours on the gunline during fire missions in my artillery battery. In fact, the only place I hadn't been able to sleep comfortably was in my own bed in my own apartment in Auckland some years before when I decided to live in the central city.

But I barely slept a wink on the boat. The problem was that every time I wanted to turn over I had to wake up and unravel my legs. I would begin to turn in my sleep, then get stuck halfway round with my knees jammed under the fixed centre thwart. To get free I had to twist back, draw my legs up one at a time, place them in the new position, swivel my hips around to match them and then wriggle down again into my sleeping bag. Eventually I grew accustomed to doing this in my sleep, but for the first couple of weeks I had to get my zzzs in instalments.

Wrecked

I HAD A definite objective for the next couple of days. It was now the 23rd of December and I had promised Adrienne that I would call her on Christmas Day. She would already have had her celebration the day before in New Zealand with her family and be back at work. I decided that I wanted to be away from the mainland when I called her. It seemed to me that it would be romantic and exciting if I called her from Key Largo. This is the first major island in the chain of keys that runs 150 miles from Miami to Key West, 90 miles from Cuba. The Florida Keys are low sandy islands that lie about a few miles off the mainland at first and then as the tip of the mainland curves back north towards the Gulf Coast, the keys continue on their own in a graceful southwest curve out into the Gulf of Mexico. There are hundreds of islands, many uninhabited, ranging in size from a few acres to ones big enough to support large towns like Key West. The waters around them are very shallow — usually less than 10 feet — and many larger boats can't negotiate them. The US Army Corps of Engineers cuts channels for deeper-draught boats to enter harbours and sail between islands but aside from these, you need a boat drawing less than five feet to make a safe passage between most places. To the west of the keys, the water is shallow for many miles and relatively few boats make long passages down this side. Sailing on the west is referred to as sailing down the 'inside'. To the immediate east of the island chain is the deeper water (25–40 feet) of the two-mile-wide Hawk Channel, which runs from Miami to Key West and which is ideal for big yachts. This is known as sailing on the 'outside'. Two to five miles beyond that is the reef. This is a line of coral that parallels the Hawk Channel and at the same time calms down some of the worst of the Atlantic seas. Big ships sail outside this reef for ecological safety. Like the Great Barrier Reef, it provides fantastic diving. My plan was to leave Miami harbour, enter Biscayne Bay, which is enclosed by the mainland and the keys, and then sail down it a few miles and call in at the small town of Coconut Grove to pick up a chartbook of the Florida Keys. Then I'd sail southwest across Biscayne Bay to Key Largo the next day.

I picked Key Largo for no reason other than it was the title of a film starring Humphrey Bogart and Lauren Bacall and was mentioned in a lovely song of the same name written by a native Floridian for his ex-girlfriend. The song was a massive hit, he got back together with his girl and married her, then adopted the high-risk lifestyle of a celebrity in the '80s and lost the money and the girl within a few years, but apparently had fun doing it. I didn't stop to think why it would be romantic for Adrienne to *get* a call from Key Largo, as opposed to *making* a call from there, but that's typical of me. Anyhow, I wanted to get there by Christmas Day – just 48 hours away.

I was all set to hoist sail and try my hand at cruising on the wide, shallow waters of Biscayne Bay but the wind was slow in coming that day. In fact, it never really came at all so I was forced to motor on calm seas out of the cove, under the big bridge at the entrance to Miami harbour and into the bay. Biscayne Bay is about 30 miles long and nine miles wide but only one to seven feet deep. Under the Florida sun the water stays about 75 degrees at all times, and frequently it's warmer in the water than out of it. The bottom is white sand with no coral and few rocks. Most of the keys are formed of sand and some mud created by mangroves. This makes the bay nearly ideal for learning to sail. Warm, fairly sheltered, and shallow enough to walk ashore in many places – and certainly shallow enough for your mast to be well above water if you sink. However, it's still wide enough to be out of sight of land at times and with strong winds it can whip up a frightening chop in no time at all. The weather in the keys is pretty predictable by New Zealand standards. Weather fronts are slim and fast, approach from the west and sometimes bring short but powerful thunderstorms with them. A front will pass over in about three to six hours and normal service (hot, dry and light breezes) will resume immediately.

This was one of those calm days that preceded a front and so I whipped the engine to life and motored off. Passing under the high bridge and into the bay was a big moment for me. Even though I was surrounded on all sides by land, much of it was out of sight and the bay is big enough to make you feel small and vulnerable in a tiny boat like mine. There wasn't much company on the water that day either. People were busy shopping for Christmas and so I was largely alone as I set off. I arranged my chart, secured my compass and set my course for Coconut Grove.

Which brings me to the only part of the whole trip that didn't scare me at all: navigation. Eight years of service in the artillery had given me quite a bit of experience with maps, compasses, instruments and navigation generally. The gunners take great pride in being able to locate themselves and their targets accurately. If they don't, they tend to drop rounds on friendly forces, so they are the master field navigators of the army. For long-range artillery weapons like rockets and tactical missiles, we will locate our position down to plus or minus one centimetre and we can find north to within a fraction of a millimetre – which is itself a fraction of a degree. Precision is pretty important to us and many artillerymen are trained as surveyors. During my time as a gunner I had completed several survey courses using ancient theodolites and tape measures to derive the raw data, and logarithms to calculate the answers. Thankfully this has all been replaced now with GPS, lasers, computers and so on, but I'm pleased to have an understanding of the basic processes that are now performed inside a silicon chip, and which many newer surveyors don't have to understand. I got plenty of satisfaction from designing, observing, computing and then closing a survey scheme. I thought this was quite atypical of me since I'm no great shakes at mathematics, but it turned out there was an explanation for this odd enjoyment. I stumbled on it in a dusty 50-year-old file.

It was genetic. Not long after my father died, and about halfway through my own time in the army, I requested his record of military service from the archives at Army General Staff in Wellington where I worked. I knew my father had been in the Pacific theatre during the Second World War but I didn't know where or what he did, and now that I couldn't ask him, I was suddenly curious. When the file arrived I settled down to read about what Daddy did in the war. He'd never encouraged me to enter the army – in fact, it was clear he disapproved. He was a long-time schoolteacher and had never talked about his army service but I knew he had a dim view of the military. It might not be wrong to describe him eventually as a pacifist, but long ago in a different era, as a lad of 19, he'd done his bit and joined up to fight 'Jerry' in 1940. I read the rest of his war record with growing surprise. As soon as I finished it I told my brother Graeme, who is the family historian, what I knew. His jaw dropped when he heard and so did mine when he told me that there was actually a prequel to this story.

My grandfather, Lionel Wilfred Hughes, had died long before I was born and so I never met him or knew much about him. Graeme told me that as a young man, my grandfather had heard the call of King and Country and had enlisted to fight the Hun in the First World War. He was an infantryman and so he wasn't trained as an artillery surveyor like me. He didn't need to be, though – he was already a trained civilian surveyor making maps and surveying land in the backblocks of the central North Island. He was just following in the footsteps of his father Hughie Hughes, who was a surveyor – just like *his* own father, who likewise did what *his* daddy had done. And old John Hughes had been making maps in Ireland in the late 1700s. Surveying the Empire seemed to be the Hughes family trade.

Maybe Lionel wanted a change of pace from technical work, or maybe the army exercised its usual skill at posting people away from their field of expertise, but for whatever reason, my grandfather spent his war in the trenches in France and so inevitably, like most front-line infantrymen in that war, he was wounded. He was duly evacuated back to a base hospital in England where he fell in love with the nurse who tended him. They married, and began to raise a family in New Zealand before pleurisy killed my grandfather. He left two young daughters and a two-year-old son – my father, Lionel Upton Hughes.

A generation later, the Germans kicked off after half-time, and so at the start of the Second World War, my father enlisted. By the time he'd done his basic training the Japs were sending reconnaissance planes over Auckland and so he ended up fighting them instead. It was all there in his record. Enlistment, basic training and then corps training in . . . Good Lord! The artillery. Well, well, well, he was a gunner like me. I never knew. But there was more. He was trained by the artillery as a surveyor too. At that point a terrible thought began to take shape in my mind. The rest of the story wasn't in his files – it was well known to me already. Like so many others in the Pacific war he was injured *and was duly evacuated back to base hospital where he fell in love with the red-headed nurse who tended him.* They married, and began to raise a family – including one son, Lee, who joined the army, became a gunner and trained as a surveyor just like his dad.

But it didn't end there – this son, while in the army, as a gunner and surveyor, met a red-headed nurse on a blind date. I didn't marry her, though. I just went out with her for a few months and then we went our separate ways for 17 years, until in a stunning coincidence, we met up again and began going out once more. It didn't take an Einstein to see how this tale would end. Six or seven generations of surveyors. Three generations of soldiers marrying nurses that they met while in the army. Two generations of artillery surveyors marrying redheads. And now, one nervous ex-artillery surveyor pondering whether there might be a hidden internal compass that was directing his course. And whether by putting a continent and an ocean between himself and the red-headed nurse that the needle pointed towards, it was possible to escape its influence. Hmmmmm.

But at least I had no fear of navigation! That was quite something, wasn't it?

~~~

AT COCONUT GROVE I put in to a marina dock and chatted to a local who turned out to own the dock and who was very interested in my trip. Like everyone I'd met in Florida, he talked nineteen to the dozen and I felt strangely tongue-tied. He gave me directions to the chandlery shop a mile away. I refilled my water bottles at his tap and set off to buy the chart I needed. Then I cast off and headed south down the bay on the western side. I planned to make some miles and then cross the bay the next day to Key Largo from where I would call my gal in the evening.

The passage from Coconut Grove was uneventful and pleasant. I did manage to raise the sails a couple of times but they didn't fill with air so I took them down again. I did some wool-gathering and the hours passed comfortably. By late afternoon I was looking for a place to anchor near Cutler Channel. I cruised into the private marina but it was a posh place with no facilities for the public, no phone and the few people I waved to ignored me. There were no shops, restaurants or gas stations, the apartments and houses nearby were expensive, the boats were immaculate and large and it didn't look like they welcomed transients, so I turned around and motored back to a side entrance that led to a shallow cove. On my chart it was called Deering Bay and judging by the signs nearby it seemed to be a wildlife refuge where pretty much everything was banned including anchoring, fishing, camping, hassling manatees, etc. But this late in the day there was nowhere else within range that offered shelter so I paddled myself to a spot in the bay that was hidden amongst the mangroves and anchored anyway. The water was black and turbid and very shallow – only about a foot deep. Almost as soon as I stopped, the no-see-ums arrived. I ignored them for a while but eventually I cracked and grabbed the bug spray. This kept them hovering in a cloud of frustration, close enough to annoy me but not able to bite. Now, in the evening heat I had added a layer of chemicals to the sweat that poured off me. I got the boom tent up and ducked under it and this seemed to help a bit but the heat increased. As soon as the sun went down, the midges retired but mosquitoes appeared for an hour or two. I battled them until they quit, while I studied my charts, listened to the weather forecast

112

and filled in my diary. I was very tired by then but I made a sandwich anyway and ate some candy. The weather was supposed to take a nasty turn tomorrow for a few hours but if I set off early I could possibly avoid the worst of it. Finally, I fell asleep in the heavy humidity and dreamed uneasily all night. In between times I woke to unravel my legs from beneath the centre thwart and turn over onto my other side. It wasn't a great night's rest and I was glad when I was able to get up at 5 am, some time before first light. It was Christmas Day but I didn't feel like celebrating anything yet. First I had to pack up, get clean, get dressed, get fed and then get the hell out of this depressing little spot. I did all of that before dawn as I wanted to make my escape from the refuge before any marine patrol spotted me and gave me grief.

By 7 am I was rowing myself across shallow water towards the channel that led back to Biscayne Bay. I listened to the forecast again on my VHF. It predicted calm seas and winds initially, rising to 20-knot winds and one- to two-foot waves with higher winds and waves in the thunderstorms that were due to arrive after midday. That wasn't ideal but it didn't sound too bad and I certainly didn't fancy staying where I was for another day. There was no phone or place to land and call my gal from, the bugs were miserable and the whole feeling was unwelcoming and lacking in the Christmas spirit. I decided to make a dash across the bay to Key Largo where I was sure I'd find a bar where I could sip rum punch while I called Adrienne. Just as dawn was breaking I motored out the channel and as I did the breeze came up into a steady northwesterly wind that was ideal for me. I was dressed in a T-shirt and shorts and lifejacket as I raised the mainsail and then the jib. With the wind behind me I was soon sailing pretty quickly towards the centre of the bay. I aimed to sail about six miles southeast to a point in the middle of the bay where the shallow Featherbed Banks had a channel cut through it for deeper-draught boats. Then I could turn more towards the south and stay in deeper water all the way to Key Largo, a further 13 or 14 miles. The total distance was 20 miles, which was further than I'd sailed or motored on any day so far, but I was confident that with 10 hours of daylight I'd be able to make it easily. And Ady wasn't expecting my phone call until later that evening so I would have plenty of time to anchor, get ashore and clean up to celebrate my own Christmas.

It was a plan with much to recommend it – and one giant flaw.

By 8.00 am it was starting to gust quite strongly, and in front of me black thunderclouds were scudding across the bay. The seas were still quite small and easy to handle – only a foot high – but the wind gusts were a little alarming. I remembered Frank's advice about sailing single-handed – *reef early*. I decided to try my hand at this now while things were still manageable. I'd only reefed a sail once before in my life – on Malcolm's boat on the abysmal night when we'd nearly run it aground – but reefing is straightforward in theory and not a lot harder in practice. I decided to begin by heaving to. This was something I had never done at all until the day before when I had practised it twice in light winds. The first time I'd got stuck in irons so I'd made the best of it and heaved to. The second time I did it deliberately.

From all my reading, heaving to was one of four things I'd decided I needed to know about. The others were reefing, capsize drills and lying to a sea anchor. I'd read the theory and studied a drawing of how the sails and tiller should look when I was hove to correctly and it didn't look complicated. It offered the immediate reward of stability, safety and comfort. I turned into the wind and let almost all the speed bleed off. I let go the main sheet, which allowed the mainsail to blow out to leeward and then I released the genoa sheet a little and pulled in on the opposite line. This left the genoa 'backed' against the wind. In effect, the mainsail was almost in irons, the boat was slightly side-on to the wind and the genoa was what was keeping it there. To keep everything just so, I tied the tiller to the same side the boom was on and hey presto! – just as advertised in Margaret's book and on the Canadian Wayfarer website, *Wanderer* came to a comfortable position and slid a little forward and a little sideways across the waves. She rode the waves easily, all the noise and commotion died away and I was able to stand up and move around her with confidence.

I went forward to release the halyard on the main and gather in the sail next to the mast. I pulled it down until the first luff cringle appeared. The sides of a sail are known thus: the side that runs up the mast is the *luff*, the side that runs along the boom is the *foot* and the hypotenuse of the triangle, running from masthead to the tip of the boom is the *leach*. (This means that the tan of the angle of the luff cringle ought to give you the cosine of a slice of pie if I remember my arithmetic.) So, the luff cringle was the metal ring around the hole in the sail close to the mast that I was supposed to secure to the mast by tying off. Instead, I had prepared a loop of rope of the correct length with a knot in the end. I pushed the loop through the cringle until the knot jammed there and then slipped the loop over a cleat on the mast. Then it was ready for me to pull on the halyard and raise the sail again ready for sailing. But first, I pulled in the lower reefing line that yanked the leach cringle at the tip of the boom down. I secured this to its jam cleat on the boom. Now I had both ends of the sail pulled down and the only thing left was to gather in the baggy bit in the middle and tie it to the boom with the reefing points that ran in a row along the sail for this purpose. At each of the four reefing points in the row, two strings, like bootlaces, dangled down from the sail – one on each side. I grabbed the ends and tied them together beneath the boom. Once all four were done, the sail was secured and about a third of its area had been gathered in and tied to the boom. This meant that the wind had less sail to push on and so I was less vulnerable to gusts that might capsize me.

All this took the best part of 30 minutes to do, so now I took a moment to think and decided that, as it was spitting heavy rain drops, I should put on a coat. The wind was strong but still warm, the spray from the sea was even warmer and so although I wasn't the least bit cold, I could see deep black clouds ahead and I knew it wouldn't be long before the temperature dropped and the thundershowers hit me. For now, I released the genoa, pulled it in on the correct side, and slowly *Wanderer* moved off. I trimmed the mainsail until we were making good speed on the wind, and then I let the main out and turned sharply downwind. In a few moments we were running smoothly along with none of the discomfort that comes from beating into wind and seas.

It never failed to surprise me how much difference it made just to turn the boat around in a storm. Beating into the wind can add almost five mph in apparent wind speed. Running downwind can remove the same amount. I should point out that a 10–15 mph wind is ideal for a Wayfarer on any point of sail – a pleasant day's sailing will be had by all. Winds of 15–20 mph are challenging but still exciting for most of us, but 20–25-mph winds are uncomfortable and are getting dangerous for the solo novice. At wind speeds of 25–30 mph it is time to heave to or come into shelter. Therefore, if you can change from danger at 25 mph to ideal at 15 mph just by turning your boat around, you can see why running before the wind is so much more pleasant than beating into it. My morale always improved with this manoeuvre, so sometimes when I was tired, scared and still miles from shelter, I'd turn onto a run for a few minutes, just to recover my nerve and remind myself that things weren't that bad out on the water. It's a question of perception as well as reality, and perception is influenced by morale, experience, confidence, knowledge etc. Initially I had bugger all of those things, so my only weapon for changing my perception and trying to bring it into accord with reality was to run downwind for a little and remind myself that things weren't actually as black as the inside of a cow.

Anyway, on this Christmas morning I was feeling pretty good about myself. The wind was strong, the seas were rising, but I'd heaved to successfully and found that things calmed down immediately. Then I'd reefed for the first time and that went well too. I had started sailing again, I was warm and comfortable, and though I was now catching a lot of spray as well as rain I had a plan for that as well.

Frank had provided an excellent Whale hand pump with *Wanderer*. It could be attached to the seat at any point just by tightening a wing nut. I had mounted it well forward where the inlet pipe could reach the lowest point of the bilge through a small aperture in the floorboards near the centrecase. I fished out the plastic inlet and outlet pipes and pushed them onto the pump flanges. Then I slid forward on the centre thwart, steered with my left hand and worked the pump lever with my right. Immediately, great gouts of water squirted over the side and pretty soon the bilge was dry again. I put the pipes back under the seat where they lived and returned to steer and navigate. It was just in time, as now there appeared in front of me a very black cloud that was pouring heavy rain down in a sheet. I figured it wouldn't be long before one of these cloudbursts struck me, and all around me thunder was booming and lightning was cracking. I decided to heave to and take in the second and final reef. I did this all right and now I had just half the mainsail exposed and I was considering furling in the genoa. It took me about 20 minutes to get all this done, and just as I did, I got hit by the first thunderstorm.

The volume of rain was surprising. The wind rose to a full gale in a few minutes and the rain poured into the boat. I furled the genoa in a flash and turned into the wind so that I wouldn't get overpowered by a gust. I lay there in irons, rocking and heaving unpleasantly until I finally decided that this was neither safe nor fun. I pulled the genoa out a fraction, a gust caught it and soon I was sailing again. By degrees, I turned the boat until I was running on course again, and as I did, the wind dropped and the rain eased as the thundercloud passed over. I pumped out again and checked my course. Now that I was about six miles from land I couldn't see any reference points so I pulled out my GPS to check my position. I was thrilled to see that all the wind had pushed me along at a good clip and I was nearing the Featherbed Banks.

Fifteen minutes later, just as I came up on the channel marker by the bank, another thunderstorm hit and this one was even more intense than the first. I managed to keep sailing as, incredibly, the wind changed direction in tune with my turns to get into the channel. I whizzed between the markers and exited the channel in fine style just as the storm blew over. By now I had shipped a lot of water and a few badly stowed items were loose in the bottom of the boat so I heaved to again to pump out and tidy up. Once the boat was shipshape I readied myself to start sailing again. I let the genoa out, trimmed the main and put the tiller over, expecting to turn downwind and move off. Instead, I suddenly rounded up into the wind. As the sails flapped and banged I yanked on the tiller again and noticed now that there wasn't a lot of resistance to it. I looked over the stern to see what had come loose and there was the problem — floating away from me was most of the rudder blade.

Shit! The rudder had broken and was off on a holiday of its own. It had broken along the dotted line I'd noticed at Geoff's place. Dammit, I thought, I should have fibreglassed it. Too late now to worry about that mistake. Time for decisive action.

In a flash I knew what I had to do — get the motor going and chase after it. But first, I had to prevent a capsize, so I let go the mainsheet and scrambled up to the mast. I untied the halyard, intending to flake the sail, but in my haste I forgot to tighten the boom vang first. Unless the vang is tight while you flake the sail, the boom can slide off the gooseneck fitting and this is exactly what happened. The boom crashed into the bottom of the boat, dragging the sail down the mast with it and somehow flicking my hat over the side too. I looked at the sail in surprise and quickly decided that this was a pretty good way of flaking it in a hurry. I flung the rest of the sail into the bottom of the boat, poked the boom forward and yanked on the roller furling line. In two seconds, the genoa was furled away, all my sails were down and I was able to clamber back to the stern. I freed the motor and lowered it into the water. Then I paused, calmed myself, and read the instructions I had stuck to the top of the cowling. I just wanted to ensure that I didn't get panicked and end up flooding the motor. I carefully set all the controls, gave a mighty heave on the starter and the engine kicked into life. I'd been keeping an eye on the broken section of rudder and as soon as I got the engine in gear, I turned towards it. It hadn't gone far and even in the rough sea I was able to grab it on the first pass. I flung it into the boat, sat down again and turned the bow into the seas while I pondered what to do. I was without rudder or mainsail in a storm, alone, on Christmas Day. No one knew where I was or what I was doing. And to be honest, neither did I.

There are drills of course that can be learned and followed for most situations, and steering without a rudder is one of them. But I hadn't had time to do this yet and I had a feeling that steering by trimming the main and jib wouldn't work too well in winds this strong. It seemed to me that it would be like steering a horse with knee pressure instead of the reins. That sort of thing works well if everything else is going fine, but isn't the kind of exercise to try when galloping a horse over jumps and around trees. And this boat was jumping around plenty as the next thunder-cloud came over me. I doubted that I'd be able to steer a safe course back to the nearest shelter either. I'd probably have to sail with the wind and that would take me towards Key Largo where there was less likely to be places that could help me repair my rudder.

So, with the engine keeping my bows into the waves I studied the chart and confirmed what I already suspected. The best shelter, the nearest shelter and the shelter most likely to have access to repair facilities was approxi-mately back the way I'd just come – directly into the weather. Bugger!

Steering by using the motor was less comfortable than by using the tiller. For a start, the handle on the motor was much shorter so I

The rudder problem – it broke right where I expected.

had to sit right at the back on the stern locker. That meant the stern dug in much deeper and the engine mount dragged in the water, which slowed our progress a little. And all the bilge water now ran backwards and that threw more weight to the rear. I couldn't steer from the port seat so it upset the lateral trim as well, and finally, there was the ever-present concern that if the engine stopped I'd be knackered until the wind went down a bit. That was all bothersome but fairly insignificant in the face of one clear fact – I couldn't see a bloody thing because of the amount of spray I was taking over the bow. Every wave crashed into the bow and threw up a bucket of water that the wind blasted straight into my face. Gallons and gallons were pouring into the cockpit as well, and after five minutes I hooked the pump pipes up again and started heaving on the handle. That worked OK, but I couldn't steer at the same time and so I had to wallow unpleasantly while I pumped. I couldn't move the pump further aft where I could reach it and steer at the same time because, if I did, there was no good access to the bilge through the floorboards. So, for the next hour I had to stop every 15 minutes and wallow while I pumped. Even so, by consulting my GPS, compass and chart I could tell we were making progress and I was feeling concerned but not scared – until the pump failed. One minute it was fine and then suddenly it created no suction. I made sure the transparent plastic inlet and outlet pipes were clear – they were. I wiggled the pump handle – it wiggled OK. But there was no suck to it. It seemed that a diaphragm had failed and though I had a repair kit deep in the bow locker, this wasn't the time to fiddle with it. I stowed the pipes and resumed motoring – except that now, as the water from the rain and spray accumulated to ankle depth at the back I was able to take my small bailer and heave occasional loads over the side. This accumulation of water wasn't too hazardous but it did slow me down even more. I really developed a fondness for my motor that day as it laboured away pushing several hundred extra pounds of burden directly into waves two feet high that were propelled by winds gusting to 30 mph or more. After an hour or so, I managed to refuel it, perching awkwardly on the stern locker as the boat rocked and rolled. Then I set off into the wind and spray again.

Funny how quickly things change. One minute I was feeling challenged but happy as I coped with rising wind and sea and made good progress towards Key Largo. One small gear failure later and suddenly I was miserable and nervous as I beat back the way I'd come just a few hours before. What made it worse was the certainty that by doing this damage on Christmas Day I'd be stuck without a rudder for a few days. Everything would be closed and that was assuming that my destination – Black Point – even had any repair facilities. If it was like Cutler Channel, I'd be knackered. I might even have to taxi back to Miami to get a new rudder made. In the two hours it took to crash my way towards the entrance to the Black Point marina channel I had plenty of time to reflect on the proposition that I might have bitten off more than I could chew.

The kindness of strangers

BLACK POINT WAS somewhere out there ahead of me. Presently it was invisible through all the spray that lashed my face but somewhere, a few miles ahead, was safety. And now, in a fine demonstration of irony, after telling half the world that I was deliberately seeking out fear and danger and adventure, here I was making a beeline for a safe harbour at the first sign of trouble. Apparently I wasn't as tough as I thought I was. I had plenty of time to think as I steered and bailed and wiped the water out of my eyes. Looking back, it seemed that I was made of sterner stuff when I was a wee tacker. Life was dangerous when I was a kid. And in every year that passed it seemed to be growing alarmingly safe. I don't think that's automatically a good thing either.

Humans like risk. Danger keeps us on our toes. Survival of the fittest does the species good in the long run, though it can chafe the individual pretty severely, I grant you. But if all the danger is removed, people (by which I mean mainly men) can't be heroic. They can't test themselves and find out if they are wanting. They can't even release tension and aggression. So I think that now, they tend to sublimate this drive and release it in socially undesirable ways. The equation probably reads something like *rugby − rucking = road rage.*

The evidence is growing, too. The second half of the 20th century, which was safer than any other for the suburban westerner, also saw the creation of scary pastimes like bungy jumping, white-water rafting, freestyle snowboarding and firewalking. Governments have caused much of this. Anything legislated by a nanny state obeys the law of unintended consequences. Thus, requiring children to wear helmets on bicycles can be regarded as a cause. Having removed overt danger from the equation, the effect tends to be boredom, resulting in glue sniffing, graffiti or skateboarding down the middle of the street in rush hour – all *sans* helmet. The common denominator is that all these pastimes are completely unnecessary and all of them provide a cheap thrill – in contrast to the unthrilling prospect of cycling helmeted in cycle lanes.

Kids know this stuff. Will Robinson didn't need that stupid robot following him round shouting warnings. Kids instinctively identify danger but push on anyway. Untainted by the absurd coddling that is enforced on us by do-gooding wankers in Parliament, they terrify their parents from an early age with their casual acceptance of risks and their determination to tear at the edge of the envelope. Put a tree in front of a six-year-old and turn your back. He'll be climbing the learning curve before you can say 'call an ambulance' and he'll emerge on a higher intellectual plane at the end, even if physically he lies moaning on the ground. As the saying goes, 'you'll be wiser after you fall into the ditch'.

Children understand that learning involves lessons. And lessons that involve pain are learned first, best and longest. The more brutal the medium, the faster the lesson is learned and the longer it sticks. If you don't believe me, ask yourself what gets the 'don't touch' message across first – a mother scolding a child in a supermarket, or a live power cable poised to give a lesson in electricity? No parent could be as firm and as consistent as 240 volts.

There are other basic physical laws that children learn early on, too. I well recall my discovery of one of Newton's lesser-known laws. It states roughly that 'given an inclined plane *in vaccuo* and gravity acting on a small child aboard any form of brakeless trolley, the rate of acceleration will be arithmetic up to a point'. This is a complex theorem but easy enough to understand if you conduct a simple experiment.

It began when the kids in my neighbourhood made skid boards. In the early '70s these were a budget offshoot from the skateboarding fever that swept more affluent areas. We had no money for expensive imported American skateboards with plastic wheels. We also lacked the athletic ability to stand upright on the wobbling boards. However, we had a genetic predisposition towards trolleys and used this inheritance to build our own substitute. When it came to trolleys we knew how to build them, tune them, race them – and rebuild the wreckage to go faster. We also healed pretty fast, too. From using them we learned minor first aid, some rudimentary road rules, and the primary trolleying law – that any hill you could run up was too slow to scare you coming down. To scare yourself you needed to labour up a really steep hill towing your trolley. Typically the trolley used pram wheels or motor-mower wheels and you steered with reins tied to the swivelling front axle. But trolleys were complex, heavy and old hat compared to the skid board. We sought bigger thrills and the new craze delivered them. Skid boards were almost lethally exciting. The sensation of speed was reinforced by the roaring noise of the wheels, our closeness to the ground and the acute vulnerability of our position. These fantastically dangerous devices comprised six elements:

- A breadboard-sized square of wood that formed the cockpit – this was the sum of all the coachwork,

- Running gear – consisting of two pieces of two-by-two with the ends whittled to approximate a round bar; one was nailed underneath the back of the breadboard to create a rear axle, the other was loosely bolted at the front to provide a handlebar for steering,

- A heavy bolt – this secured the handlebar and allowed it to pivot,

- Three old ball-bearing rings of equal size – two for the back wheels and one for the front,

- Many nails – for running repairs, and

- A small boy – fulfilling the dual role of pilot/casualty.

The victim mounted up by kneeling on top of the tiny board grasping the handlebar with both hands. We took care to ensure that our thumbs were lying parallel with our fingers. No one ever used the 'opposable thumb' grip on the handlebar since the steering mechanism had a well-known defect. Because the handlebar pivoted so freely and was bolted flush beneath the breadboard, it formed a blunt guillotine. If the front wheel struck a small stone at high speed it would sometimes jackknife the handlebar and this would mash your thumbs.

When mounted about two inches off the ground, the pilot would crouch tightly, lean forward and lower his head like a jockey – or a buffalo about to charge. This reduced the wind resistance but also gave the skull the secondary function of a bumper. The pilot was then pushed down the pavement at top speed by his launch crew of friends until he exceeded their best sprint and was cast free like the last stage of a moon rocket. A good push crew was fit, fat and mildly retarded. The fat ones added power at the start before collapsing winded on the pavement. The fit ones kept pounding along until the last moment, and the dense ones would do their bit time and again without asking for a turn in the trolley. After giving their all, the expired propulsion units fell away to the grass verge to await either a meteor shower of gravel that signalled an abrupt departure from the critical path (definite mission failure), a terrified scream (impending mission failure), or the fingernails-down-the-blackboard sound of a skid board being flung into a magnificent 40-yard three-wheel drifting skid with sparks flying up from the steel tyres (complete success).

Crouched down on the skid boards we would power down the path – a shrieking blue streak of optimism – our soft-boiled heads carving a slipstream as we flew down Union Road. Sadly, our aerodynamic posture also carried risks. Pre-stressed with nerves and fear we would generate even more cringing tension as we rocketed past blind driveways like a missile. Because, occasionally, the worst happened. Mission Control would register a distant dull thud as a hurtling pilot pounded headfirst like a bowling ball into the side of an emerging car.

This was the exact point at which the arithmetic of acceleration ceased in accordance with Newton's law.

The confused vehicle driver would hear an unhealthy WHUMP! and might feel a modest vibration through the heavy steel frame of his early 1950s V8. No evidence of a problem would be immediately apparent. The skid board would have slid underneath the car and run quietly onto the grass. The silent child would be semi-conscious on the path and a cursory glance around at eye level by the seated driver would detect nothing wrong. (No flying cyclist skidding down the path gathering concrete burns, and no shower of wood chips from an exploding trolley. Parents were familiar with these.) Those old post-war cars made many unusual random noises and this one could safely be put down to just another engineering mystery. We, of course, were not about to associate ourselves with any culpable victim no matter how badly injured. Displaying good common sense and a clean pair of heels we would have fled the scene of the accident before the echoes died away.

Most parents would at least get out to see if something important had dropped off the car – say a wheel or third gear. Then they would discover a dazed or unconscious nipper and only a barely perceptible dent in the car to indicate that the child hadn't just fallen out of a passing plane. As soon as the pilot was hauled off for first aid, the eldritch shriek of steel on concrete would resume, but it would only be a few days before another motorist would accidentally trap a pilot like a hockey puck.

So danger wasn't just something we lived with – it was something we actively courted. Occasionally we wooed it too successfully and then got bitten. I experienced this during the Mighty Crash. Marshall Hogg was the test pilot. He was my next-door neighbour and his father actually *was* a panelbeater. He made his son a metal trolley and it was a work of art. It had rubber tyres on all wheels and – in an unequalled feat of leading-edge technology – *all* the wheels were the same size. It had a padded seat and a real cockpit and even a curved perspex half-windscreen. It looked like a 1928 Bentley racing car. It weighed about the same, too. It was built like the truck that hauled the shithouse bricks. It didn't race – it lumbered.

Normally this meant that it was too slow a runner to be used when compared to our flimsy sprint trolleys, until one day when all our trolleys were wrecked and we were forced to use it. That was the day we accidentally discovered its full potential. Normally a trolley-pusher can instinctively judge just when to stop pushing, straighten up and let go, allowing the driver to accelerate by the power of gravity alone. On this occasion, the pushers were plentiful and we got off to a tremendous start, but as one of the pushers, I lost my head for a moment. I was far too enthusiastic and I failed by an enormous margin. Long after the other pushers had detached, I just kept running – way, way past the point where I had control of my balance. Instead I just clung to the back, almost horizontal, as the trolley gathered speed. I tried frantically to keep my legs spinning so that I didn't collect a dose of gravel rash from my neck to my knees. It was hopeless, of course.

I yelled at Marshall to slow down, but he had no brakes and so I trailed behind him like a briskly flapping banner – my body weight adding cruelly to his momentum. Marshall did really well to keep control all the way down Cook Street and around the two corners at the top of Union Road. Beyond that there was no safe run-off – there was a steeper slope that ended in cross traffic on busy Moore Street, so we had a solid chance of dying if we didn't take action soon. With me shrieking instructions from behind it looked like we might survive if he elected to turn onto the wide grass verge outside his own house. It had luscious, deep, soft kikuyu grass that would slow him down, and if that didn't work, then in the middle of it was a solid post that would do the job. By now the steering rope was humming like a phone line in a hurricane and there was an ominous wobble in the front wheels. Trolley reins are savagely quick to react to any outside influence. You need sensitive hands for the job. Even a stone can throw the wheels into a full-lock turn. I could feel that Marshall was about to lose control. On most trolleys the emergency brake was applied by wrenching the reins one way or the other. Below a certain speed, the front wheels would turn so sharply that the inside one would bite into the side of the trolley and jam. Then we would skid safely sideways until we stopped. But above that certain speed, the trolley wouldn't skid – it would flip and crash, and sometimes, one wheel would roll off – just like in the movies. So, in cases of doubt, we tried to skid onto some soft grass before we hit the gravel on any of the unsealed driveways further down. This was Marshall's sensible plan and he got so very close to bringing it off.

Only a couple of feet before the escape route he struck a stone chip. In a savage flash, the wheels locked solid against the side, we slammed into a leftwards skid off the pavement and the leading wheel dropped into a grating over a drain. Instantly the front end bit into the ground. I tried to let go, but at the crucial instant I tripped and lurched forward, awarding him a generous but completely unneeded dollop of energy. I then detached myself and skidded face first onto the cool grass. Marshall and the Bentley, meanwhile, flipped straight up into the air, rolled over sideways – *still in the air* – and then smashed upside down onto the grass. I have no idea how Marshall managed to scrunch himself up into the cockpit of the trolley, but he did and it may have saved his life. The trolley's skid sheared off the half-windscreen at dashboard level and would have broken his neck at the same time if he hadn't gone foetal in the bottom of the cockpit. As it was, he carved a good deep groove in the soft grass with the top of his head and only stopped doing it when the trolley hit the post.

Yeaaahhhh! Whorrrrrrrr! Mighteeeeeee! The applause from behind was intense and sustained. From inside the trolley I could hear muffled sounds that indicated Marshall was having some kind of breakdown, but I made no sound at all. I just concentrated on retching up grass.

Life was a canvas painted in bright colours in 1972. Mainly red.

~~~

THIRTY YEARS LATER, though, I wasn't so overjoyed at the sight of disaster approaching, but I was determined by now not to let this setback stop me. If I could survive disasters like the Mighty Crash, I could surely survive teeny upsets like a broken rudder. And now, as Black Point channel markers appeared ahead through the lessening rain, I hoped that once again I would be able to depend on the Christmas spirit or at least the kindness of strangers.

Puttering up the channel to the town's public marina I passed a fisherman on a dock. That was unexpected as it was now about noon on Christmas Day and I figured that everyone would be at home opening presents or whittling a turkey or arguing with relatives. Since I had no idea what the town of Black Point had to offer, I drew alongside the dock and asked him. His name was Bob, and he said it wasn't all that likely that I could get a rudder fixed here. Behind him was a large workshop and I had the feeling that even if they reconditioned refrigerators, they'd have a saw and some plywood so I'd be able to fashion a temporary rudder to get me to a proper boatyard. Bob and I chatted for a while about his own small boat that he was restoring – a Drascombe lugger. He went on to say that I could dock around the corner and the dockmaster would drop by the next day to collect a fee. Since I was a vessel in distress at present, no one would object to me tying up overnight.

Five minutes later I was tied to a dock next to the marina office, pumping out the bilge. It turned out that a seashell had got stuck in the outlet valve and jammed it open so that it wouldn't suck. As soon as I removed it, the pump worked fine. I reset the boom, flaked the sail, stowed loose items, sponged down the boat and set things out to dry on the dock. The thunderstorms had passed and the sun was out. After half an hour of busy work, I looked up to see Bob approaching. In his hand he carried a piece of plywood, a saw, a drill and some hand tools.

The kindness of strangers continues.

'Thought you might be able to rig up something temporary with these,' he said with a grin.

I made a mental note – total time from declaration of disaster to complete stranger and arrival of said stranger with repair equipment – 35 minutes. Americans have never disappointed me in this respect and

Bob was unconsciously upholding his country's reputation.

I hastily stripped my rudder down and then laid out the two pieces on the dock. Sure enough, it had broken along the line of the crack as I thought. I pulled out all my hand tools and repair gear and it looked like I had what I needed to make a replacement. Bob's sheet of plywood was thinner and shorter than the rudder blade, but it would work until I could make a proper rudder. I drew the outline of the rudder on the plywood and cut it out, then drilled the big hole for the pivot pin and the small hole for the lifting string, after which I filed open the pivot hole so that it would take the bolt.

An hour later, I had told Bob all about my trip, he had told me all about his father's boat, I'd told him about my girlfriend and he'd told me darkly about hurricanes and septic tanks and what a mess they had made of things in recent years. I also had a pretty good temporary rudder ready to be fixed to the rudder mount. Bob stood up and excused himself, saying that he had to get home for Christmas dinner. He wished me luck and I thanked him for his trouble and wished him well with his lugger project. I said I'd make him famous if I ever wrote a book about this trip and he said that'd be fine by him. We smiled and shook hands, both happy that we'd improved each other's day by quite a bit.

Not long after he left, while I was smoothing the edges of the blade with a file, a voice hailed me from the shore. A solid-looking man in a khaki shirt asked how I was doing. I held up the broken rudder pieces and said, 'Not real well this morning but I'm doing OK now,' as I held up the new rudder.

'Well, that's a good place for you to stay tonight – I'll come by tomorrow,' he said and waved as he climbed into his truck and drove off. I guessed he was a security guard or maintenance man pulling a little overtime.

Once I had the rudder installed, I packed up my gear, and began setting up my boom tent and bed. As soon as that was rigged I burrowed into the bow lockers and extracted my Christmas presents and laid them out around my tree. Adrienne had damnably included a 12-inch Christmas tree in her Christmas parcel to me and I'd felt obliged to haul this thing all the way across the continent to Canada on a Greyhound, then down to Florida in a U-Haul and, finally, to Black Point by Wayfarer. At last I could put it up, celebrate the happy day and then get rid of the darn thing. I'm not the least bit sentimental about Christmas. I actually prefer to spend the day alone with some nice delicatessen treats, a bottle of Bushmills whiskey, a cigar and a good book, so the lack of company for my Christmas dinner didn't upset me in the least. It was nice to set out my gifts, though. I knew what all of them were, since I'd had to unpack Adrienne's gift box on the ranch when I packed them into my duffel bag for travelling.

On this Christmas Day, my treats included a bag of chocs from Sandy, Adrienne's mini Christmas pudding and a bottle of Elaine's Mad Dog 20-20 wine, part of my leaving present from the ranch. It was real wine, too – said so right on the label – 'Red Grape Wine'. A touch of class there and it didn't taste that bad actually. I had some mini-pud and then some elk jerky. Another gulp of wine. It had a port-like quality – obviously it was fortified for the discerning derelict. I noted that it had no voltage on the label but I reckoned it to be about 25 percent alcohol by volume. More pud, one of Sandy's chocs,

Christmas Day.

some wine, some jerky, some more pud, wine, a cigarette, a gulp of Cointreau orange liqueur from my own hip flask – ah, this was more like it. A mellow feeling of accomplishment came over me with the prospect of a real treat still to come – I'd call Adrienne soon and talk to her for the first time in weeks. I missed her quite badly already. I had last spoken to her from Geoff Orr's house in Fort Lauderdale, but only briefly to arrange this phone call. Now I wanted to talk to her for a good long while.

Having finally got the boat in order and satisfied the inner man, I decided it was time to look for a telephone. Just beside the dock was an administration building and next to that was a bar and grill and a small dockside shop. They were all served by toilets in the centre, and despite the fact that the whole place was deserted, the toilets were open, the lights were on and, best of all, they had hot water. On my way back from them I passed a public telephone on a wall and spotted a garden chair nearby. It looked like I could make my call in comfort. Half an hour later I had taken a hot sponge bath, washed my hair, shaved, and cleaned up the water I'd sloshed all over the floor. I was in clean clothes and I had done some washing and hung it up to dry. I took my calling card and rang Adrienne's home number. I got hold of her sister, Mary, who told me Adrienne was at work until 10.30 pm, which equalled 3.30 in the morning my time. Oh bollocks! Her cellphone wasn't working so I decided I'd have to get up in the middle of the night to call her. Oh well, I'd probably be awake anyway – unravelling my legs – so it wouldn't be any great trial. I settled into my bed on the boat and updated my diary. It had been a busy day already and tomorrow it looked like I'd have another challenge – either trying to find a place where I could make a proper rudder or sailing *Wanderer* with my improvised one to another town. That *would* be fun.

My call to Adrienne went well and lasted nearly an hour. I'm not much of a gossip on the phone – I like to just get to the point and then finish – but in this case, talking at length was the whole point of the call. My news about my sailing was a bit irrelevant to her, and her news to me about the progress of the house she was decorating and her little homestay business was equally unconnected with anything

I was doing, but for once in my life I was happy just to chat. She sounded like she missed me a lot and I certainly wished she was with me. On so many occasions I wanted to nudge her in the ribs and point to something strange or funny. I wanted to show her the huge houses on the shore, the dolphins swimming alongside me, and the neat new place I'd found to stow the flare box. Little stuff like that, but important to me at the time. Instead, all I could do was take indistinct photos, make cryptic entries in my diary or try to remember a month's worth of incidents when I phoned. Not quite the same.

By 5.30 I was back in bed, just as the sun came up. I dozed until 7.00 am and then got up again and fixed some cereal for breakfast. By 8.00 am a few people were arriving at the marina and I was preparing to ask for advice from them when the security guard from the day before walked up and introduced himself. Turned out he was the dockmaster and he ran the whole show. His name was Jesse and he said he thought he could help. First, he said that the large workshop across the marina did mainly metalwork but might have some tools I could use. He knew someone there and would ask on my behalf as soon as they opened up in an hour or two. Meantime, I should just hang tight and wait. He had a good look at my boat and admired the roller furling. We chatted away; turned out he had a small yacht – a 19-foot Bristol – and he was refitting her so he could take his son out sailing. I said I'd stop by the office and pay my dock fees and he said there was no hurry.

When he left I walked to the marina shop and bought gas for my engine. After that, I dried out my tent and then began packing up my gear and was halfway through it when a shadow fell across the boat. On the dock next to me was a tall, slim guy in shorts, shirt and a baseball cap with a frown on his face. Behind him was Jesse, who stepped up to make the introductions.

'This is Gary, I asked him to take a look at your rudder. He's not from the workshop – I'll get to them later,' he added. Gary looked down at the two halves of my broken rudder laid out on the dock. Without shaking hands or saying hello he scowled at the rudder as if it were offending him.

'Plywood, huh?' he said with disgust. 'Wouldn'ta happened with mahogany. Or aluminum.' He examined the two pieces of plywood. 'Yeah, what you need is a nice piece of mahogany.'

Instantly I was niggled by this. Who the hell was he to criticise any part of my *Wanderer*? And sure – mahogany would have been stronger, but it was a bit late for that wisdom now. I was pretty pissed off so I enquired with false curiosity, 'Mahogany, eh? You got some?'

'Nope,' he said slowly, 'but I got some plywood. Close up your boat and get in the truck.' And with that, he picked up my broken rudder, turned away and walked back towards the shore. I stood there, not intending to go anywhere with this git, until he noticed I hadn't moved. He turned back and smiled for the first time.

'C'mon, get in the truck. I got some plywood and fibreglass that'll fix that. I got a wood-shop, see. I fix boats.'

Mightily surprised, I turned towards Jesse, who grinned and said, 'Go on. He'll fix it for you. Gary's my friend. I just called and told him about your boat and asked him to come take a look.'

Two minutes later, *Wanderer* was closed up, I was in Gary's truck and we were heading for his house to repair my rudder. It was about 9.00 am and I'd been in Black Point marina for 18 hours and was on my way to getting my second rudder made with the help of a total stranger.

Ten minutes later, we pulled into his garage. Inside was a complete home handyman's woodworking shop. Saw bench, drill press, lathe, hand tools and a whole wall of wood stock. On the way there he'd explained that he used to live aboard his own boat, which he'd restored from scratch. Now he ran his own company that built marinas but he still fixed up boats for himself and his friends in his spare time. In no time at all he had selected a sheet of plywood from his store that was one-sixteenth of an inch thinner than my rudder.

'We'll build it up with fibreglass at the top and put a layer all over the rudder. That'll last. So how'd you break it, anyway?'

For the next couple of hours we worked away at cutting and shaping the blade, while I told him how I broke it, how I came to be sailing a dinghy and what my plans were. He was a good listener too. Every now and then he'd chip in with a good entertaining story of his own that would lead us into a new conversational stream. He was one of the first Floridians I'd met that understood that a good conversation isn't a competition, it's almost a team event. About the time we set the first fibreglass layer out to dry, Gary's wife appeared with cold drinks and two plates of pasta and meatballs for lunch. We ate them standing up in the garage, drinking from time to time to get rid of the sawdust.

In between applying layers of fibreglass, I helped Gary work on his current project. He was installing a new deck in a friend's motorboat. It was made of a South American hardwood and required some intricate measuring and cutting. The end result was beautiful. Once he had applied the penetrating oil finish instead of varnish, it glowed softly with a rosy brown colour. I held parts in place while he measured, I steadied bits of wood while he cut them, I remembered to bring the pencil each time we walked back to the boat to measure a new component, and I held up my end of the conversation. In short, I did bugger all except enjoy myself.

We finished up with a beer each and then watched Gary's son racing his new Christmas present — a remote-control car. It was a wonderful day in comparison with the one I had imagined when I was motoring

Jesse and Gary — the Samaritans.

to the marina the day before. Instead of gloomily traipsing around town on foot, knocking on closed shop doors looking for wood and fibreglass and tools, I had made a new friend, I'd learned how to apply fibreglass and I'd had a bloody good yak. Total cost for the transport, use of supplies and tools, lunch, beer and advice — $0. So at 6.00 pm when Gary ran me back to the marina, I had in my hands a freshly fibreglassed rudder that would slot into my rudder head once I had sanded away the excess the next day. And Gary went back home with the only thing I could give him — a signed copy of *Straight From The Horse's Ass*. It was all I had to thank him with, except for the promise that when I wrote a book, he'd also be world-famous in New Zealand.

Sitting pretty

I WAS PRETTY chuffed when I sailed away from Black Point. Aside from the mild weather, the glow of friendship and the confidence that came from surviving the thunderstorm and the de-ruddering manoeuvre, I'd also spent far less money than I had expected. That morning I had mounted the new rudder and paid my bill to the marina – a very reasonable 75 cents per foot per night. For my 16-foot boat that came to $12 times two nights. Then I'd seen Jesse again and gone to admire his little Bristol sloop. He'd seen me using a scrap of foam cushion as a seat and pillow and so when I stepped aboard his yacht he casually mentioned that he was going to redo the upholstery and he wondered if I wanted this spare old seat cushion that he was planning to throw away. It was white with red beading and there was nothing wrong with it. In fact, it was perfect for my boat. I didn't feel the need to refuse out of politeness and that cushion became one of my most valuable fittings. It even matched the colour scheme that was evolving for the boat. It was the luxury that I needed to sit out seven to nine hours of sailing per day. And it was a gift from a friend, so that gave it extra meaning. Along with the hat from Geoff Orr (which was now elevated to daily use after the loss of my other one in the thunderstorm), these two objects became the most treasured of all the items that might be swept overboard, and for months afterwards I took special care to see that I didn't lose them. I am conscious that it sounds daft – a grown man with a security blanket – but hey, when you're alone for so long you take your comfort where you find it.

I gave Jesse a wave as I motored out of the channel and into the bay. It was nearly ideal for sailing – a following wind at 10 knots that jostled me across to Arsenicker Key and then to Pumpkin Key, a tiny dot of a private island just off the shore of Key Largo. I got there in the mid-afternoon, anchored in a sheltered spot near larger yachts and decided that I had finally earned myself a proper day of rest. It had been a busy week and I had a list of small chores to complete – I needed to sew up a small tear in my boom tent, replace a couple of broken rivets with nuts and bolts on the catches of my stern locker, cut my boom crutch down by an inch or so, reorganise the lower locker, spend a few hours reading my guidebooks and charts, and finally, just get some sleep. I decided to cook a good meal, lie in the next day, do my chores and go ashore as a treat in the afternoon. And, very importantly, I wanted to tie a string to my stove and my lantern.

Two nights previously, I had experienced difficulty getting the lantern to burn properly after refilling it. Flames had leaked out of the glass and lapped against the metal handle. I turned down the pressure and eventually controlled it but that was nothing compared to the antics of my pressure stove. The previous night, I had refilled it and lit it while sitting on the dock. Immediately, it had shot up a volcano of flame three feet high. I'd managed to cover it with the billy and choke off the flames. I assumed that I'd just spilled some fuel on it, so I wiped it dry, and tried again. WHOOOMMFF! Another blast of flame until I slammed the pot on top. While it cooled, I reread the instructions, fiddled with the controls, released some pressure and applied another match. More volcanic activity but this time I was ready with a pair of pliers to hold it while I plunged it in the water. Eventually I calmed the bastard down and got it lit without any accidental welding of my cutlery but I wasn't confident about it. I decided that if it did this sort of thing habitually then I wanted to have a long string tied to it so that I could just fling the bastard overboard and then reel it in when the fire was out. Even though I had a fire extinguisher, I didn't want my boom tent to have burn holes in it.

KEY LARGO HAS several small towns and I was anchored near one called Ocean Reef – it should have been called Creepyville. I had no idea of this as I sailed up a canal towards what I hoped would be a pleasant little seaport with maybe a burger stand and a grocery store.

Right away I should have spotted that something was up. It is hard to find a public landing for a dinghy in Florida. Most of the foreshore is privately owned and there's no such thing as a Queen's Chain or any other riparian access laws. Consequently, every boatie has to constantly search for places to dinghy ashore and do shopping or sightseeing. I was no different in this respect but it was a little harder for me since it required a charitable interpretation by the dock owners to regard my 16-foot live-aboard boat as a dinghy tender. Mostly I got away with tying up next to the other ducklings, but at the start I always felt vulnerable with all my gear stowed on a boat that was tied to the shore in easy reach of thieves. I had no secure locker and there wasn't an easy way to fix a padlock to any of the compartments, so apart from putting a bicycle lock on my outboard when I went ashore, I just took my cash with me and hoped for the best. I was never disappointed either. In all the time I sailed I never had a thing stolen, and after the first month I quit worrying.

Anyway, here on Key Largo it was the usual story – all private docks. I motored fruitlessly up several canals before I spotted a section of floating dock that was next to a public road and not at the bottom of a private garden like all the rest. Thinking that this was the public dock I tied up to it behind a mammoth motor cruiser and got my day pack loaded for an afternoon ashore. As I walked down the road in the direction of what I hoped was a town I noticed that the house on the other side of the street where I was docked had no access to the water. That seemed odd and then I realised I was tied up to his dock just across the road. Oh well, too late now. There was a lot of space behind me for another boat so I walked smartly away. I hadn't gone more than half a mile along the side of a golf course when a mini-van pulled up and a uniformed driver lowered the window and asked where I was headed and whether I wanted a lift. I had no idea where town was, so I said yes and he opened the electric sliding door.

'I'll just drop off this gentleman and then I'll take you to the fishing village,' he said. I looked at the other occupant. He was a very preppy 14-year-old with a set of golf clubs. Holden Caulfield's obedient brother. I looked at the driver and saw the *Ocean Beach* name on his epaulettes. Hmm, I guessed he must work for a resort hotel and had taken pity on me.

'So what's in town?' I asked.

'Oh everything, shops, bank, marina. I have a map here if you'd like.'

I took it. It showed the town and surrounding streets and *four* golf courses, as well as a small airport. On all the streets we passed, golf carts were buzzing to and fro – some with golfers, but many with people and kids just out travelling in them. Odd. There was very little regular vehicle traffic. The map had a ritzy look to it. Clearly Ocean Beach was a prosperous town if they could give these away. After we had stopped to drop off the teenager I asked the driver who lived here.

'Folks who like to golf – and rich people mostly,' he said bluntly. 'We had Denzel Washington here the other day – we get a lot of celebrities who like privacy here.'

'What's it like to work here?'

'OK,' he said guardedly. 'I mean, they like us to dress well – no bare stomachs, no visible piercings, no bare feet.'

Us? I thought. Who was *us*? The last time I had heard a workforce referred to as 'us' by one of the *us*, I was at a ski resort that treated its staff like serfs. Maybe this was one of those places. He stopped at the entrance to the little town and pointed out the book store to me. I thanked him and hopped out onto the main street which didn't look like any fishing village I'd ever seen.

Right away I got a creepy vibe. It looked exactly like Main Street in Disneyland. The buildings were all part of a single complex built in faux Victorian style with pastel shades and perfect street furnishings. The pavements were expensively paved, there were no litter bins, the streetlights were expensive decorative cast-iron structures and every-where you looked you saw perfect teeth, blond hair, light tans, Prada, Armani, and Abercrombie & Fitch. This was clearly the holiday home of the ruling elite. These WASPs all buzzed around in golf carts and

139

Creepyville, USA — Ocean Beach, Key Largo.

the range of carts was scary. There were Rolls-Royce lookalikes, Cadillac lookalikes, Mercedes lookalikes and plenty of other expensive toy cars. Young kids and old grannies wheeled these around with aplomb. The only proper vehicles were the real thing – Cadillac Escalades, Lincoln Navigators, the occasional Lexus or BMW. The golf cart thing rang a bell though. Where had I seen something like that before?

I walked on a little further and saw a street directory. I stepped up to read it and orient my map. As I did so, a cop cruiser pulled up and the cop leaned over to ask what I was looking for. Suddenly I was conscious of a worrying lack of Ralph Lauren in my clothing – I had a grubby T-shirt, grubby shorts with a hole burnt in them, ancient sneakers covered in paint and my sunglasses were $2 Shop specials. I was unshaven and too tanned. Clearly I didn't belong here amongst these lords of the earth.

'S'okay. Found it. Just looking for the grocery store. Right over there, eh?' I said, pointing across the intersection to the parking lot of a small store 100 yards away.

'I'll give you a lift,' he said.

'No, I'm fine. I've gotta go to the book store first, but thanks,' I said and walked smartly away from him. Walking smartly away was becoming a habit. As he drove off I saw on the back of his car *Department of Public Safety*. Yikes – they don't even have cops, they have Public Safety Officers. Orwellian. I passed a bank that had a lane marked *Drive up window for golf carts*. The marina had luxury yachts of the kind you normally only see in James Bond movies. Another courtesy van discharged its occupants in front of me. On the back, it had *Am I Driving Leisurely? Call 1-800 343 2300*. Shit sakes! Am I driving *leisurely*? Oh, this place was creeping me out. A flock of golf carts came towards me and suddenly I knew where I was.

I was on the set of that 1960s mystery cult show *The Prisoner*!!

It was all too similar – the same sharp clothing, the same bungalow houses, the same over-controlled, immaculately ordered streets. With golf carts instead of mini-mokes. This place was like *The Prisoner* with a dash of Disneyland architecture, and a cast of *Stepford Wives* and children. I stood out like a tartan wedding dress. I waited for the giant beach ball to come and herd me back to my cell.

Oh well, too late to do anything about it now. Instead, I took a couple of snaps of Main Street and then set about my shopping. I browsed the book store, bought some groceries and watched a 10-year-old pay for chewing gum with an *Ocean Beach* charge card. The grocery store, like all the other shops, was way too upmarket for me and the prices weren't bashful either. I bought a copy of *Time* magazine, a bottle of 7-Up and a banana and began walking back to the boat. Along the way I studied the Christmas decorations on the houses. Every one was the same – a single identical Christmas wreath on the front door. Nothing else. In America, that's seriously strange, since most streets have at least one house with more Christmas lights on the lawn than a Las Vegas casino. The only other external decorations appeared to have been provided by the town council and consisted of bland wreaths on the streetlights. Clearly, no unauthorised happiness or random seasonal joy was going to creep into Ocean Beach. I reckon the Public Safety Officers would use deadly force to stop anyone hanging washing on a Hills Hoist in this town.

It wasn't until I walked past the corner of Gatehouse Road that I realised why everything was so freakishly over-ordered. This was a gated community for the rich. If I hadn't snuck in accidentally by sea, I'd never have got past the border guards. I was just too raggedy-ass poor-looking to mix with the quality. And frankly, looking at the way they lived, I knew that was the best thing, too. You couldn't imagine anyone throwing a football in the street or crashing a skid board, let alone hauling the engine out of an old Chevy under a shady tree. Nope, this was a Nightmare on Palm Street. Despite the friendliness of the residents, it was the creepiest and most unlikeable place I've ever been in and that includes slums in Asia, hospitals in Africa and army camps in Australia.

I got back to my boat, found it undisturbed (I was half expecting it to be clamped or ticketed – or decorated with an approved wreath), and motored quickly a half mile offshore to Pumpkin Key, where I dropped anchor again. From the back of a Canadian yacht near mine, a friendly arm with a beer can in the fist waved lazily to me. The arm had tattoos on it. Good. I was back with my own kind.

~~~

I TIGHTENED THE shrouds to stop them knocking, spent another restless night and on the following morning I was able to sail calmly under a broiling sun down Card Sound, through a channel into Barnes Sound and then into Jewfish Creek. Here I had to wait 20 minutes for a bascule bridge to open and then I resumed sailing on Blackwater Sound. That narrowed into Dusenbury Creek, which had definite overtones of *The African Queen*. Mangroves either side, just a puff of wind to keep me drifting along, and all around me, water birds of every kind. Herons stood out on the shallows around every corner and even passing motorboats slowed down to avoid disturbing them with their wake. Progress was slow but comfortable. I played with the genoa and main, trying to achieve the perfect aerodynamic shape, but the winds were too light for much success and the day passed peacefully. This was the type of sailing I had imagined when I was planning the trip all those months ago and so I was quite content to only make 15 miles by the time I anchored in Tarpon Basin, a sheltered cove off Key Largo.

As I sailed into the basin, a bearded fellow sailed through the boats at anchor in a tiny dinghy with an oar for a mast. I found a spot to drop the pick, and as I did, he sailed up and hailed me. We got chatting, and it turned out that he was waiting for a wind change before heading outside the keys to make for the Bahamas. He invited me on board his 40-foot yacht for dinner and I was quick to accept. Steve Axon and his wife, Helen, had a summer home in Idaho but spent their winters cruising. Their sons were at college and they kept in touch with them by email.

On the stern of his boat was a portable Weber barbecue grill and on this they whipped up roast chicken, rice and zucchini, that we washed down with a lemony beer. They showed me a very useful guide to the ICW. It was one of a series published by Skipper Bob and his wife. Copied on plain paper and spiral-bound, it had none of the annoying bullshit recommendations about where to eat expensively ashore. Instead, this one described all the anchorages and places to land and shop on the ICW as far north as Canada. Skipper Bob had a simple four-star rating for six categories at each location: *holding, wind, current, wake, scenic* and *shopping.* He also identified those places where nearby public libraries provided free email facilities and places where pets could be exercised, laundry done and mail forwarded. I made a note to buy it as soon as I could. Skipper Bob was to be my faithful guide for the rest of the trip. At last I could see where I could buy gas and food and avoid paying a bundle for dockage. Skipper Bob understood the limitations imposed on sailing craft that averaged only 6 mph under power and less under sail. Brilliant. That was me to a tee.

I said good night to Steve and Helen and retired to my boat, which I had tied up to their stern. I felt mellow and well fed and sleepy. I dropped off quickly and didn't wake up until morning and my legs were still on the right way round when I sat up in bed.

The wind had shifted round to the south overnight so I was glad I'd decided to take the day off and go shopping. I started up and motored off to a deserted dockside restaurant. It provided good access to the strip malls running endlessly in each direction along the side of the main highway that ran down the islands all the way to Key West. The

Deserted dockside restaurant – ideal berth for a small cruiser.

restaurant had been a popular nightspot for years but its owner had been caught laundering drug money and was doing a wee spell as a guest of the governor so the dockside was deserted and shabby. It was perfect for me to tie up to for half a day, so I landed myself, put my gear away and marched off for another of my many shore explorations.

Now you have to know a couple of things about urban America to appreciate the whingeing that follows. Firstly, strip malls are the name given to the sprawling rash of shops, restaurants, gas stations, outlet stores, supermarkets and roadside entertainments that begin on the outskirts of a town and spread for miles beyond it. The keys were blighted more than most places in this respect because the islands were long and narrow and only had room for one main highway – US1 – running down the spine. All development spread along the road and directions to any place on it were given in terms of mile markers; i.e. '*Get your Booger burger at Burger Baron on Plantation Key, Mile marker 44¹/₂*'. The miles were measured from Key West all the way north to Miami. The islands themselves were connected by dozens of bridges and long causeways that took the place of a famous railroad built at the start of the 20th century by Henry Flagler – a well-known East Coast mogul and entrepreneur. The railway was a huge boost to the economy of south Florida as it drew in hordes of North Easterners looking for a warm winter vacation spot, but it was terribly vulnerable to destruction by hurricanes. It survived a few, but in 1937 it was comprehensively blasted by a hurricane that sent a tidal surge right across many keys, simply sweeping away everything in its path. It took hundreds of lives and prompted Franklin D. Roosevelt's government to replace it with a public highway. The highway, like the railway before it, is a marvel of engineering and a fine example of Yankee spirit. Rather than mess about with too many manned bascule bridges that would have to open and close to allow boats to pass from the inside (Florida Bay) to the outside (Atlantic Ocean), they built the bridges 65 feet above the water to give ample clearance to all but giant yachts. These beautiful arches of white concrete rise like small hills in front of the motorist as you drive the 150 miles down to Key West. The view from the top is terrific and the cost must have been enormous – but that's never stopped US engineers from building yet. North of Miami, the same thing is happening as small, low, expensive bascule bridges are replaced by tall, gracefully curved, multi-lane fixed bridges. In Florida alone there must be 200 or more of these bridges connecting islands to each other or to the mainland, each span being about half the size of the Auckland Harbour Bridge. It's an impressive highway to drive on or to sail past.

Anyway, US1 is the backbone of the keys and all along it are strip malls designed for vehicle access only. Walking between shops is quite time-consuming and the scenery is grotty – signs, car parks, inter-sections, etc. – but if you head off in either direction eventually you'll come to what you want. In fact, as you move from town to town you experience a type of déjà vu as you start to repeat the cycle of con-venience stores, chain stores and fast-food outlets. Americans call this repeating landscape *Generica*. All I had to do now was pick a direction and start walking and eventually I'd find all the things I needed – even if I had to walk to Miami. I started by heading south a couple of blocks to a Publix, an upscale supermarket in a mall. Nearby were a K-Mart and a public library. First I emailed Adrienne and checked on the news from home.

I got my groceries, bought a better lock for my outboard and then set off looking for a one-gallon can of white gas fuel for my lantern and stove. I headed north, dropped off my purchases at the boat on the way past and then began calling in at a number of places suggested to me by boaters and others. After an hour and a half I was several miles north of the boat, getting tired and hadn't found what I wanted. I plodded back to the boat, untied it and motored back to a quiet nook where I anchored in shallow water near to the mangrove shore. It was boiling hot again and the wind had died away. The spot was well sheltered and there were no waves so I lazily ate a sandwich on a flat calm sea and soaked up the sun in my swimming togs.

I spent the afternoon installing a reinforcing plate to the transom to better support the engine mount. I'd kept the rudder blade made with Bob's piece of plywood so I fashioned two overlapping plates that fitted the shape of the transom. Lapped together, these gave an inch-thick reinforcement to the thin area of fibreglass at the stern. They fitted perfectly and the job looked quite professional. I should have painted them too but they were well out of sight inside the locker and they wouldn't get wet or sunburned. I was very pleased with myself and I enjoyed the whole process of working away steadily with my hands and my limited amount of tools and carpentry knowledge. It was only a small challenge but it was all part of the adventure. To celebrate, I fried up half a pound of bacon and made cream cheese and bacon sandwiches for dinner. Delishimo.

The forecast warned of a strong front coming through on New Year's Eve, so I decided to stay put and complete my shopping. I could call Ady from the phone box at the library, too. Once again I tied up at the deserted restaurant dock, locked things away as best I could and headed off in search of lantern gas. After another long search in the wrong direction, I found it – at the K-Mart. I called Adrienne and she warned me that she didn't think she was going to be able to afford to fly back to the US in May to visit me when I reached Washington DC. That was a real blow to my plans since I had figured on sailing up the Potomac to the city and seeing the sights and museums with her. I managed to convince her not to rule it out completely, but to wait a few months to see how our finances lasted. Aside from that unwelcome news, we had a lovely time talking and I felt pretty happy when I hung up.

In the afternoon I took Frank's big multi-band radio and set off again. I'd seen a pawnshop nearby and since I wanted to get rid of the big radio, I decided that this was the time. After a lot of paperwork and fingerprinting I got $10 for it, which I used to buy a little transistor at Radio Shack back down a mile next to the K-Mart. It was a lot of walking again, but now I had plenty of spare space in my electronics bag to stow all my expensive, delicate electrical things and my spare batteries, camera, film and torch. Now that I had standardised all my appliances on AA batteries I donated the other sizes to a boat that had tied up their dinghy behind me.

Then I set off to motor around the basin looking for the ideal spot to anchor that night, but in the end the dock provided the most shelter and convenience so I tied up and listened to golden oldies on 103 FM while flares and fireworks whistled up into the night sky. The wind blew, the rain passed quickly, the Mad Dog 20-20 got sampled again and then I was asleep as *Wanderer* rocked me gently into a new year.

Blue skies

I HAD DONE a few days' sailing now but had still to really enjoy the experience. On New Year's Day I set off into a moderate southerly wind and butted against it all day. I started out double-reefed in case the wind rose and then tacked in and out of the basins and channels until 5.00 pm when I finally made it into Little Harbour on Tavernier Key – only about nine miles from my start point. On the way I lost a reefing string from the sail and discovered that my roller furling needed to be tied down to the foredeck in two places instead of just one. Without the second tie-down, it tangled at awkward moments. Then, as I was flaking the sail before anchoring under jib power, I dropped a flaking cord as well. That gave me a couple of chores to do the next day while I waited for the wind to come up. It never did, so in the end I spent the morning at a laundromat and finally I motored out of Little Harbour in the early afternoon on a completely flat calm, oily sea. There was a mist that gave the sea an eerie look but nothing odd happened and I made 11 miles before deciding to anchor in Little Basin off Islamorada Key. This was a shallow basin – perhaps three feet deep outside the main channel – so I was surprised to see dolphins hunting in the evening light. Sometimes their fins would stick up above the surface and I could follow their progress as they chased small fry. Their occasional bursts of speed were astonishing. I'd seen dolphins cruising along at boat speed on many occasions already, but when they stepped on the gas I could understand how the force of one of their strikes could stun a shark.

The forecast that night was for a powerful northerly to whip through with thunder and heavy rain. To be safe, I threw out a second anchor and buttoned my boom tent up tight. Sure enough, about midnight, the wind rose, lightning flashed and the rain came down in sheets. Some leaks appeared and I covered my sleeping bag with plastic but the tent stayed secured to the boat and did a good job of keeping the wind out as well. I slept intermittently until just before dawn and then I finally gave up and started breakfast.

The weather forecast predicted 25-mph winds all day but at least they were northerlies and I was keen to make some miles after the piddling progress of the previous week. I motored down the complex winding channels to get into open water and then hoisted a reefed mainsail. The following seas and wind made for fairly fast sailing but I was nervous of the gusts and didn't enjoy the sloppy steering that you get in these conditions. Fortunately the waves stayed small so that I didn't surf down them or risk a broach, but I was still relieved to spot a small harbour where the national Scouting organisation had a sailing school. I put into it and tied up to a dock while I asked where it was OK to anchor. The answer surprised me – it was a private harbour and I could stay only as long as it took me to untie and get out! I could see there was no shelter ahead of me for a good few miles so reluctantly I motored back about two miles and found a corner of a private canal that had room for me to swing at anchor. There I spent the night, comfortable enough but a bit ticked off that the owners of a half-empty harbour would send a small boat back out into the sort of weather that had kept every other boat home that day.

Next morning it was noticeably cooler, so for the first time I put on Frank's wet weather gear and sea boots. Immediately I felt twice as good a sailor. I packed up the boat and readied her for another wet day but first I tied up to an empty berth near a fishing factory and went ashore to buy milk and bread. I stayed there for an hour or so, waiting for the wind to stop bending the coconut palms over. I was nearly ready to cast off when a fellow came over and told me sourly to get off his dock. I had no choice but to apologise for occupying an empty space and since it was about 11.00 am I decided to give sailing a try. Lower Matecumbe Key did seem to be full of unfriendly natives. I motored down the channel and quickly hoisted sail. And, boy, was I glad I did.

Yes, the wind was a bit strong at first and the sea and sky were grey and unattractive, but before long I got a feel for the conditions and soon I was letting out the mainsail and pulling out the genoa and within an hour I was absolutely flying. I was quite nervous being out all alone on this lumpy sea but I was well prepared: I was never more than a couple of miles from land, I had a lifejacket on, a safety rope attached to the boat, and I had all the safety equipment I needed. For two busy hours, as occasional blasts of spray soaked me, I steered by compass, making the changes in course that the channels and islands dictated. I passed by Matecumbe Key, the eight-mile Long Key viaduct, Long Key, the Conch Keys, Duck Key, Grassy Key and Fat Deer Key. The wind began to die down a little and by late afternoon I was once again cruising under blue sky and mild winds. The front had passed over, I had gained confidence, and in just four hours I had made 22 miles. That was more than I'd made on any two sailing days previously and I was bursting with pride as I neatly tacked into a sheltered spot behind a tiny unnamed island near Vaca Key. In honour of my gal, I drifted up to an overhanging mangrove, grabbed it, stood on the bow in an exploring pose, faced a floating pelican nearby and grandly named the little island 'Adrienne Key'. Then I ate an apple to celebrate.

This was a big important day for me. I had sailed well and fast in conditions that originally I didn't want to sail in and it had done me nothing but good. I guess I had to thank the man at the dock for kicking me out, just like I had to thank the people at the Scout harbour for moving me on. It seemed that even the bad things that were happening on this trip were turning out for the best. I had got over another little bit of fear and that was what the trip was all about.

~~~

THE VHF RADIO station that broadcast my weather forecasts was out of range now – a pleasing sign of progress – so I switched to a new one. It wasn't as friendly. Both of them used dispassionate computer-generated voices to read the weather in a stumbling inept way that placed the emPHARsis on the wrong sylABBles, but I had grown accustomed to the first voice and it seemed to me that the new one was a little bit more abrupt. It occurs to me now that this was one of the first signs of loneliness that I recorded on the trip – affection or disapproval for a robot weatherman is an indication of a loosening in the hinges. But the weather was clearly the dominant force in my life now. I listened to the forecast last thing at night, first thing in the morning, and sometimes during the day as well. They covered several land and sea areas for up to seven days in advance, broken down into morning, afternoon and overnight predictions. Then they gave masses of other information as well, such as tide times, tide heights, flood warnings, summaries of the previous day's weather that stated the actual temperature, rainfall, humidity, wind speed and direction, and then compared it to the record for that day of the year in history, as well as to the average for that day of the year. All this was replayed continuously on a loop that took about 15 minutes to go through. If you switched on a moment after your forecast finished, you had to wait for the cycle to repeat.

Frequently, as I moved along the coast, I wasn't even sure where the sea areas lay, since I had no idea of the local geography. Sea areas were described in relation to capes, islands, rivers, cities, towns or even counties up to 100 miles north or south of me, so often I'd have to pull out my large-scale Rand McNally road map of the USA to identify the landmarks before I could work out which section of the forecast applied to me. Then I'd have to listen to it again to actually comprehend the details. Sometimes it would take me an hour to finally discover what was going to happen tomorrow and then, unless I jotted down a note, I'd get it confused with what was supposed to happen the next day and the day after that.

And I needed to know it all because I had to plan my cruising about three days ahead. If not, then I ran the risk of getting stuck somewhere grotty while unfavourable weather passed through. I would often have to plan to sail like hell for two days, just to be in a comfortable place when bad weather arrived a week later. If I missed out on my chance to gain a good anchorage, I might get stuck for a day or two while rain poured down or waves bounced me around. And 48 hours spent stationary under a boom tent with nowhere to go ashore was a prospect I didn't look forward to. In short, listening to the weather was a hassle and living by it was an even bigger inconvenience. When I started sailing I knew in an academic way that the weather was critical to the completion of the trip as well as my enjoyment of it, but I had no idea what it meant in practice. In fact, rest days were granted to me only by the weather gods – good sailing days were too precious to waste.

~~~

FEELING PRETTY CHIPPER the next morning, I sailed off towards my next destination – Bahia Honda Key – where I paid for a berth in the marina. It cost $20 but it gave me access to a shower and a chance to shop in Marathon. Half an hour after landing I was cleaned up, had my second-best shore clothes on and was in a taxi heading 12 miles back to Marathon ($22). I found what I'd come for – *Skipper Bob's Guide to Anchorages on the ICW* – in a second-hand book store ($18). The owner was a lady in her fifties and she talked to me about *Wanderer* and even looked it up in an encyclopaedia of boat types.

'Wow, that's small – and I thought our 20-footer was tiny.' Then she added, 'But I can stand up in the head in ours.'

'Well, so can I – as long as no one's looking,' I replied.

The book store-owner's husband gave me a lift another two miles up the highway towards the airport where I could grab a bite to eat and catch a bus back to the marina for $8. By 5.00 pm I was on board my boat again, about $80 poorer but still pretty happy with my excursion. That shows the cost of moving around on shore on a holiday like this. But the bus trip back down to Bahia Honda had one unexpected benefit. From high up on the Seven Mile Viaduct that I'd sailed alongside earlier in the day I could compare the Gulf waters with the Atlantic side. There was no doubt that the Atlantic side was far smoother. The bookshop owner had also said I'd have plain sailing on the Atlantic in these northerlies. The keys, which curved around to the southwest, gave shelter, and looking at the two options I decided to risk a day on the Atlantic Ocean. Now *that* was scary.

Early the next morning I lowered the mast at the dockside, but I forgot to first undo the tie-downs for the roller furling and as a result I nearly broke the mechanism. I spotted the mistake in time and did no lasting harm and a few minutes later I was motoring quietly out of the marina and up to the bridge. I glided easily under it onto the Atlantic and hauled the mast back up. Once I was confident I had it rigged snugly again, I hoisted the mainsail and eased through the shallow reef and out onto the ocean. Right away, things got good. The wind was steady and strong but not gusty and it didn't vary in direction at all. The longer Atlantic rollers were far smoother and less frightening than the short choppy Gulf-side waves. And best of all, there were no islands or channels or reefs or shallows to dodge. I set *Wanderer* on course, trimmed the sails, leaned back comfortably on my pillow and with the genoa and main sheets in my right hand and the tiller in my left, I settled down to enjoy the ride. Behind me, the clouds were thin, high and unthreatening, Ahead of me, the headlands appeared with regular precision and all morning *Wanderer*'s bow cut through the waves with a keen hiss as we made 4½ miles per hour. This was even better than the previous day. I was amazed to discover how much less work there was when you barely had to navigate or worry about gusts of wind. I just steered the same course for four hours and suddenly, there we were, right off the point that marked the entrance to Newfound Harbour.

I'd picked this as my next stop because my new Skipper Bob's guide said there was a library with email facilities within walking distance, as well as a supermarket. I tacked around the point and headed up the harbour into a short chop. Immediately I got soaked with spray and it stayed that way for the three-mile beat up the channel towards the town on Big Pine Key. This happened quite often – I'd have a lovely dry day's sailing and then get drenched coming into the wind on the last half-mile to an anchorage. Oh well, I didn't mind it now – I was still on a high after sailing the mighty Atlantic!

I know I was only two miles offshore and that hardly counts as sailing on the ocean, but it was a big psychological boost to me to get out onto it anyway. Now all I was looking for was a place to tie up near town. Skipper Bob reported some canals nearby that provided good shelter, and as there was another weather front due the next day, I nosed into the first of these and looked for a vacant lot where I could stop for a day. I found one pretty quickly so I tied up to a tree, pumped out the bilge and spread my wet weather gear out to dry. With everything as tidy and secure as I could make it, I set off to find the library and do some emailing. It was only a mile or so to the library so I got there in good time to discover that it was closed on Mondays. Rats. I bought a few groceries at the Winn-Dixie supermarket and headed back to the boat. On the way there I spotted an office services business so I paid $12 for an hour on their email connection and sent off a news bulletin to everyone I knew that was interested in the trip. I had done this three times before and I called them my 'Hughes Nughes' letters. It was an easy way of keeping everyone informed. Geoff Orr, Stan Murdock, Brian McCleery, Adrienne, my family and a couple of friends in New Zealand were the core of the list. I sent the letter to Ady and she then forwarded it to all the names on an address list that she kept for me. It was easier than retyping all the names on each new computer I used in every little town. Writing the bulletin took about half the time – deleting my spam emails took longer.

When I got back, there were neighbours standing around looking at *Wanderer* and I chatted with them for a moment or two while I stowed my food. It seemed as though they didn't really approve of transients staying there overnight so I untied and puttered off in search of a more private berth. A few minutes later I found one that looked just right. So right that someone else had tied their motorboat up to it as well, but there was room for me behind it. I motored past it to check the space in front and then turned around and went back. As I made my final approach, I got distracted looking for a tree or something on shore to tie up to and I didn't throttle down soon enough. As I cut the engine I drifted speedily towards the stern of the motorboat and I had no choice but to turn the bow into the bank to avoid a collision. It looked like solid clay but actually it was rock and I hit it with the towing eye on the stem hard enough to bend the little steel fitting. I ran up the front to see what damage I'd done and when I saw it I said loudly, 'Bugger!' No great harm – but it was a stupid thing to do.

'What's the matter?' said a voice from behind me. I looked around at the speaker. He was about 50, with a ponytail and he was dressed in

Phil De Clue – another member of the bloody good blokes club.

sneakers, T-shirt, head bandanna and shorts. He looked like he was in the middle of painting something. I explained that I am a bear of little brain who could only do one thing at a time.

'What did you hit?'

'Just the bank – I missed the boat,' I said as I held onto the shore while reaching for a mooring line.

'Planning to stay long?' he asked.

'Umm no, just overnight if no one objects,' I said, as I leaned down to find a line. 'I'm on my way down to Key West tomorrow or the day after.'

'Uh huh. So you're not planning to live there?'

'Well, no. I mean, I live aboard but I'm not here for long.'

'Oh. Well that's OK I guess. Why don't you tie up over here? You can use my dock.' He had a nice little dock to tie up to, whereas the bank behind the boat lacked any place to secure a line.

'Well, that's very kind of you, but I live on board and you don't want some drifter littering up your dock, do you?' I asked.

155

'Hey, if it's only for a night, I don't mind. I just don't want anyone tying up permanently. You get that around here sometimes. People think they can stay forever. I had a guy try that once.'

The dock would be more convenient and I did plan to leave the next day if the weather was OK, so I thanked him for the offer and paddled *Wanderer* backward to his dock. A few minutes later I had my fenders over the side and was neatly secured.

'I'm Phil De Clue,' he said, putting out his hand and smiling.

'Lee Hughes, captain of this mighty vessel and piss-poor pilot too. That piece of land snuck up on me and I bent the towing eye on the bow. Can't believe I did that,' I said, grinning.

'Gotta watch out for that land,' he agreed with a smile. 'OK, you're welcome to stay here and use the bathroom if you want. Do you need water or anything?'

'Well, thank you, I'm OK for water and I've got all I need on board here. I'm just going to cook up some tea, do my diary and stow my groceries.'

Phil said to sing out if I needed anything and then he went back to sawing pieces of wood for some construction project that was going on inside the house. I rigged my boom tent, made some sandwiches for tea and ate a packet of potato chips and half a packet of chocolate bridge mix candy and guzzled a Vanilla Coke. On shore, Phil hammered and sawed away, occasionally glancing in my direction. Around dusk, he went inside and left me to read by lamplight. Secure in my little world, tied up legally to a sheltered dock, I finally slept like a log.

The forecast predicted a weak, fast-moving southerly front for the next day so I decided to stay a day longer and do some more emailing and also plot my course properly using GPS. Because the GPS would drain my batteries pretty quickly if I left it on all the time, I tended to just turn it on for a minute or so every few hours when I wanted to check my boat speed; or in fog, or when out of sight of land, I'd refer to it about every 20 or 30 minutes. I wasn't using the full suite of functions that included plotting waypoints and navigating to them using the GPS the whole time. It wasn't necessary or economical, but for the next leg, I decided to practise doing it so I could remember how to do it later if I needed to. I also wanted to update my chart tracks so far by drawing them in pencil on the chart, highlighting them and recording all the locations where I spent a night. A pleasant day in the library beckoned, but before I got away, Phil leaned out his back door and invited me in for a cup of tea. Sure enough, inside the house he was relining the walls, repainting it all and retiling the floors. He said he'd just recently bought the house and the adjacent plot of vacant land where I had planned to tie up the day before. He was doing it up as a holiday home. Phil was a glazier with his own business and various properties in St Louis, but he was comfortable enough to think of semi-retiring to Florida. Then he thought he might buy or build a catamaran and base it here so that he could cruise the Keys and then the Bahamas and the Caribbean. Clearly he was a man with a plan and he was already carrying it out. I liked the cut of his jib. He agreed that it was a poor decision for me to push on into a southerly and he recommended that I stay another night. We nattered away pleasantly for an hour and then I set off for the library.

The library was closed. Didn't open till noon on Tuesdays. Instead I visited an information centre nearby and found out all about the miniature deer of Big Pine Key. They were the chief cause of all the vacant lots in the canals and elsewhere. It seemed that these deer were isolated after the last rise in water levels many thousands of years ago. Now, they formed a distinct sub-species unique to Big Pine Key. They were all protected and so was much of their habitat. They wandered freely around the streets and the pine scrub in between. To save the key from overdevelopment, there was a pretty comprehensive ban on building new houses. Even expanding an existing dwelling was a problem. One way around it was to own an undeveloped lot next to your house. Then, by some quirk in the rules, you were permitted to spend as much as half the taxable value of your home on further improvements to it. That was why Phil had the vacant lot and why he was busy doing up his main dwelling. He wanted to get the taxable value up before it was next inspected. That valuation would give him the ceiling he could spend on developing the other lot. Or something like that. The end result was that there were many vacant lots, little improvement of existing dwellings and the whole island had a relaxed charm with the noise of traffic drowned out by the sound of chippies' hammers. It also meant that Big Pine Key had a healthy supply of two things – miniature deer and hippies. The hard-core alternative lifestylers (who are to hippies what stockbrokers are to the rest of us) hadn't moved in yet – these were simply hippies. Mellow, friendly, slightly weird and fairly trusting. Phil might have had a hard head for business but he was just as laid-back as could be socially.

By late afternoon I was back on *Wanderer*, charts all neatly updated and GPS loaded for bear. I tucked them all away as Phil called me over to meet his friend and occasional carpentry assistant. Bernard was what you might call a character. Or what you might call a flake, depending on how judgemental you want to be and how confident you are that we didn't all spring from the bastard offshoot of a race of space aliens who built the pyramids, colonised the world, left us to go back to some distant star and who looked like giant lizards. Of course, I didn't find this out all at once. And that summary is a pretty brutal description of some of Bernard's ideas. But, with some sotto voce explanations from Phil, I was gradually clued in to some of Bernard's weirder beliefs. Aside from that, he was great company. Bernard was about 80 years old, German by birth and upbringing, but New Age flaky by inclination. He was well educated, a pleasant conversationalist and didn't seem to mind being gently teased by Phil, who of course had heard it all before. Bernard lived aboard his own boat moored in the harbour nearby and occasionally came ashore to help Phil and pick up a little spare change. He refused to have anything to do with the authorities (and that included refusing to register for the social security cheque he could have claimed) and he lived a life of apparent self-sufficiency. Anywhere else you'd write him off as a semi-derelict nutcase, but if you stopped and thought about it for a second, his beliefs and lifestyle were no more primitive or impractical than those that were held and practised by 90 percent of the western world as little as three hundred years ago. In fact, in some of his grumpy opinions about the 'world going to hell in a hand-basket' he reminded me of my late brother Malcolm. Phil in turn reminded me of my other brother, Graeme. Sitting in Phil's lounge that night eating pizza and drinking beer provided by Phil, I was completely at ease. We chatted away about anything and everything and the conversation never laboured or lacked traction. I didn't want to overstay my welcome so I called it quits at ten o'clock but I could have sat and yarned away for hours. It was quite the opposite of the manic speed of conversation in Fort Lauderdale. At last, I was in synch with my surroundings. On land at least. Now I just needed a good day on the water.

The end of the beginning

THIS WAS ONE of those days that exceed your expectations. Clearly, Santa had belatedly put in a word to the Great Pumpkin himself and on this morning I got the kind of perfect day that would have had Lou Reed singing in key.

After a breakfast of coffee with Phil in his kitchen, I motored out of the canal and into the head of the harbour. Passing Bernard's boat I hoisted the main and started tacking down the harbour towards the Atlantic. As I came out past the headland, the wind was a steady, warm northerly at about 15 knots. No gusts, no veering or backing, just the warm breath of the God of Small Boats pushing me along at about 5½ mph. I raised the genoa, trimmed my sails, sank into my cushion on the starboard seat, and with the wind on the beam I concentrated on steering a nice crisp course. Occasionally, as the sun warmed up, I discarded a layer of clothing until I was sailing in just shorts, sunglasses, cap and a lifejacket. Headlands and beaches slid past me to starboard, waypoints and reef markers to port. Long Atlantic rollers passed easily beneath *Wanderer*'s keel. After a while I tuned in the radio to a golden oldies station and snacked on an apple and some muesli bars. I sang along to Simon and Garfunkel and the Bobby Fuller Four and I whistled the ending to 'Dock of the Bay'. Above me the sun hammered down; below me the clear water showed a white sandy bottom 30 feet down with occasional long strands of kelp. Dolphins visited for a few minutes and then left on their own urgent business. Far off, big yachts made the passage south outside the channel markers, but I gave them a run for their money before their long hulls drew them ahead of me. And all the time, *Wanderer* surged up one side of the waves and slid down the other. She ran on, hour after hour without missing a beat, like a big V8 gobbling up small hills.

Occasionally I'd go forward to stretch my legs and to get another chew of tobacco from the packet of Red Man Gold Blend ('America's Best Chew') from the green canvas bag beneath the coaming. I never smoked cigarettes while sailing and I only had an occasional one or two Camels or Lucky Strikes in the evening, perhaps twice a week. I kept track of the number of packs I bought and over the whole holiday it was only seven, so that would just see me in the beginner's cancer ward, not up there in the Humphrey Bogart high rollers' suite. Very rarely – say four times on the whole trip – I smoked a cigar, but every day when I was sailing I'd pop in a chew of tobacco. Oh sure, the occasional spitting might look pretty gross to a bystander, but that was the whole point – there weren't any bystanders on this trip, so I could enjoy my small pleasure without disapproving glares from the righteous. Chewing was one of the few pleasures on this trip that involved no great expense or inconvenience. It wasn't fattening, I could do it in any weather and it left my hands free for sailing at all times. In short, I recommend it to anyone working outdoors who cares not a jot for the opinions of do-gooders, doctors, or bleating PC nanny-state nosy parkers with their chatter-chip hard-wired for auto-nag. When you're alone on a wee boat you can say hock-ptooey to the lot.

After only five hours of perfect cruising I could see the next island just ahead and it was Key West. After 17 days' sailing I'd almost reached the official start point of my journey. I rounded Fort Taylor at 1.30 pm and began the slow tack up the channel towards the entrance to the small old harbour of Key West Bight. I'd read my guidebooks and knew that dockage for a small boat would be scarce and expensive, but I hoped I might be able to find a wee nook where I could tie up and go ashore. The weather forecast didn't predict any nice southerlies to blow me back up the coast in the next day or two so I was mentally prepared to spend some time sightseeing ashore. If I couldn't find a berth in one of Key West's three crowded harbours, I'd have to anchor off one of the islands and get rocked around by the wake of the dozens of boats that passed in and out of Key West every hour. And that included the 400-foot-long cruise liners that docked at the sea wall half a mile away. And even if that was an acceptable option for anchoring at night, it still left me with the problem of getting ashore each day. My boat was too long to qualify for the dinghy dock (fee $5 per day) so I'd either have to blow up my inflatable and row in, or else catch a water taxi. I didn't like the idea of using the inflatable in case a wind came up and blew me out of the channel into open water. It wasn't a very good boat for fighting the wind in because it rode high in the water and was very light. And a water taxi was expensive and not always readily available.

It took an hour to tack a mile up the channel to the harbour entrance. Then I had a half-hour of motoring around the berths amongst the super yachts before I got advice from a relaxed-looking bloke on a shabby 25-foot yacht. He said I should wait until after 5.00 pm and then tie up to the harbour master's pier in front of the fuel dock for free and leave before he came back at 8.00 am the next morning. I didn't want to waste the two hours of daylight until then, so instead I visited the harbour master's office and explained what I was after. He was very obliging. First he quoted the official price for a berth for me there.

'We have a minimum length of 30 feet at $1.80 a foot which would be about $60 a day for you to tie up.' Too much, says I.

'Well, I'll call the marina in Garrison Bight, they're cheaper.' So he did, and they said, '20-foot minimum – cost you about $36 plus tax per day.' Not a chance, I said.

He contacted the other harbours and they quoted the same sorts of fees. I could have tied onto a mooring ball in the channel much more cheaply but that left me with the problem of getting ashore. So, in the end he looked at his watch and made the kind of suggestion I hoped he would.

'Well, I finish here at five and that's two hours away, so how about I charge you $10 to use the fuel dock till then, and after that, what I don't see won't hurt me. As long as you're gone from here by 8.00 am, you'll be fine. Don't worry about security, those guys will drop by about eight o'clock tonight but if you're not around to answer questions, they won't bother you.'

Twenty minutes later I was snugged up to the fuel dock in front of a giant luxury yacht that looked like a minesweeper, with my boom tent up and secured. I grabbed my camera and headed off to see the sights of the Town at the End of the Road.

Key West was famously home to Ernest Hemingway in the 1930s. Now, though, it's home to a fair assembly of hippies and bums, who are crammed into a couple of square miles of prime Florida real estate and slowly being crowded out by more expensive homes and accommodation for tourists. Businesses cater to cruise-ship shoppers keen to whack down wads of money for designer labels and any sort of witty T-shirt or knick-knack with *Key West* on it. It isn't yet a hideous tourist trap – there's still plenty of ordinary and some extraordinary folk around – but it's a stretch to call it laid-back.

Snugged up in Key West at a discount berth.

It's getting to be like the tourist quarter of New Orleans, with which it shares many features. It has its own Mardi Gras festival after hurricane season and it changes character in the summer when tourism goes down as the temperature goes up. All in all, if you've seen any seasonal tourist town at the far end of a peninsula, then you've seen most of Key West too. I enjoyed it, but having been there before, I found that after just a few hours I'd seen enough. I knew that if I stayed around I'd spend a bundle of money and I'd do things I didn't really need to. I'd end up with something that was a hamburger in every respect except that it cost twice as much and couldn't be eaten with your fingers. You know the kind of thing – two buns served separately on a plate, with too much frilly mutant lettuce, aioli, beef patties, peanut sauce and something that might be a grated radish. The whole thing is too big and sloppily constructed to be eaten with your hands, so you have to sit down and eat it with a knife and fork and you still spill sauce on your new Key West T-shirt. Then you need to wash it down with a stupid drink sporting a paper umbrella and the whole thing tastes no better than a Chicken McNugget meal and costs as much as a case of beer. But for the time being I was very happy to be here.

It had been the most perfect sailing day and, importantly, it was the first time I had felt truly at ease sailing alone. Instead of the nagging concern that the weather or sea might start to toss me around, or that something might break on the boat, I'd accumulated just enough experience with boat handling and weather reading to know that all would be well on this day. I knew I could fix almost any problem with the boat or motor so I'd just been able to lean back and enjoy the sensation of sailing a good boat on a great day. I was certain that nothing troublesome would brew up, but even if it did, after the difficult, finicky and sometimes stormy sailing conditions I'd had since Christmas Day, I knew I could handle anything short of a full-blown gale. That confidence was the big difference. And that new-found feeling only lasts a short while. Soon after that, you take it for granted and you find that instead of enjoying the moment, you start to worry about how long conditions will last before something upsets them, or you fret about whether you can go faster some-how. In other words, you look too far ahead.

There was another key to this day, too. It was the last time I'd have to sail south. Now I could finally turn north and begin the long run, 2500 miles, up the coast to Eastport, Maine, on the Canadian border. I wanted to start from a particular landmark, so I tried to find the giant concrete nun buoy that marks the southernmost point of the USA, just 90 miles from Cuba. It used to be

South Pier, Key West.

on a street near the sea in Key West but though I found a point that was labelled the southernmost tip, there was no nun buoy, just a long pier with lots of tourists taking photos. I persuaded a lady to take a picture of me, then I shouted myself a toasted sandwich and a beer for dinner – my first cooked meal ashore in nearly three weeks. Piles of designer lettuce bulged out the side of the toasted sandwich and it cost more than my mooring fee but it was still a treat. Afterwards I strolled back to my boat. All was well with *Wanderer* and as I lay in bed I listened to the inevitable rendition of Jimmy Buffet's 'Margaritaville' from a bar band nearby. But though I could think of worse places to be wasting away in than Key West, all of a sudden I was seized with a powerful urge to get moving north – back to see my new friends Phil De Clue and Geoff Orr and then north as far and as fast as I could go. Right there, I decided to abandon my plan of two days' sightseeing and then sailing back via the western side of the keys. Instead, if the winds would cooperate I'd go the whole way back to Miami on the Atlantic and I'd start tomorrow. A fast passage was what I wanted. I had things to skite about to Geoff. I had new stories to tell and I wanted to show off. I'd sailed nearly 200 miles already and by the time I got back to Fort Lauderdale it would be double that. I could almost call myself a sailor then. Now if the bridge tenders called me Captain, I wouldn't feel like a big imposter.

MOTORING BACK UP the coast to Newfound Harbour took me almost the same time as sailing down it. The wind never came up and I roasted all morning and half the afternoon as I puttered along. I used $2\frac{1}{2}$ gallons of gas and covered the 28 miles in $6\frac{1}{2}$ hours. All the way I indulged in recreational thinking instead of trip planning. For instance, when a pelican landed in the water astern I thought of the rhyme my father told me – 'A curious bird is the pelican, his beak holds more than his belly can'. Which led me to other silly childhood verses, like my sister's favourite: 'The elephant is a graceful bird, it flits from bough to bough, it makes its nest in a rhubarb tree and whistles like a cow.' That would immediately lead me to the alphabet duet:

'AB, CD goldfish?'

'MNO goldfish!'

'SAR! CD BD Is?'

'OS, IC.'

Now the pelican had a fish, sooo – what was that one my mother sang about a little fish 'that swam and swam all over the dam'? How did it start? Was it 'One fishy, two fishy, three fishy, four'? No, that was the start of the Banana Bunch song from TV – 'One banana, two banana, three banana, four. Five bananas make a bunch and so do many more.' Never mind, I'd ask her how it went when I got home. But I did know her other nonsense song: 'Maresy doats and doesy doats'.

Now what was I doing before I got carried away with silly rhymes? Oh yes, thinking about why a pelican looks as rumpled and ugly as the average French President. As I said – you have a lot of time to think when you're sailing alone. Maybe too much. There was never a ripple on the water and the sky was the blue of a Chinese bowl overhead. By three o'clock I was back alongside Phil's dock and he and Bernard were tying my mooring lines to the cleats. I was smiling and happy as I told them of my fantastic day's sailing down to Key West and they were suitably impressed with my achievement.

'Glad you're back, Lee,' said Phil. 'I'm just going to finish cutting the timbers for this wall with Bernard, and then I think I'll put something on the barbecue. Have a wash in the bathroom if you want.' I declined, since I'd managed a shower at Key West the night before and so I put

Wanderer in order and tackled a bit of the busywork that always seems to need doing, even on a boat as small as mine. At about 5.00 pm I strolled down the road to the gas station, filled my fuel tanks and bought a dozen Miller Lite beers. I'd already enjoyed enough of Phil's hospitality to feel that I should be contributing to it myself. Half an hour after that, he and Bernard downed tools and cracked open a cold beer. Phil pulled out his Weber barbecue and fired it up. I have to admit, based on my experience of his cooking over the next three days, that this boy could do anything on a barbecue that TV cooks do in a studio kitchen. He could seriously fly his little Weber. We are talking test pilot skills. On this occasion he hauled out a chicken and started stuffing it. Once the Weber was burning nicely, he put the central pipe in place (sort of like a chimney stack) and leaned the whole stuffed chicken against it on one side and the sweet potatoes and sweetcorn on the other. Then he covered the whole thing with a domed lid and picked up his beer.

'Roast chicken, huh?' I said.

'No, more like baked or steamed, actually,' he replied, and to my amazement he was right. It was baked not roasted and it tasted gorgeous. I'm not a big fan of sweetcorn because it's so messy to eat, and I've never liked sweet potatoes or kumara, but I could have eaten Phil's vegetables every day for a month. He bought them at a local open-air vegetable market and they tasted so much better than anything else that if I could have fitted a Weber on my boat I'd have bought one then and there. We ate sitting on the back steps in the evening sun. It was another one of those serendipitous evenings when everything came together. We'd each been pleased with our good work over the previous two days, the weather was perfect, the beer was just right and the food was divine. Even Bernard was mellow and entertaining. He didn't talk about his theory of how humans came from space aliens – instead he told us about his time in the Hitler Youth. Bernard's mother did not approve of the Hitler Jugend and neither did Bernard.

'Effrybody in a uniform, you know,' he said, in a way that made the words 'in a uniform' sound like 'interfered with livestock'. It was obvious that there was no greater insult he could deliver about the organisation.

ONCE AGAIN, THE weather forecast said there was no southerly. I got up early the next day to hear Phil calling me to come and have a cup of coffee. Over breakfast, with Phil's persuasion (it didn't take much), I decided to stay another day. I spent the morning doing chores. I took down the mast and then bandaged and taped the ends of the spreaders so that when the sail was let fully out in a following wind it would have something soft to rub on and wouldn't chafe. Then I reorganised and restowed the dirty locker, repacked my food bins, and finally, washed down the hull around the waterline. By then it was lunchtime and Bernard and I ate cold chicken and salad with Phil. I yakked away to Phil while he cut and measured trimmings for the woodwork in the lounge until the sun was almost under the yardarm and then I made us a couple of gin and tonics. After dinner, cooked by Phil, we ate ice cream and watched a couple of cable movies. There was a George Clooney marathon on – we'd missed *Three Kings*, but we were in time to see the end of *The Peacemaker* and all of . . . *The Perfect Storm*. Oh joy. A story about a small boat being sunk in a freak Atlantic hurricane. *Just* what I needed.

Late that night I listened to the weather forecast and it predicted no winds at all for two days followed by northerlies arriving on Monday. I didn't want to spend an entire week at Phil's with only an overnight trip to Key West in between to show for it, so I decided that I'd leave on Monday regardless and just tack into the wind if I had to. For the next two days, though, I planned to help Phil paint the interior of his house in return for his hospitality. I thought that might even the balance a little, but I'd made a chance remark earlier in the evening and I didn't realise that Phil had plans to get ahead of me again. I'd mentioned that I'd seen some T-shirts in Key West which said 'Not only am I perfect, I'm a redhead too'. Adrienne's birthday was a week away and I had planned to get her something like that. It seemed an ideal present – a nice little gift from an exotic island. However, I'd left in a hurry from Key West without buying one and now I didn't know what to get her from Big Pine Key. I also mentioned that I hadn't found the nun buoy and Phil said that this was just too bad. I didn't realise that he'd already decided that I wasn't leaving Key

West without a T-shirt and a picture of a big concrete block.

The undercoat went on in just a couple of hours and before lunch-time Phil said that since we couldn't do anything more while the paint dried, and since he had important business in Key West, why didn't I jump in his truck and catch a ride down there this afternoon? He could do his stuff and I could get a T-shirt for Adrienne and a photo of my chosen start point.

'Well, that's great, Phil – suits me like Armani,' I said and 10 minutes later we roared out the gate in his pickup truck. I freely concede that I can be a bit slow on the uptake at times. Phil's important business turned out to be the pressing solution to the mystery of where the nun buoy had gone. Eventually we found it and I took my pictures and shopped for the T-shirt. I bought a New Zealand flag decal for the stern of the boat and we grabbed an ice cream and drove back to Newfound Harbour in time to whack a marinated steak and some more sweet potatoes on the Weber and chisel open a beer before sunset.

The next day we slapped on the topcoat then shopped at the local flea market before I sent out my weekly Hughes Nughes email from Phil's computer. For dinner, Phil invited Bernard over and we yakked away for hours, solving the world's problems over G&Ts and pork chops, yams and roast seasoned tomatoes. Delicious as always. Bernard was in a worried mood – he'd been listening to talkback radio and it was full of empty-headed discussions about whether the US should march into the Middle East and start kicking ass and taking names. This is a perennial topic for the chattering classes and though Bernard would have shit a brick if you'd described him that way, he couldn't resist bringing the subject up.

'It'll all turn out fine, Bernard, it always does,' I said.

'How can you say that, Lee? Look at all the terrible things that have happened in the world,' he replied.

In the kitchen, Phil groaned a little – he didn't know the trap I had set for Bernard and no doubt feared he'd be off on one of his gloomy rants about the state of humanity. But I wasn't afraid of setting him off. Over the years I've met a few people like this and I've developed some arguments that generally floor them. And if they don't work, I'm not above making up a few false scientific facts to bolster my case. It works like this. First, I begin by stating that bad things are always predicted and never eventuate, so we should stop worrying about the things we know, and secondly, that the things that do go horribly wrong in the world are always unforeseen, so we can't even start worrying about them. Thus, we have no rational cause to worry. Then I give examples.

About the time I was born, the world population was less than three billion and the following disasters were predicted by every loudmouth in the world. There would be rampant overpopulation resulting in fascist governments exercising forcible population control. Or, rampant overpopulation resulting in mass starvation of the developing world by 1970 and food riots and revolution in the west by 1980. But definitely overpopulation. Plus, there was no hope for a rational or peaceful end to the Cold War, so we were certain to face a nuclear winter after the obligatory missile exchange some time after 1985. Or else war would be triggered by some computer accident. If that didn't get us, then some germ would escape from a laboratory and we'd all die in a pandemic. Pollution was irreversible, we'd all choke on smog, and rugby would never turn professional without wrecking the game.

Whereas what we actually got was the exact opposite. The population is now over six billion (and is seriously self-limiting in most countries that lack a government subsidy for breeding). We have food in such abundance that we have butter mountains and grain islands and wine lakes that we can't give away. Communism caved in, the missiles are rusting away in their silos, and when the anthrax bug got out of the lab recently it killed less people than will be riding on the roof of the average Pakistani bus before it next falls into a river.

And the totally unexpected things that we never worried about because we never imagined them included AIDS, the greenhouse effect, match fixing in cricket, and the Internet (which is actually penicillin for fascism, communism and fundamentalism). In short, by the end of the 20th century everything the doomsayers in 1960 thought they knew for a fact turned out to be a load of bollocks. They couldn't have been more wrong if they'd tried. Turned out they didn't even know the half of it. It seems humans have a surprising capacity to avoid foreseeable disasters and even survive the unexpected ones. In short, we're good and getting better.

So that's why I am so surprised at the persistence of talkback radio. I can't understand why it hasn't gone the way of Sunday trading laws and six o'clock closing. I do respect the right of talkback callers to have an opinion. All I ask is that each caller cease to worry about every problem in the world, and instead just pick one and worry it to death.

Bernard luckily still had the soft courtesy of an older generation and so he listened patiently to my summary of the previous 40 years and said nothing while I demolished his house of unreason. Instead he derailed my entire train of thought by reaching into his backpack and handing me half a dozen delicious ripe starfruit that he'd picked for me on his way to dinner.

'I have some for you too, Phillip,' he said.

I felt like I'd kicked a kitten, but from the kitchen I could see Phil making notes for future use.

I've got that
sinking feeling . . .

ON THE DAY I left, Phil fried a whole pound of bacon, made me a breakfast of bacon and eggs with half of it and then, as I was leaving, he handed me the rest of the bacon in a bag to snack on. What a nice guy. I made good sailing on the Atlantic right through to Black Point, where I was able to meet up with Jesse again.

Sailing out of Black Point on Friday, it was dead calm but with 15 to 20-knot winds predicted for later in the day. I pootled along, having fun, listening to the radio, getting a tan and trying to rig self-steering gear with a bungy cord. Soon it began to puff, so I stopped fiddling about and started sailing. I was making six mph or so, but after a while I decided to take in a reef as it was gusting strongly. I left it a little longer than I should have and was just bringing *Wanderer* around to sail on the opposite tack, when I guess I held the mainsail in too long and a gust got me and tipped the boat up. Suddenly there was green water pouring in over the side! I got a real surprise but managed to flip the mainsheet out of the cleats, fling myself over to the windward side and as the gust passed and the sail went out, she righted.

There I was — in the middle of the bay — swamped! I guess the Biscayne Bay Sailing School hadn't rung the bell for the end of class. It was blowing hard so I dropped the boom and mainsail into the bottom of the boat and grabbed a bucket. The water was a foot or more deep over the floorboards and I guess I had 200 gallons on board. I bailed away and then pumped until all the water was back in the bay where it belonged (I'm a tidy chap).

Then I stowed things and hoisted the sail, got back on the horse and rode it into Miami Harbour. I was double-reefed by then, but near me, people were racing their little boats with full mainsail and jib, so I wasn't in a storm or anything. It was quite a mystery to me how I managed to swamp the boat, but at least I was well prepared for it and didn't lose anything. Plenty of stuff got wet, but nothing that couldn't stand it. I dried out in the wind as I motor-jibbed across the harbour and under all the bridges on the ICW.

All in all, it wasn't a too-scary experience – just puzzling. The next morning I made it back to Fort Lauderdale, into the New River and up to Geoff's. Geoff made me welcome again and I moved my gear into his spare bedroom and washed and dried all my wet-weather gear, air beds, etc. For the record, I'd sailed 389 nautical miles, which is about 430 statute miles.

The break at Geoff's was very welcome, not just for his company but also because it gave me a chance to recover from the tiredness I was feeling at this time. In order to make the miles I needed to each day despite the predominantly northerly winds, I was sailing long hours. I'd wake at 5.00 or 5.30 am each day and listen to the weather. I'd either skip breakfast or eat just a bowl of cereal. Not once on the whole trip did I brew a hot drink for myself – it just seemed like a lot of work for not much reward – so after eating, I'd clean my teeth, wash my face and pack up my bed. By 6.30 I was hauling up the anchor and heading out to the ocean. Then I'd settle down to sail for the rest of the day. That meant nine hours of continuous helmsmanship. I never stopped for lunch. It was much easier to keep sailing and just whip up a sandwich or eat muesli bars, fruit, biscuits or cold fried bacon followed by a drink of water. By 4.00 pm I'd be looking for an anchorage. It got dark just after 5.30 so if I could find a sheltered spot, I'd anchor with at least an hour of daylight left. That would give me time to set up the tent and dry out anything that had got wet from spray or rain during the day or from dew the previous evening.

Every second day or so I'd heat water up and have a hot shave and sponge bath. It felt tremendous to get rid of the layer of greasy sweat and to have clean hair. Usually I'd be too hot and tired to cook so I'd just make a couple of cheese, ham and pickle sandwiches and snack on candy and do my reading by lamplight until I fell asleep at 7.00 pm. Now and again it would be cool enough for me to feel like cooking a can of stew and noodles. Very rarely I'd have a cigarette while I studied my charts to work out what I could achieve the next day. If I had done a good day's work, I'd reward myself with at least an hour of recreational reading – on a topic unconnected with the ocean. Generally I was pleased with my sailing – my best day's run was a healthy 39 miles.

I really enjoyed snuggling down into my lovely, soft, warm bed because it meant I didn't have to get up again for any reason until dawn. I could eat and drink and even pee lying down, so unless the anchor dragged, I was set for the night. Because *Wanderer* was so small, I could tuck in behind tiny outcrops that sheltered me from small waves that would otherwise have bumped me all night. On one or two occasions I beached the bow and tied up to a tree or planted my anchor on shore, but I was always cautious about checking the tide height before doing that. I didn't want to wake up the next morning and find myself stranded. That would mean a long delay while I waited for the tide to come in. Luckily it wasn't hard to predict – if there was water under me when I lit the lantern, there'd be water under me when I woke up the next morning. If I beached her, I didn't like doing it on a sloping shore at any time because then I'd wake up in the middle of the night, jammed in a corner of the boat where I'd slipped as the hull settled on a lean at low tide.

The Florida Keys were the perfect place for me to learn about things like this. The tides were small – not more than three feet at most, and the currents were very weak. All in all it was a very gentle and safe introduction to cruising. The only thing I would have really liked was some informed advice on how to sail *Wanderer* better from another Wayfarer owner. Strangely enough, that was about to happen.

AL SCHONBORN IS a bit of a legend in Wayfarer circles. He's been a champion sailor of these boats for many years but he also runs the Canadian Wayfarer Association website. It's called the Whiffle and you can find it at www.angelfire.com/de/whiffle/. This was where I'd seen Frank's advertisement for *Wanderer*, and ever since then, Al had been keeping in touch with me. He had posted all my Hughes Nugheses on his weekly bulletin page along with some photos of me. One lovely feature of Al's work was that he answered all the letters to the editor in great detail. People from all around the world regularly wrote to him asking his advice on everything from the market price of a used plywood hull, to the correct tension and angle for mast spreaders. He had an answer and a recommendation for everything. When I described my occasional battles with wind or tide or gravity or whatever, he would insert his excellent advice into the text that he published so that other novices could learn from my mistakes. I had already read plenty of his comments like these before I started sailing and learned useful things like how to heave to, how to reef and so on.

Now he had another surprise for me. He and his sailing partner, Marc Bennett, were coming south in a few weeks' time to compete in a Wayfarer racing tournament on Lake Eustis in central Florida. At that time, I'd be near Cape Canaveral, just an hour or two from where he was racing. He suggested that we meet so we could go for a sail and he could take some more pictures to post on the website. I was delighted at this because I planned to pump him for more information about how to sail. I emailed back and started calculating when I'd have to leave and how fast I'd have to sail from Geoff's in order to make the rendezvous.

First though, I had some serious maintenance to do on *Wanderer*. I sanded the floorboards and then gave them a thick coating of cream enamel; soaped and sponged out the bilge, finally removing all traces of a gas spillage that had happened at Black Point; dried out the centreboard and fibreglassed it; and spent three days getting the old varnish off the seats before applying three fresh coats. It was worth the effort. The dark mahogany gleamed and shone. Then I worked on the rudder and sanded and varnished the boom crutch, the hand paddle

The seats are all varnished and ready to go.

and the rudder head and tiller. I was about to mount the rudder back on the boat when Geoff came by with some more white paint.

'Can't put it in the water like that, mate. Spoils the whole effect. Put this paint on it so it matches the hull.' He was right, and when it was back in the water it looked great. When I finally put the seats back in the whole effect was dazzling. With her smart white hull and floors, her gleaming brown woodwork and her nifty red trimmings, *Wanderer* looked suddenly upmarket. She resembled one of those enormously expensive vintage wooden boats that have a fortune spent on them by indulgent owners. Admittedly the shine would wear off in a few months, but for now she looked terrific. Too good for the likes of me.

I had already given the engine its 50-hour service and so all that remained was to stow everything back on board and do the ropework. I pulled out my little book of knots and splicing and sat down to make a few things that I needed. I'd done some splicing before but only with much larger ropes so I was really struggling with the small whippings and joins until Geoff took pity on me and handed me a fid. (If you plan to do any ropework, save yourself some heartache and buy this tool

In the end Wanderer *gleamed.*

right at the start.) Then he showed me some tricks to make it easier and pretty soon the fid was flying. By the end of the day I had knotted and spliced and lashed everything I could, and for the first time, I had *Wanderer* set up the way I wanted. A good deal of thought had gone into it and it worked because I never changed any of it later on. Frank had set things up differently, but now *Wanderer* was mine and I felt free to make a few changes.

All that work occupied a week, but in the evenings I had plenty of free time. I cooked my entire repertoire of four dishes and did a bit of house-cleaning; it wasn't much, but at least I managed to repay *some* of Geoff's limitless hospitality. Geoff and Sandy and I went out to Waxy O'Connor's for a few beers with Geoff's mates and now I felt comfortable talking about sailing. Before, I was just an idiot with a few big plans, so I didn't want to shoot my mouth off too much. Now I was less of a navigational hazard and I had a few good stories too. The night before I left, Geoff and Sandy invited a bunch of their friends around for a Super Bowl party. I didn't have a clue about the game, but I knew they usually scored in multiples of six or seven, so in the sweepstake, I tried to fill in the boxes that had those numbers. I had a wonderful time that only got better when I won the $40 sweepstake after an astounding touchdown against the run of play by ummm, well . . . the team that were playing from left to right on the TV.

I'd planned to leave on Monday morning. I had spent nine nights ashore at Geoff's and he'd been a terrific host. He'd taken me into his house, he'd helped me with advice about the boat, he'd loaned me his tools and run me around shopping in his pickup truck. He'd bought me things with his chandler's discount. I'd borrowed his bike, met his friends, drunk plenty of his beer and eaten lots of his food. Mostly, though, I'd made a good friend who right from the beginning had been completely willing to do anything to help me get this trip off to a good start. The fact that I'd never met him at all until I parked my truck in his driveway just made it more astonishing. I finally asked him why he invited me to stay and he just shrugged and said that he owed my sister-in-law a few favours because she'd been good to him when he was a nipper. I'm sure that was true, but mainly I think he did it because he's a bloody good bloke and it just came naturally.

Ebb and flow

THE ICW NORTH of Fort Lauderdale is heavily civilised for about 100 miles — all the way past Boca Raton, Lake Worth and ritzy Palm Beach where the old New England money used to come for winter holidays. I sailed and motored through it smoothly in three days. The only liveliness happened one night when I anchored near mangroves and found myself sitting on mud in the middle of the night after the tide receded. I floated the next morning so that was no problem, but it was a reminder to be more careful in future. By now I was able to sail through even the smallest bascule bridges. I'd call them up a few minutes before I arrived and then tack around in circles while they opened. If I saw that I had 24 feet of clearance then I'd sail right through them without asking for an opening. I had even graduated to gliding under them by lowering the mast with the mainsail still hoisted. It wasn't too difficult as long as the wind or current was sufficient to carry me forward. It certainly impressed the powerboats that had to queue up for an opening. Fortunately, most bridges opened on demand and I didn't have to use this trick more than once or twice a week.

Each night I found a secluded spot to anchor but it was still a rather urban environment. The shores of the waterway bloomed with expensive houses and occasional apartment buildings. There were fleets of power-boats tied up to docks on the dozens of side canals that connected to the waterway. The predominant vegetation was a mixture of palm trees and traffic lights. But north of Hobe Sound and the St Lucie inlet it quickly opened out into the Indian River. This body of mostly salt water runs parallel to the coast for about 150 miles from St Lucie, north to Mosquito Lagoon and the adjoining waters around Cape Canaveral. The Indian River is one to three miles wide, fairly shallow and well protected by a low foreshore that guards it from the Atlantic. Roads and towns are built on the sandy ocean shore, but these are in constant peril from hurricane tidal surges. Most houses facing this risk (which is every house within five miles of the shore in Florida) are built with an open concrete basement, sometimes used for garaging, but mainly created in order to lift the living areas above the level of the expected waterline if a major storm hits. In the previous 10 years two major hurricanes had devastated populated areas of south Florida. In coastal towns all through the south you occasionally come across warning signs showing hurricane evacuation routes and others showing the expected height of a tidal surge if a hurricane hits. In Brunswick, Georgia, I came across one when I was walking down one of the main streets. It was seven feet high, which was a tad troubling to consider, but what was really alarming was that Brunswick is located 10 miles inland on a river.

Probably the only thing I was insulated against while travelling in *Wanderer* was the danger of flooding. Later in the trip I would sail through areas that were having unusually wet weather and the rivers and canals were well above flood level. For me, it was no problem at all – I just cruised on by the flooded fields and swampy forests. It was the only time I got one over the weather.

On the Indian River though, I was still able to enjoy the best weather and some of the loveliest scenery. Small creeks created meandering passages through uninhabited islands with fields of tall, waving wild grass. The bird life was prolific, and judging by the abundance of dolphins, so was the fish life. There was very little traffic that moved at my speed so what powerboats did pass me by were quickly out of sight and sound. Only one threw up a wake that jostled me more than was fair – it was out of Fort Lauderdale (which I considered my home port) and sadly its name was *Wanderer*.

The climate was still mild and sunny, the civilised areas on the shore reduced the number of buggy nights, and since I had called Adrienne on her birthday before leaving Geoff's place, I wasn't feeling homesick or lonely. I even had something new to look forward to. Just before the Indian River narrows down again is the small town of Cocoa on the mainland shore. This is not to be confused with nearby Cocoa Beach, which is the oceanside resort on the Atlantic closest to the launch pads at Kennedy Space Center. My only appointment now was to get to somewhere near Cape Canaveral within seven days so that I could meet up with Al Schonborn. On the map Cocoa looked to be a good spot for that. Then I could get a sailing lesson. My first. That would be good.

Meantime, as I neared Jupiter Inlet, 70 miles south of Cape Canaveral, one Sunday morning I turned the radio off so that I could listen for the sonic boom of a space shuttle returning. I'd always wanted to see a rocket launch, but I'd never been near Cape Canaveral when one was happening, so to see a spacecraft fly low overhead just before touch-down would be a nice bonus for me on this trip. This part of Florida called itself the Space Coast and motels and businesses had put 'Welcome Home *Columbia*' on their illuminated signs a few days previously.

At about 10.30 I sailed into a marina to refill my fuel can and buy groceries and that's when I heard the news. *Columbia* was destroyed, all the astronauts were lost and another tragedy had blindsided America. Within hours, the thousands of flags that flew over homes and government buildings since the outpouring of patriotism that began in September 2001, were being lowered to half-mast. Motels began changing their signs to read 'God Speed *Columbia*, God Bless the families' and the media began its relentless coverage of the enormous scavenger hunt for clues. I didn't want to wade through coverage of the disaster, and on my little boat I was able to avoid a lot of it. For once, I was happy that no other country took public pleasure in the blow to American confidence and pride. It's a rare day when some sorry son of a bitch isn't dancing in the street if the US suffers any sort of tragedy, but this time no one was taking credit for causing it, so after a while, as terrorism was ruled out, the public let out their breath and began to mourn their loss. A week later, on the day I sailed past the launch pad at Kennedy Space Center they held a memorial service on the runway as NASA jets flew the missing man formation overhead. I was anchored nearby and I saw them come thundering over the water, rocking a little in the morning heat before the missing man turned and flew up and up and out of sight. As fine a farewell as anyone could wish for people who just wanted to go further and faster than anyone else. But on this morning, soon after I filled my fuel can, the man on the dock saw me looking at a street map searching for a supermarket.

'I'm going for lunch in a few minutes,' he said, even though it was barely 11.00 am. 'Hop in my truck, I'll give you a lift to the mall and back.'

In America, some things never change.

~~~

I REACHED COCOA a day before Al was due to arrive so I had a little time to reconnoitre the town. I exchanged some books at a second-hand store, shopped for a little food, bought my first ice cream of the trip and wandered around the skinny streets of the tourist part of town.

Uncle Al Schonborn — yet another B.G.B.

Like so many coastal towns, there was an abundance of antique shops, but these ones looked like they were doing healthy business. They had a big shiny library so I caught up on my emails and checked the news from home. Adrienne sent me some pictures of her at a Christmas picnic. She looked gorgeous sitting in the afternoon sun surrounded by her nieces. Once again I wished she could be with me.

That night I called Al, gave him directions to meet me in the town square and spruced myself and my boat up with a quick wash-down. I motored in to the dock next morning and just before noon as I was walking past the park in search of another ice cream I saw a dusty little VW Golf with Ontario plates. Two men got out and one looked slightly familiar.

'You must be Al,' I said, and indeed he was. He introduced his sailing partner, Marc, and we shook hands.

'If you need a minute to get settled, I can meet you on the boat in a wee while,' I said, but Al had other plans.

'I've got beer,' he confided. 'Good Carolina beer from the Outer Banks.' Marc nodded solemnly.

'Outer Banks beer. Travels well but doesn't keep. Best get it open,' Marc said.

'Crime to waste it, but we can't drink it in public. Would it travel as far as my boat down there on the dock?' I asked.

'Yep.'

Lee and Marc sailing hard on a malty sea.

And so a few minutes later, we knocked the scab off as fine a bottle of rich liquorishy beer as I had tasted since I left New Zealand. Al settled into the bottom of the boat with a cushion behind his head and stretched out his legs. He looked instantly at ease. He was about 60, a retired teacher, and he has that permanently tanned look that sailors get. Marc was about 30 and was originally from Jamaica but now lived in Canada. Al and Marc were a racing team that had knocked off plenty of trophies at races in Canada and the US and I was sure I'd get good technical sailing advice from them. For the moment, though, they just looked glad not to be driving. We chatted about our respective journeys and by and by the beers dried up and we began to get restless for some sailing. First though, we set off to find a motel for them, and once that was done, Al gave Marc his digital camera to take photos of us while we went for a short sail. We left Marc to walk to the spit of land that launched the bridge across the narrows of the Indian River, while we cast off and sailed out into the bay and then north underneath the bridge. The pictures Marc took are the only photographic proof I've got that I ever sailed my boat. I had a good selection of pictures of me on land next to my boat or of me sitting in it, but none of me driving her under sail. I would have liked a few more of me leaning out and going fast in rough water, but once again, the wind was light and barely enough to fill the genoa. We tacked along for a half-hour and then set off to sail a couple of miles up to the next bridge before turning for home. On the way, Al showed me all sorts of tricks and answered many questions about rigging and trimming the sails. He strongly recommended two things – switching to a centre mainsheet that would move the position of the mainsail rope from the tip of the boom to the centre. Presently, the mainsheet would sometimes catch on the head of the motor when the rope went slack as the sail crossed over to the other side. I could keep an eye on it and easily free it, but it was a bit of a nuisance and could be unsafe in strong winds. He also recommended swapping my heavy mainsheet for a lighter, longer rope that would run more freely through the blocks and allow the sail to swing out further. At this time I couldn't let the sail go out as far as it could because the rope was a bit short and it was sticky with salt and didn't run freely – especially in light winds when the sail barely filled. I didn't realise this because I had no knowledge of how far out a sail should be allowed to go. Al said that if it went out so far that it pressed on the shrouds, that was fine, but for that I needed a longer mainsheet.

The only evidence that I can sail – albeit with a crew.

From there the sail would drive the boat better and it was less likely to accidentally gybe. I agreed in principle to these things but I had a huge reluctance to change anything that Frank had set up because I worried that, while they might be good ideas for a weekend racing dinghy where fragility can be accepted as the price to be paid for speed, they might not be good things for a long-distance cruiser where strength, simplicity and reliability were better. So, despite agreeing with Al at the time, I secretly planned not to make the changes.

For now, though, we put back into the dock where Marc was waiting. It was knocking on dinner time so they headed to the motel to wash up and I did the same on *Wanderer*. We agreed to meet back at a restaurant called Murdocks that was highly recommended to us by the lady at the information centre who had found the motel for us. She had told me where the supermarket was and even offered to drive me there later on if I wanted, but instead Al said he would take me. She knew her restaurants too, because it was a great casual bar that served darn good food.

Unusually for me, I picked a seafood dish – a spicy catfish sandwich with grits on the side. It was yummy and I gobbled it all down. I still don't know what grits actually are and I can't remember what they looked or tasted like but I'm glad to say I tried them and I liked them. They sure beat okra, black-eyed peas, and hush puppies. On TV you hear about a lot of foods that aren't available in New Zealand – everything from Cherry Cokes and raisinets to lox and cream cheese bagels. Whenever I'm in the US I try whatever familiar-sounding exotic food I can, just to see what the fuss is about. Of all the types

I've had, Amish souse was the best and Amish scrapple was the most disappointing. The scrapple cost $2 a pound (that was a clue right there because it was even cheaper than ceiling insulation). I fried it up as directed and it tasted like fat sawdust. So I seasoned it with some Tabasco and fried it some more. Now it tasted like fat, shellacked sawdust. So I progressively poured in a bit of everything I had in the way of spices – Worcestershire sauce, salt and pepper, more Tabasco, grated cheese, tomato sauce, beef Oxo cubes and Mad Dog 20-20 wine. By the end it tasted like a hangover. I threw the remaining half-pound over the side and went ashore for a burger. When I came back there was an oily slick around the boat.

Cocoa seemed to me to be a very well-set-up little town. Al and Marc planned to stay an extra day, so since it had good bars, the folks were friendly and because the weather wasn't great for sailing yet, I thought I might stay around an extra couple of days too and take care of something that was nagging at me like a sore tooth.

It was, in fact, a broken molar. I'd been trying to untie a rope knot at Black Point a few weeks before when it broke and though it didn't hurt at all I felt I should take care of it before it gave me any trouble. I had inquired about a dentist and found one not too far away that could see me immediately; so the next morning, after a big cooked breakfast at Denny's in case my visit to the dentist prevented me from chewing much later on, Al and Marc dropped me at the dentist. While I was poked and probed and eventually divested of a tooth, Al went shopping. Since we'd had such a good time the previous night, we agreed to meet for dinner again. I got back to the boat at about 5.00 pm and Al picked me up and took me to their motel, where I had a long hot shower. First, though, he dropped off 50 feet of 8mm white nylon rope.

'Just what you need for centre sheeting,' he said. Of course I tried to pay him and of course he refused. I can understand why now. It was exactly the same as if I'd seen someone on a horse trying to rope a calf with a piece of regular rope. You just know they're not doing it right and it offends your sense of propriety and you want them to enjoy the success that usually comes when you use the right tools for the job.

For roping, that means a stiff, slick, hard rope that can whip out of the coil in a flash and retain the shape of the loop as it drops over the calf. A regular soft rope barely works at all and the calf just keeps galloping into the distance while you untangle the rope from your horse's feet. Al must have looked at my main sheet and heard the sound of galloping hooves too. He dropped the new rope into my boat and refused any payment.

'My contribution to the trip,' he said.

'Thank you, Al, and I hope you'll let me buy you a beer.'

Dinner was a more dignified affair than the previous night's excesses, and since I couldn't drink anything with bubbles in it on the orders of the dentist, I settled for a couple of glasses of a good red wine. Al let me buy him a drink, but you can guess who insisted on paying for the food. The meal was terrific and worth every one of Al's dollars. Afterwards we visited a seashore bar with loud music, pretty waitresses and a noisy group of very short-haired women all dressed in flannel shirts, jeans and heavy work-boots. The nearest lumber camp was several hundred miles away and they weren't filming a *Home Improvement* special episode either. We concluded that they were so over-the-top stereotypically dykey that they had to be taking the piss. Surely real lesbians didn't dress like that any more. I mean, they hang around with gay men, so some of that fashion sense must rub off, surely? I wanted to ask them what the story was but Al said I was missing a tooth already and did I want to lose another? I said I'd taken bigger girls than that down to the carpet before and he said yes, but there were eight of them and only one of me. I said those were the odds I liked best. Al looked at Marc and said, 'See, this is what happens when you spend too long on a boat.'

We finished our drinks, said our goodbyes and they dropped me off at the dock. They had to head for their regatta the next day and I had another 2000-odd miles to sail. It was time to move again.

A perfect day

AS I WORKED my way further along the Indian River, I accumulated a little more experience. Some of it was unremarkable to report but important for me. One of the first things I discovered was that Al was right about centre sheeting. I knew when he dropped off the rope that I'd have to try it since he'd inevitably see photos of *Wanderer* later on and if they showed I hadn't adopted his method, he'd wonder why. So, the morning after he left, I changed the rig over. When I set off towards the NASA Causeway bridge at Addison Point about 12 miles north, the wind was from the south and I was able to trial the new system. It worked like a charm and I felt much safer knowing that I'd reduced the chances of an involuntary gybe by about half. The next morning I saw the fly-past in honour of the *Columbia* astronauts before I sailed towards Titusville.

After an extra day there due to weather, I battled north to a snug anchorage in a tiny cove dug out of the Haulover Canal. This connected the Indian River to Mosquito Lagoon, but I spent nearly a day cooped up in it waiting for more bad weather to arrive and pass. By mid-morning the next day I ran out of reading material so I poked my head out to have a look at the sea. It wasn't that bad, so I hurriedly packed up my bed and pulled up the anchor intending to make a few miles before the wind got up. Instead, when the front arrived I found myself reluctant to stop and make camp in the cold and rain, so I kept on sailing. It was a fast, exciting reach right through the bad weather and I made a good 22 miles in half a day. I finished up in New Smyrna, in a terrific little spot near the town docks but completely secluded and too shallow for anyone else but me. That was a good lesson not to be afraid of a bit of wind and rain.

North of Cape Canaveral I soon entered the cooler part of Florida. Orlando and Disney World are near to the cape and these mark the border between reliably hot and humid south Florida and slightly cooler central Florida. For the first time, I found myself cold at night and I occasionally wore a woollen beanie to bed. By day, as long as I had on a thin cotton turtleneck sweater and my foul-weather clothing and boots, I was plenty warm. My tent wasn't leaking too badly at this point but I was finding that I had to sew up small tears regularly. That was ominous, since it suggested the material was going to give up and tear in half soon. I started to think about a replacement.

I learned not to tie up to unused docks that had large numbers of pelicans and other birds roosting on them. When I did that at a Daytona Beach marina I returned from my shopping trip to find a solid dusting of guano all over the boat. Took ages to sponge it off.

And finally, I discovered how to flake my sail perfectly when I packed it away at night. I'd begin at the mast end but as soon as I had the reefing lines pulled in tight, I'd slip one of my purpose-built toggle ropes around the stern end to hold things in place before returning to the mast end to flake the rest of it. Little things like these pleased me immensely — the only wonder was that it had taken me 700 miles and nearly two months to discover and perfect them.

~~~

THE NEXT FEW weeks were about the smoothest sailing I was to experience on the whole trip. I'd finally got the boat in order and I'd learned enough about handling *Wanderer* to be able to switch off and daydream while I reacted to changes in the sea and weather instinctively. I'd mastered the interpretation of weather forecasts and the reading of charts. I could anchor firmly in a sheltered spot with confidence that the wind and tide wouldn't shift me. I knew how to anchor so that if the tide left me beached I'd be sitting level and able to float again when I was ready. Because I was still sailing on the sheltered parts of the ICW, I didn't have to worry about wild waves and sea monsters too much, so the overriding fear of the trip was safely in the background for the time being. Though the climate was cooler, there were no bugs to pester me and no pests to bug me. Most days were warm enough to allow sailing in just shorts and lifejacket and the nights weren't too humid or sticky any more. I slept well from 8.00 at night to 5.00 in the morning. I'd lost 20 pounds, gained a tan, and now that my tooth was fixed I felt I was in the best shape I'd been in for years. I'd learned how to minimise the hassle and time taken for chores like shopping and emailing. My finances were holding up OK; I didn't feel deprived of company and I wasn't missing Adrienne too badly.

I have some pictures that pretty much summarise how good it was at this time. I took them one afternoon when I anchored to the bank of a small creek that wound through acres and acres of tall waving marsh grass. This wasn't a swamp – if anything, it was like boating through the middle of a cornfield. When I lay on my back that day and stared up, the sky really was a limitless blue that grew from the colour of a Bombay Sapphire gin bottle just above the horizon, steadily deeper and darker until it was saved from becoming the colour of deadly nightshade only by meeting the ascending blues from the other horizon. Underneath, it was nothing but golden grass as far as the lens could see – except for *Wanderer*'s clean white hull and slender mast rising up from the symmetrically blue waters of the creek. In one of the pictures, her reflection plunges down into the limpid water. The thing is, shallow creeks like this are supposed to be muddy and brown. Swamps are supposed to be unpleasant and humid. And even blue skies are supposed to have a smudge of small white cloud to give them definition. But here, everything I could see was raw, undiluted colour and the pictures I have are proof.

I have a clear memory of a day when I was four years old or younger. I was lying on my back in our front yard, on freshly mown grass one baking-hot afternoon. I was looking up through the branches of a tree,

The perfect day.

past the outrageous explosion of white peach blossom to the bluest sky my wide child's eyes had ever seen. Even at the time I knew this was special. That was the first absolutely perfect moment I can recall and it will last forever. That occasion was so sublime and unique that it pinned itself in my memory immovably. It is the benchmark of perfection for me for all time. Green grass, white blossom, golden heat and blue, blue sky. When I'm old and dribbling into a bib, it will still be there and so will that glorious afternoon in Florida decades later. I lay there for an hour just drinking it in and fixing it in my memory. Golden grass, blue sky, blue water and dazzling white boat. It was one of those moments of absolute perfection, and even better, I knew it at the time, so I was able to wring every drop of satisfaction out of it.

~~~

ST AUGUSTINE BILLS itself as the oldest inhabited city in North America. Founded by Spaniards in the early 16th century under Ponce de León, it was primarily a fort that dominated a fairly unsatisfactory harbour on the Matanzas River. Around St Augustine's fort, a small town sprang up that was repeatedly razed during the various wars of the American colonial era. Five different nations have ruled it over the years (Spanish, French, British, American Federal and Confederate), but chiefly the Spanish. As far as city sites go this was an odd choice and it was not a great success for many years. The harbour is a little shallow, exposed to many winds and subject to powerful tidal flows. The land is not good for farming, it doesn't dominate any strategic feature, and virtually every town in Florida that was founded after it has better natural resources nearby. The climate was tough on the early settlers, but the natives were assimilated into the population more effectively than in most other European settlements. Eventually the stone fort was completed and the town was also ringed with a city wall, providing a less precarious existence for the inhabitants. Under the guns of the fort, the harbour provided some refuge for Spanish bullion ships from British pirate ships, but it is not a naturally defensible site. It survived, though, and even more unusually, much of its original architecture is preserved, making it the only Spanish city of its type in the US. The centre consists of about half a square mile of small shops and houses laid out around a couple of squares on the original grid plan dating back over 300 years. Just outside what remains of the old town wall is the fort, which is the major tourist attraction. Across the Matanzas River is the quaint, ornamental and busy Bridge of Lions. I approached St Augustine from the south, intending to anchor near the bridge and visit for a couple of days.

My approach was pretty impressive. I was blasting down the river with a strong following wind that had pushed me 15 miles from Fort Matanzas in just two and a half hours. As I neared the city marina just before the bridge, the wind came up. A lot. In the last half-mile it rose to well over 20 knots and with the sail full out I didn't have much to do except hang on. I weaved my way safely through the anchorage and towards the marina where I would anchor for the night. The marina is right beside the Bridge of Lions and I planned to hurtle down towards it and then turn sharply back on myself and into the wind so I could bleed off some speed and gently nudge into the dock. That was the plan.

Instead, as I neared the marina I could see that there might be an area where I could later anchor between the bridge and the docks. I sailed down to look at it, which put me very close to the bridge. It was unsuitable so I made my turn into the wind and prepared to slide grace-fully to a halt by the dock just 20 yards ahead. As soon as I turned though, I found myself blown to a halt about 10 yards away from the dock and then shoved smartly backwards by the wind and the current. I tried tacking but it was hopeless. I only had about 30 yards before I would be swept under the bridge and dismasted, and at the rate I was going backwards I hadn't enough time to get sailing on a tack anywhere. A powerboat that was leaving the marina saw me cross his path going backwards. He slowed down to watch me get jammed against the bridge and lose my mast or capsize. In these situations I am good at one thing – making a decision. I decided in a flash to quit sailing and start driving. I whipped the engine into life and gave it full throttle. By the time the prop bit into the water and started to push me forwards I was about 10 feet from the bridge, and the motorboat I had impeded was also being swept sideways into the bridge by the current. I roared ahead, mainsail flapping and banging, as he gunned his big engines, lifted his bow and came rocketing across my wake.

Incredibly, my racing engine now propelled me at a goodly clip toward the dock. I yanked the kill cord and dashed up to fend off the bow. I hit the dock fairly solidly and managed to jump out with a mooring line in my hand. But the sail was still up, the current was strong and I only just managed to get the line around the cleat before the boat blew briskly off the end of the dock. I stumbled back aboard and did what was becoming a habit for me in all my nautical emergencies – I loosened the boom vang, undid the halyard and once more sent the boom and sail crashing into the bottom of the boat.

Would I never stop having to do that?

I spent an hour wandering the streets and discovered that it really was worth the effort. It was bigger and older than I expected, and best of all, in the early 20th century when St Augustine had another mini-boom as a stop on the railway line that Henry Flagler built to take vacationing New Englanders to Key West, the new buildings were constructed in a style that complemented the original architecture. Using poured concrete walls, they built tall, turreted hotels in a neo-Spanish style. A hundred years later, they had weathered and aged and blended very well with the original tiny adobe-type buildings of 300 years earlier. Now, the larger hotels were transformed into a museum and a university and were attractions in their own right. All in all I gave

The Bridge of Lions – which I did my best to hit.

the town fathers high marks for not screwing things up over the years.

The town was very busy with tourists and yachties. The large city marina was well run and tolerant of small fry like myself. Many public and private marinas actively discouraged live-aboard boaties like me – especially when we preferred to anchor out and avoid paying overnight dockage fees, but here in St Augustine they took a longer-term view and I'm certain that it paid off.

When I got back and collected my washing, the wind had gone as the thunderstorm that caused it had dumped its rain and blown out to sea. *Wanderer* was drying out nicely and I was stowing clothes when a fellow walked by and stopped to chat.

'Good-looking boat. She yours?'

'Yep,' I said, because for once I knew the answer.

'Where d'ya come from?'

'Key West, bound for Maine.' He nodded and continued to closely examine my boat. He was in his twenties, lean, muscular, bearded and tanned. He was wearing battered old boat shoes, a tie-dyed T-shirt and shorts.

'You'll like it in Maine. I'm from there. It's a good place for a small boat. You live on her?'

'Yep.'

He rolled a smoke while he studied *Wanderer*.

'You got your Whale pump and your roller furling. Got your kicker and your oars. Where d'ya sleep?'

'Right here. I just take this out and put down my bedroll,' I said, pointing to the port-side seat. 'With a boom tent, of course.'

'Uh huh. Goin' up to Maine. How far?' He paused to light his cigarette. I finished stuffing clothes into my duffel bag and started stowing some food I'd bought.

'Eastport.'

'Uh huh. Well, this town's got about everything you need here. Good second-hand chandlery about a mile away if you want fittings. Here, gimme your water can.'

I passed the empty can to him and he refilled it from the hose on the dock and handed it back.

Aaron Clarke – practical hippy and B.G.B.

'If you need to go anywhere I'm sure we can fix you up with a bike if you want. The market's about a mile away if you want a Publix. You staying long?'

'Well, maybe long enough to get a new boom tent made up,' I said, deciding on the spur of the moment that I might as well not wait until it collapsed completely.

'I'll walk you up to the guy that's making my new sails. Ed'll do it.'

'OK, sounds good.' I packed my pockets with wallet, sunglasses and camera.

'Name's Aaron, I'm on *Cushnoc*, that Vega out there second from the bridge,' he said as he pointed to a trim-looking 30-foot yacht. He put his hand out to shake mine. And that was how I met Aaron Clarke and came to stay a week in St Augustine.

~~~

THE QUOTE FOR the new boom tent came to $300, which was exactly what I'd figured. I'd have paid $400 if I had to though, since rain leaking on my down sleeping bag and dripping on my face wasn't a good feeling at all. A down bag is very warm and light, but it's a bugger to dry if it gets wet. I explained to Ed the sailmaker that I wanted a decorative strip of nice red canvas on the spine of the tent and underneath it I wanted a reinforcing strip of strong vinyl to stop the chafing against the sail from making fresh pinholes in it. I left the old tent there for a pattern. Aaron immediately invited me to sleep aboard his boat that night since I no longer had a roof over my head. Since the forecast was for rain, I was happy to accept.

The next morning I rowed ashore intending to do nothing but visit the library to check my email and then see the sights slowly. The library was closed for Presidents' Day so I walked all over the town and around the fort and then visited a museum. I got some film developed and shopped for a couple of pieces of chandlery on the way to pick up my new tent. It looked terrific – a light tan colour with a snazzy red stripe. Ed hadn't joined the stripe to the sides of the tent as I had expected. Instead of laying the stripe on top and sewing it down like the capping on a roof, he had laid the sides of the tent on top of the stripe and then sewed them down onto the stripe. It was too late for an alteration but I guessed that with the additional vinyl layer underneath it would be waterproof. Actually, I was dead wrong and for weeks afterwards it leaked like a bastard while I tackled the problem with repeated applications of seam sealer. Eventually I got it whipped, or so I thought, but then, after folding the tent a few times it would start leaking again. Sometimes it would be two or three weeks between leaks so I never knew if I'd solved it completely or not. I could have had it resewn but that would have meant a long slog to find a sail-maker that could do it immediately and it would have cost money, so after a lot of bother I finally lashed out $2.40 on an 8 x 12-foot blue plastic tarpaulin which I could slip under the tent as an extra layer. With a little bungy cord to hold it in place, it worked perfectly. Anything that got through the canvas just ran down the plastic and over the side. Only then could I really enjoy the sound of rain on the roof.

I was in no hurry to leave St Augustine and since the town's annual birthday festival was coming up in a couple of days, I decided to stay and watch the parade and regatta. In the meantime, Aaron and his friend Bryan took me to meet a couple they'd met while sailing one day. Howard was a New Zealander and Sheera was his American wife. In his early forties, Howard had been stood down by the airline he worked for as an electrical engineer after it nearly went into bank-ruptcy, and so they decided it was a good time to sell their home and go sailing. Like many of the yachts in St Augustine, including Aaron's, they were slowly making their way down to the Caribbean and on to South America. For Howard and Sheera it was a shakedown cruise in a very large boat that was entirely new. For Aaron it was routine sailing in a boat he'd owned for years and which he was now sailing without an engine because he found it was a hassle and he hardly ever needed it. Given my choices, I'd have opted for the boat with the engine, but one thing was sure – I'd rather have done it all on

Wanderer despite my lack of amenities. The reason can be summed up in one word – consequences.

If I screwed anything up there were no repercussions. For instance, if I ran aground due to inattention, lack of navigational skill, poor charts, adverse conditions or dumb luck, the consequences were nil. I'd just step over the side and she'd float again and away I'd go. For anyone else there'd be damage and tow bills or possibly hours of labour and delay. If I dragged my anchor in a crowded anchorage and hit another boat, the consequences were nil too. I'd just apologise, rub the mark off the other guy's hull and reset my anchor. No harm done, no lawsuits or repair bills or fights with insurers or visits from the harbour master. Even if I wrecked *Wanderer* completely and sunk her with all my gear on board I'd be out of pocket by no more than $10,000. That wouldn't break the bank. If Howard lost his boat though, he'd be out a lifetime's savings and the family home. If I misjudged the weather and couldn't make port when I should have, I could just beach *Wanderer* and wait it out on semi-dry land. I wouldn't try that with a 55-foot keeler. All in all, for what I was doing, I felt that I was now freed from a lot of the worries that must have given bigger boat owners sleepless nights. Best of all, I didn't have to stop and find work all the time to pay for dockage and maintenance and fuel. Aaron was doing that now, Howard and Sheera would have to do it some time in the next few months, but I could run my whole adventure on about $100 a week. That wouldn't fill the main gas tank on any powerboat I'd seen yet and precious few yachts either. Admittedly, I might have more daily discomfort than those on larger boats and possibly a greater risk of drowning if I attempted to do what they did, but as long as I was sensible about where and when I tried to sail, I felt that as a beginner I had the advantage over them. Most of all, this little boat was doing something my old horse did when I rode down the Rockies. It was acting as an introduction to all sorts of interesting and generous people. That was something that bigger-boat owners didn't get so much of and some of them told me flat out that they wished they could do what I was doing and meet the people I was meeting. That made me feel good, even when my tent leaked.

Stranded

THE ST MARY'S River was a waypoint for me in more ways than one. When I reached it, two days after leaving St Augustine, it marked my departure from Florida and arrival in Georgia, the start of the prolonged bad weather, my first serious sailing in fog, my first defeat by the weather and my first deliberate stranding.

I waved goodbye to Aaron and Bryan on a windy grey Sunday morning, weighed anchor and tacked out of the harbour, across the St Augustine inlet and into the Tolomata River. The wind died away, the sun came out and I spent several hours slowly tacking back and forth like an overlocker until I anchored in a quiet stream just 12 miles north of the city. The winds were kinder the next day and I made a good 20 miles to Jacksonville Beach and 28 miles the next day. That put me at Fernandina – just south of the Georgia line.

The next day was important because I would cross the St Mary's River and enter beautiful Cumberland Sound where several people had recommended that I stay for a day or two. But when I cast off the next morning, I was plunged into heavy fog. The wind was blowing at about 15 knots and the river was tossing up two-foot waves. I pushed on, and by and by, after I crossed the river, the wind steadied and the waves smoothed out and as I sailed into the sound I found it was pretty peaceful. The only problem was the fog. A lot of big ships pass up and down the river and the sound so I fished out my gas-powered foghorn and slipped it into my lifejacket pocket. I came up on a freighter anchored in the river – it was at least 200 feet long and 40 feet high and I was within about 70 yards of it before I saw it. Luckily it wasn't moving, but other smaller craft were occasionally making sharp changes in course as they came up on my stern. After a while I was able to get to a wider part of the ICW where I could sail to the side of the main track and not worry about a collision. It seemed to me that I was navigating very well. I was using my GPS to check my position in relation to the channel markers and I found that I could sail accurately by compass at five mph between markers and come up on the buoys and cans like clockwork. Since the markers were evenly spaced I could time myself, and every 12 minutes or so I'd start looking for a marker. Amazingly, every time I did this, one would loom out of the fog about 70 yards away and it would be the one I was expecting. I just used the GPS for reassurance. I didn't have to allow anything for leeway as I was sailing upriver and there was no cross-current and I had a following wind. As for magnetic variation, I just applied an even five degrees through Florida and Georgia. For compass deviation I allowed nothing at any time on the whole trip and never had a problem. I always kept metal away from the compass, and since I always stowed the boat in exactly the same way, I never had a problem. I didn't use my boat compass, for taking bearings by eye so I had no problems with parallax either. I used my hand-held Silva orienteering compass, which was tied to my lifejacket, for taking occasional bearings to landmarks and found that I could roughly plot these on my chart while sailing along. The resulting resections gave nothing like the accuracy I was used to on land, but it was good enough for my purposes. All this navigation gave me something to do on a day when there was bugger all to see and it did mean that I only turned the GPS on about once an hour for a minute or so. Because of this, I was still using the batteries I'd installed before I left Phil's place a month earlier.

Sadly, the fog meant that I missed the scenery of Cumberland Sound, but since the winds were fair, I pushed on and made good time to the US Navy installation at Kings Bay where they have a boomer base. A picket boat patrolled the entrance as I sailed past the degaussing range. (Degaussing is a means by which metal ships are protected against magnetic mines.) I hoped I'd see a nuclear submarine but nothing was stirring so I sailed past with a wave to the guard boat and entered the Cumberland Dividings.

Now the wind dropped some more and soon I was struggling to make progress, but I tacked and tacked and by 2.00 pm I had made 20 miles. I was still in the Cumberland River, at the point where it began to widen and flow into St Andrews Sound, which had a mean reputation. But it was only two miles wide at the mouth and I thought I could get across it, even if the wind died and I had to motor.

Inexperience, however, caused me to overlook an important weather sign. The forecast had predicted northeasterlies at 15–20 knots but I'd had 10 to 15-knot southerlies early on and now I had variable winds at five knots. I assumed that the forecast weather was a trifle late in coming, and indeed it was. What I didn't realise was that the variable winds were a sign that the front was right upon me and that very shortly the promised winds would arrive. When that happened, I would face opposing winds and waves and I'd be trying to beat five miles down a river and across two sounds (St Andrews and Jekyll) before I could gain shelter.

When the southerly wind finally petered out, I started the engine and motored two miles down the river and turned northeast to make my run across the sound. As I neared the turn, it began to rain and the wind began to puff into my face for the first time. I ignored the signs. I was only about five miles from my intended anchorage, I had two and a half hours of daylight left and I was confident that my motor would take me where I wanted to go in about half that time. The only uncomfortable thing I noticed was that in a nor'easter, there was absolutely no shelter or anchorage worth a damn on the whole Cumberland River until I got all the way back to the Cumberland Dividings – and that was 10 miles behind. The wind came up quickly and by the time I reached the mouth of the river, only two miles away, I was catching spray in my face and had already had to pump out once. That took me almost an hour, but by then I just had a three-mile crossing of the two sounds and I'd be in Jekyll Creek for the night. The wind came up a little stronger and I felt the swell of waves from the nearby Atlantic Ocean as they rolled in through the heads. The result was an endless series of steep short waves on top of longer rollers. The fog had changed to mist and visibility was only 200 yards. In an hour of crashing into this weather I made only one mile. I was about one-third of the way across the first sound and it would be dark in less than an hour. At this rate it would take me two to three hours of hard motoring to make the crossing, and if my little engine stopped for any reason I'd have no choice but to turn and sail all the way back to the start of the Cumberland.

I turned and ran downwind for a minute or two to see if that improved my morale, but all it told me was that it would be easy to beat a retreat. The moment I turned back into the wind I knew I would be silly to attempt the crossing. It was raining heavily and I had pumped out twice more in the last hour. Getting over the sound would require that everything stayed as it was or got better, and even then I'd get in well after dark. If anything got worse, I might not make it at all. With an hour of light left I decided to quit and look for a place to beach *Wanderer*. All I needed was a tiny dent in the coast about the size of a double bed. If I could find that much protection from the waves I'd be fine. I ran down the windward shore of the river which was bounded by Little Cumberland Island – a private reserve with tall trees and a few houses on it. The other shore was just swamp-grass that offered no protection from the wind or waves. Within a mile I found what looked like a small dry lagoon no bigger than a single-car garage in area.

I ran *Wanderer* onto the sandy bar and took the anchor line ashore and planted it above the high-water line. For the first time that day I was on land, so I took a moment to walk up a path that began at the lagoon. Just behind a screen of trees was a partially built holiday home. No one was around so I went back to *Wanderer* and tried to ease her up the sand bank and into the shallow lagoon. There was enough water in the lagoon to float her and there was hardly a ripple on it, despite the medium-sized waves that were crashing onto the rest of the beach. But I couldn't pull or push the hull over the sand bar. I did get her high enough up so she wouldn't get swamped over the stern, and then I jockeyed her around so her bow was facing out into the waves. For the next hour I watched as the tide crept up but it never floated her over the bar and then it began to recede. All the time *Wanderer* was jostled and bumped by wave action and I could see that this would happen again in twelve hours' time. But if the tide didn't come this high in the morning, I might be stranded. I decided to push her off the bar and down the beach a few yards to another spot that was deeper. There she would be sure to float the next morning, although it meant she would get jostled by the waves for a lot longer. I managed to get her moved and set out two anchors — one on shore to hold her to the land and one out as deep as I could throw it so I had something to kedge the boat off the beach with early next morning when the tide returned. And it would stop her from getting pushed further up the beach if the wind and waves started to crash onshore. Then I set up my tent, took my wet-weather gear ashore and hung it to dry on the verandah of the house and returned to my boat to make dinner. *Wanderer* was still being rocked uncomfortably by swells when I went to sleep. It wasn't the best way to go to bed and I knew that if I wanted to get off this shore I'd have to pull myself off the beach on the morning tide by 5.30 am. If I didn't do that, I'd be stuck until the afternoon tide. But at least I was safe for the night and not out in the middle of the sound bailing out my swamped boat and flooded engine in the dark. That felt good.

I woke again at about 10.00 pm when rain dripped onto my face. I looked out to see where the tide was. I was high and dry, on an even keel and the rain was pouring down in sheets. The radio predicted coastal flooding. I went back to sleep.

At around midnight I woke to check that my sleeping bag was still dry and to take a pee. All was well except for a trickle of water that had soaked my towel pillow. I went back to sleep.

At 2.00 I was woken by the unpleasant rocking action of the waves as the tide returned. It was quite random and seemed to consist of hard shoves that jerked the hull and made nasty grinding noises. I looked out to check my anchors; they were holding well enough but all the slack in the seaward anchor was taken up and it strained to hold me from being pushed up the beach and sideways into the roots of a large fallen tree. I could reach out and touch the roots, but so far the mast and rigging were free of the tangled wood and the hull was nudged into sand that had piled up around the base of the tree. I didn't like the look of it so despite the rain I went on deck and tried to pull myself into deeper water away from the roots. I was still stuck fast, though each wave rocked *Wanderer* from side to side. There was nothing to do except go back to bed.

At 3.30 I checked the tree roots and they were still just clear of the hull. At 4.00 I did it again. *Wanderer* was floating freely, and though the tide had risen much higher than high water the previous night, I decided that with the rain still falling and the waves still crashing, this was no time to put to sea. Since the seaward anchor was holding me clear of the tree I went back to sleep.

At 6.00 I finally got up, fished out some biscuits and considered my situation over breakfast. It was still raining, the sea was too lively for comfort, and the weather was forecast to improve late in the afternoon – possibly. It was still dark and I didn't feel up to the idea of setting sail yet, so I mopped up the leaks, cleaned my teeth and decided to wait until the rain stopped before leaving. As the tide receded I could see I was on a gently sloping sandy shore. When it came time to float her again, if the tide was well out, I planned to unload *Wanderer* and lift her bow and stern onto the big roller fenders. I'd bury an anchor in the sand down by the water's edge. Then I'd use the mainsheet block and rope to rig a 3:1 tackle that I could use to pull her down to the water. By the time I packed all that back up and rigged her for sailing, the tide should have come in a little and she could float off. It would be hard work and it would take plenty of time but it was nine or ten hours till the next high tide and I wanted to be long gone by then. If I waited for the tide to come and get me, I'd be casting off at dusk and then I'd have to sail across the sounds to Jekyll Creek in darkness. And also, the weather was forecast to get grotty again overnight, so I really wanted to be sailing by midday or early afternoon. That would give me time to motor or sail all the way to Brunswick where I could buy a berth at a dock and get a shower and use the laundry to dry my damp clothes and sleeping bag.

The rain lifted at about 9.00 am and five minutes later I was piling stores on the sand behind the boat. I could see now how much the morning tide had shoved me up the beach. I was some 20 feet further up and the debris left on the beach was higher than the previous high-tide mark. Clearly, all that rain, added to the flooding on the three rivers that spilled into St Andrews Sound, had created a flood tide of unusual height. Alarmingly, the waterline was now quite a long way off and it was still three hours from low tide. I had just finished piling stores and was about to lift the bow onto a roller when I saw a man approach from the little path leading to the beach house. He was about forty and he had solid work-clothes and a gun on his hip.

'Are you Colin Newman?' I asked. That was the name on the building permit for the beach house.

'No, I'm Steve McDonnell, the superintendent here. This is a private island reserve, you know.'

'Yeah, I saw that on the chart but I kind of got stranded here. Literally. I didn't want to push my luck crossing the sound last night and I didn't want to sail all the way back down the river to find some-where to anchor, so I beached her.'

'Uh huh. I saw you here when I was coming to work. We get people coming ashore sometimes but it is private land. Well, at least it's private above the high-water mark. So you're all right, I guess. We just don't want people camping here is all.'

'Well, I went on land to see what was here and saw the house there. I left my gear to dry on the porch overnight, but that's all I did. I'll be off here just as soon as I can get her down to the water. I want to get to Brunswick today if I can get floated early enough.'

'Brunswick, huh. That where you're headed?'

'No, actually I'm going to Maine, but I've got mail to collect in Brunswick.'

'You're going to Maine in that thing? Hoo boy, that's a way off. Where'd you start?'

'Key West a couple of months ago.' And at that he smiled for the first time and held out his hand to shake mine. And with the ice broken, we went through the usual questions that everyone asked when they met me. Where did I sleep, how far did I go each day, what possessed me to do it, what did I do for a living, when would I finish, how much sailing had I done beforehand, why such a little boat and was I an Aussie? To which I gave my usual answers. By the end of all that, he was looking at the boat and complimenting me on my good sense in not pushing my luck.

'The sound isn't very wide but it can eat your lunch for you. I met a guy once when I was crossing it who we had to tow in. He was paddling one of those little inflatable canoes you give to kids. Going from God knows where to Key West. It was so small, he had to sit in it near the water's edge, then pile all his stuff on his legs and lap and then wait for the tide to float him off. When we found him he'd been paddling for nine hours non-stop and his hands were all raw and bleeding.

'Well, I'll leave you to it — unless there's anything you need?'

'No, I'm fine, unless you have a tow truck in your hip pocket,' I said jokingly.

. . . I had a long haul back to the water.

'Well, I gotta truck just up there that'd tow you if you want,' he replied. 'I can't pull you all the way into the water 'cause I'll get stuck, but I can haul you out of that hole you're in.'

After 15 minutes of careful pulling, we had *Wanderer* within 40 feet of the water. I unhooked the anchor line, and with a cheery wave, Steve drove off. I looked back at the blue antifoul that was streaked on the sand where *Wanderer* had rocked back and forth overnight and then examined the hull. It seemed that only a little of the paint had been lost and nowhere was it sanded through to the fibreglass hull. Looked like I'd got away with it.

For the next two hours I pried and shoved *Wanderer* down the beach chasing the receding tide. I stopped every 10 minutes for a rest and in one of the breaks I took a picture of how far *Wanderer* had been dragged and shoved. It was clear that without the truck I'd have eventually got her down the beach to the water – but only by late afternoon when the tide was coming back to meet me and only after busting a gut. Thankfully, it was still only about noon and I could see the tide was turning. The bow was within six feet of the water and the muddy sand was nearly flat so within an hour we would be afloat. I began to gather up the stores and restow them. Sure enough, by the time everything was packed, *Wanderer* was partially afloat. I shoved her gradually into deeper water, plonked the motor halfway down and carefully held the propellor up until it was safe to drop down. The wind was still pushing me back to shore so I gunned the engine and powered out into the sound as fast as I could.

Stranding myself had been an unusual and slightly uncomfortable experience but I'd learned a lot from it. Mainly, I'd learned that while it was undoubtedly a prudent choice, and one that I thought I could do again with fewer complications, the need for it could be eliminated by paying more attention to the weather forecast. For now, though, having motored smartly into deeper water, I was happy to cut my engine, raise the sail and contemplate the luxuries awaiting me in Brunswick, where I intended to squander a few dollars on my first overnight dockside marina berth since Key West.

Georgia on my mind

BRUNSWICK WAS THE nicest place and yet it was another of the many large coastal towns I would find that seemed to be barely hanging on. From here, all the way to the New Jersey shore, most of the ports were changing radically. The wharf areas and centres of the towns were half-empty. For Sale and For Rent signs were sprinkled along the main street. The only places that were unambiguously thriving on the water were those that had invested heavily in revamping their waterfront to make it attractive to recreational boaters. Even the small fishery towns were having a hard time as declining catches reduced fleet sizes. On the Chesapeake, in towns like Crisfield, this was a little painful to see, but here at Brunswick, the shrimping fleet was still sizeable.

I sailed by it as I made my way to the marina. All the way up the river I passed pairs of boats rafted up to a winter dock. They were smallish boats, not more than 50 feet long in most cases, and looked top-heavy with their nets and trawling gear. They had the solid, grubby, unbeautiful look that working equipment and vehicles get when used by an owner-operator with thin profit margins. Behind them was the deep-water port that served the big ships that came to collect timber and wood pulp. It didn't seem like timber country, but it smelt like it. It wasn't unpleasant – just distinctive. As I motored the two miles upriver to the marina, I reflected on what I knew of Georgia. Not a lot really and most of it came from the lyrics of pop songs.

From these impeccable sources I decided that I would probably see 'bright red Georgia clay', 'peaches on the streets' and 'a rainy night in Georgia'. It was drizzling and grey as I sailed into the marina and before I'd gone a hundred yards from the marina I would see red dirt. Two out of three ain't bad (as another song says) and I was happy that these songwriters knew what they were talking about.

I berthed at the marina for a fee of $12, which wasn't too bad since it included free use of the laundry and the warm TV lounge. The lady at the dock was very helpful and gave me maps of town and explained where everything was and even offered to charge up my VHF radio overnight. Later, while putting my sleeping bag in the dryer I got talking to another yachtie who was wintering over at the marina and he invited me for dinner. Bob and Sally Burnette took me onto their massive 50-footer and served up red beans, rice, salad and ice cream. Over a beer I explained what I was doing and they told me how they'd retired early, decided to sell their house and go sailing and had now been cruising the US and Caribbean for five years on their yacht. Well fed, comfy and dry, I was pretty impressed with Brunswick so far. Outside it rained like a big fat bastard.

And the next day. And the next and the next, but the day after that it only rained like a medium-sized son of a bitch. I stayed at the berth the whole time, paying my $12 each morning and hoping for two things – fine weather and my parcel. Adrienne had posted a package containing a small New Zealand flag, a few packets of Throaties and a card. I had been searching for a flag ever since I first arrived in Fort Lauderdale but they were all too large or too small. The big ones were half the size of my genoa and the small ones were the size of a pack of cigarettes. I've never been a big flag-waving patriot, but it was clearly the custom to fly a flag on the stern so I'd asked Ady to find one and post it off. As it turned out, she'd been delayed and I'd been sailing fast and the flag had left New Zealand the day after I had left St Augustine. It probably would take several more days to get from Christchurch to Georgia.

To kill time while I waited for the flag, I walked the streets admiring the Georgian (what else) architecture, scoured the second-hand book store, made my ritual five-mile pilgrimage to a supermarket, resealed the leaking seam on my tent and talked to other boat owners. Mostly I visited the local library and emailed everyone, especially Adrienne. By now, we had agreed that she couldn't really afford to take more time off work to come away for another expensive American holiday. She was also busy trying to sell her house and run her homestay business. It seemed best that I didn't drag her away to meet me in Washington DC.

I had got my charts wet when I battled the weather on the day that I beached *Wanderer* on Little Cumberland Island, so on the second day I took them into the laundry and spread the ICW chartbook and my Skipper Bob guidebook out to dry on a table. That evening when I came to get them they were gone. Yikes! I put up a note on the door asking for them back and pointing out that I hadn't discarded them, I was just drying them. I suspected that someone thought they were being given away – a common thing in most marinas, especially ones where there were plenty of people staying for the whole winter on their boats. Here, there were about 60 boats moored and perhaps 20 had permanent live-aboard couples who were wintering over or working in Brunswick. People exchanged surplus goods and gave away old charts frequently. I'd given Aaron my bulky rescue flare and smoke generator which Geoff had donated to me. It was just too big and I doubted I'd have time to operate it if I sank anyway. I waited a day for the books to reappear but they didn't show up.

This was a serious problem for me. Brunswick isn't a town that has a whole lot of chandlery stores and the ones that did stock charts didn't have an ICW book, only local coastal charts. No one sold any Skipper Bob books either, since these are marketed directly by Bob to just a few dozen places on the east coast. Tom, another boatie who was wintering over with his wife, took me the next day in his car to a chandlery shop several miles away but they didn't have a suitable book. We stopped at a K-Mart, though, and I bought more canvas waterproofing compound for the tent, so that was a good result. That day I emailed Skipper Bob and found that the nearest source was in Savannah, 102 miles north, but to get there I had to sail and I couldn't do that without my ICW charts. Chicken and egg. Driving to another town for shopping wasn't an option. By the time I'd checked local phone directories it was obvious that I'd have to either go to Savannah or return to Jacksonville, Florida, 100 miles south. Renting a car, buying gas and spending a day doing that would cost about $100 all up. Ordering an ICW chart by mail from the West Marine catalogue would cost $87 and would take three days to arrive. That added $36 in dock fees. Any way I sliced it, I was looking at a $100 bill at least. I reluctantly placed the order with West Marine and went to the Post Office to check for the third time if my parcel had arrived. It hadn't, but when I got back to the marina that afternoon, my ICW chart was back on the table with no sign of where or how or why it had disappeared. Yahoo! Skipper Bob was gone for good, but that wasn't a problem. I had my chartbook with its invaluable record of where I'd sailed and where I'd anchored overnight. Best of all, I was mobile again. A boat without charts just cannot sail. Now all I wanted was my mail and I'd be able to start cruising again.

When I wasn't at the library I would usually make a sandwich snack on *Wanderer* and take it to the lounge and eat it while reading a book. That was how I met Laurent and Eliane, a Swiss couple who had heard my tale from Bob and Sally and who then invited me aboard for lunch one day. They cooked a delicious seafood chowder and then roasted chickens and made salad and finally served pears with melted chocolate. Laurent had some extraordinary tales to tell. As a young chap he had left Switzerland for Africa and decided to drive a 2CV across the Sahara. He made it too and had amazing adventures including giving a lift to a hitch-hiker in Niger who turned out to be escaping from the scene of a murder.

The police arrested them both and charged Laurent with being an accessory to the murder. He had to talk his way out of it and even managed that so successfully that the police loaned him some gas to get to the next village. At the end of the trip, young Laurent decided he'd seen enough of the desert and wanted to go sailing. Now, 20 years later, he'd had two boats sink beneath him in storms and the one he was on currently had been struck by lightning the previous summer and he was only just finishing the uninsured replacement of all the electrical equipment. I listened to his stories and those of Eliane with real delight. The best of all was Laurent's tale of cremating his hang-glider when he crashed it into high-tension lines in France. 'Poof – burnt,' he said with a huge grin and then indicated with his hands how he instantly plummeted to the ground in the wreckage, sustaining a small but educational concussion. I was in fits. It was nice to be entertained by someone else rather than have to tell my story for the umpteenth time.

Outside, it had stopped raining over lunch and my spirits rose, but it was just catching its breath. The next day it poured so hard I could almost have floated *Wanderer* on the rain and the spray it threw up from the surface of the water.

I made my way to the Post Office splashing in the puddles and saying hello to everyone as if they were old friends. The people in Georgia and both the Carolinas were extraordinarily polite and friendly. Everyone, even the few town derelicts, would make eye contact, say 'Hi they-uh' or 'Harr are yew t'day' or 'Iddn't this rain sumpin'. Once, a little old lady held the door open for me and called me 'dear'. I could see why so many couples brought their boats back to this odd little town that had seen better days, miles off the ICW and a world away from the flash Florida marinas that had so much better weather.

This time though, Sarah at the Post Office had a big grin and a parcel for me. I tore it open and there was my flag and my favourite candy.

'Have a safe one,' Sarah said as I left.

'How'dja know I'm leaving?' I asked her at the door.

'Written all over yo' face, Lee,' she said and she was right. Brunswick was a neat place to stay, but it had been six days with no movement towards Maine. The next day was dry and I went sailing.

~~~

WITH A MILD wind pushing me along under grey skies, I managed to make an excellent 42 miles by the time I anchored in darkness. I took a short cut through some creeks near the town to avoid the long dogleg down the Brunswick River and across St Simons Sound. Then it was up the Mackay River, into tiny Buttermilk Sound, across the big Altamaha River, along the Little Mud River, across the junctions with the Darien and North Rivers, and then up Old Teakettle Creek to Creighton Narrows where I dropped the pick by the side of the channel, just out of the way of the late-night barge traffic.

Now sailing up a river sounds like hard work but, in fact, it isn't in this part of Georgia. Firstly, Georgia has a low coast so rivers run slowly to the sea with no raging power behind them except in a few localities where the tide helps things along. Also, well before they reach the Atlantic the rivers cross many creeks that are tributaries. These creeks connect to other rivers to the north and south as well, forming a lazy, slow-moving spaghetti-grid of waterways that connects everything with everything. After that the rivers and creeks discharge into a sound. Here they average 10 miles long and two to five miles wide. The ocean entrance to them may be as narrow as half a mile. They are frequently much deeper than the rivers that fill them. The sounds in Georgia are usually filled by more than one large river plus up to half a dozen creeks before these combined waters escape through the headlands of the sound into the Atlantic. These sounds, with their great volume of water and narrow headlands, are what make ICW sailing in Georgia so challenging. When masses of water have to exit a narrow aperture in just six hours of falling tide they generate a high speed as they flow out – maybe three to six mph – about the same speed as I could sail. Once the water is gone, it has to come back when the tide turns, so the tidal flow is almost as strong again in the opposite direction, but this time the tide is opposing the flow of the rivers and this can occasionally throw up lumpy water. In any event, crossing a sound is best done at low or high tide when flows are slowest.

In Georgia, a lot depended on the tides. When you might enter six or eight creeks or rivers and cross perhaps two sounds in a day, the issue of tides and timings becomes complex. Tides turn at different times at different places and finding out when a tide will turn on a particular sound isn't easy. For a sailor like myself, who was new to all the areas I sailed in and who didn't know even the names and locations of most of the places mentioned in the weather and tide forecasts, or the places named in the pilot guide, calculating tides for my next destination was a major effort. I sometimes had to shuffle through a pilot guide, a road-map, a guidebook and my ICW chart to finally decide when it would be high tide tomorrow, 20 miles away. And once I planned my day to get there at the right time I'd often find I was late or early because on the way I'd picked up a boost or a setback from a river or tidal flow somewhere, so my timing was all shot to hell anyway. Eventually I solved it another way entirely. I just got up at the same time each day, then sailed all day at whatever speed I could make and then quit at quitting time with no regrets about how far I'd got. But if I felt I had to make it to a particular anchorage for some reason, I'd fire up the motor towards the end of the day and just fight the tides. I had just enough power to beat any tide I encountered.

In retrospect, this was a lazy and inefficient and possibly unsafe way to plan my sailing (if you can call it planning) but it worked for me because I had no rigid timetable to adhere to. I had no particular port to reach at any given time and I was entirely self-contained and could easily spend three or four days afloat before I ran low on water or food or gas. If I was late, who cared but me?

Rain

CONTRARY TO EXPECTATIONS, the weather was still crap. I rather expected some warm spring sunshine by now but instead I was getting Biblical rain and barely enough therms to elevate the mercury beyond 50 degrees. The weather was at best changeable and I got a taste of it the next day. The forecast suggested sunshine early on and thunderstorms later in the day followed by a front that would drop heavy rain for another day or two. I began sailing in T-shirt and shorts with light southerly breezes and quickly crossed Sapelo Sound, but about noon when I had re-entered the tangle of rivers and creeks, the breeze became a strong gusty wind that knocked up whitecaps even on sheltered water. Eventually I hove to, double-reefed and put on wet-weather gear. I set off again, surprised at how far the wind had pushed me when I was hove to and rather glad that I'd taken in two reefs. A couple of hours later the wind dropped significantly and I had trouble making progress as I tacked back and forth up a winding river. Above me, black thunderheads darkened the afternoon and I watched them closely, ready to drop the sails.

Just after 4.00 pm I felt a sudden drop in temperature – it was so quick and so large that I knew what was about to hit me. I flew into action, starting the motor in case I needed it to keep from being blown aground, and then lowered the mainsail. I had just got it into the bottom of the boat when the rain and wind struck. While I fumbled with the sail to get it flaked, the rain pelted into the boat. The quantity of water was so much that as soon as I had the sail away I pumped out the bilge as I motored up the river. After a couple of minutes of this, the hail arrived. By then I was ready for it with my polar fleece jacket, woolly hat and fingerless gloves on, my wet-weather gear all zipped up and my charts folded safely in a plastic bag. When it hit, the noise of ice bouncing off the hull was so loud that I couldn't hear the motor. Luckily I was in the Bear River, a winding waterway about two hundred yards wide at the most and so there was no danger of being turned over by waves thrown up by the wind. I wouldn't have wanted to be on a sound at this time, though. I decided to anchor for the night as soon as I could find a suitable spot and my only option appeared to be three miles ahead. There, just before the Ogeechee River, was the shallow Queen Bess Creek which had a dogleg in it. On the point of the bend was a deep hole with room enough to swing in any direction. The chart indicated trees on one shore, too, and it looked as if they would give shelter from the expected winds. Everything else was either too shallow or too exposed.

Just as I finally eased into Queen Bess Creek, the rain stopped and I was able to anchor and set up my tent in relative dry. I put down two anchors as I knew there was a fairly strong tidal pull and there was a lot of floodwater too. The creek was well over its usual level and the marsh-grass was flooded and impassable on foot now. I got *Wanderer* all sponged out and unrolled my bed, and an hour later I was able to relax. The rain returned as I cooked my dinner and lit my lantern. The radio predicted flooding and continuous rain for the next day. I spread my wet-weather gear out to dry around the lantern and then dug out my selection of books, spread my poncho to catch most of the drips running steadily through the faulty seam of the tent and settled down to read.

I spent the next day like that, too. It rained heavily all night as far as I could tell and my sleeping bag got soaked at the foot. Next morning I sponged out, breakfasted and updated my diary. I read as much of my cruising guides as I could and studied my charts to plan the next week. I tried to restrict my candy intake and occasionally smoked a cigarette, but I only had six of them to last me until I got to Savannah so I rationed these as well. That evening I pulled out a pen and wrote the only longhand letter of the trip.

It was, of course, to Adrienne and in it I told her the reasons why I enjoyed her company so much – even why I loved her. That wasn't the first time I'd told her but it was the first time I'd said why. I had to rewrite it after it fell onto a damp part of the floor but that gave me a chance to improve it and by the end I was pretty happy that it said everything. Luckily I ran out of writing paper so I was saved from long-windedness and had to confine my admiration for her to just two sides of a sheet of paper. But that's quite a lot of space given that Shakespeare only ever needed about 14 lines to state his case. I'm no poet but I know what I like and this trip had given me plenty of time to think about Ady and to decide that I liked her easily as much as Ranfurly Shield rugby and possibly as much as test footy. Only time would tell if she was as wonderful to me as a series win away against the Springboks. I knew I wouldn't be able to post my letter for a day or two, so I would have time to reread it and revise it if I'd said any-thing that was over the top. Being trapped in a 10 x 5 x 4-foot tent for hours and hours can amplify feelings of loneliness and result in an excess of commitment to all sorts of strange ideas. I didn't want to send off a letter to the other side of the world that made any wobbly emotional declarations which wouldn't stand up to scrutiny in the light of a normal day but I was pretty sure that this letter was one I wouldn't regret writing.

That night, the weather forecast was for more fog and rain, possibly clearing later in the day. I decided that whatever happened, I would sail away. Another 12 hours under the tent were unavoidable, but I didn't like to think of spending another 36 hours there. I was fast run-ning out of nibbles and was reduced to arranging my four remaining cigarettes, one cigar and 30-odd individual pieces of candy in a com-plicated sequence along the edge of the seat. I took into consideration the taste of each item, the size and amount of time they would take to consume and the calorie value when determining their positions in the sequence. I allowed myself one item every 15 minutes, be it a low-value pink jellybean, a high-value whole cigarette or best of all a throat-soothing lozenge from Adrienne. I didn't like to think what I might do if I came to the end of the line before the weather cleared.

Alone on my boat at times like that, I usually had no great trouble occupying my mind. I could let it off its leash to wander through whatever thoughts surfaced, listen to the radio or read. Second-hand books were ideal for this type of journey – I'd buy them in one town then trade them in further up the coast. The big problem with being stationary in weather like this was that I had few ways to exercise physically. With the tent up I could walk no further than three careful steps forward along the edge of the deck before I was standing on the bow. But getting to the bow, where I could at least stand and admire the view, meant I was treading on the canvas tent where it bent over the side and was secured to the line that encircled the hull. Footprints on the canvas impregnated it with dirt, through which water leaked. The only cure was to scrub it clean and then reapply waterproofing compound to the material and let it dry. That wasn't possible on rainy days so if I dirtied the canvas I risked an immediate leak. Treading on the edges of the tent wasn't so bad as mostly the water just ran through the canvas and landed on the six-inch-wide strip of deck that ran down either side of the cockpit. From there it was easy enough to brush it over the side underneath the canvas.

So, as the second evening drew in with more rain on the roof, I just climbed back into a fresh dry sleeping bag, spread my damp down bag over the top as an eiderdown and dipped deeper into *Angela's Ashes*, the autobiography of Frank McCourt. At the end of each miserable story of this feckless Irish family I thought once again how lucky I was to have had a happy childhood with everything I needed right around me. And it was still true. Warmth, shelter, food, drink and transportation. *Wanderer* had it all within arm's reach. Except, of course, my girlfriend. She was half a world away.

Next morning dawned like an execution. No sunbeams leaked through the fog but the blackness became grey enough to read a compass so I began to pack up. An hour later I was motoring off into the fog, dressed for the worst – long johns, fleece jacket, gloves, hat, waterproofs. The weather didn't get violent, though it stayed cold and rained plenty. The greatest problem came at the start when I was motoring down Queen Bess Creek to join the Florida Passage on my way to the Ogeechee River. I was supposed to go a few hundred feet, turn right out of the creek and then follow that bank of the passage to where it joined the river. I started by following the right bank of the creek, past the trees on the island and then along the marsh-grass. However, I stuck to the curving marsh-grass bank too long and by the time I realised that I was heading east instead of north, I was technically lost. It only took a moment to fire up the GPS and set a course for a nearby channel marker in the Ogeechee River, but it was a powerful indication of how difficult it can be to fly by eye instead of by instruments. After that, I pulled out my hand-held compass and used it to calculate courses between markers. Then I steered by the boat compass and found that I didn't need the GPS again that day. Within an hour, as the fog reduced to mist, I was nearing the mouth of Moon River and I was able to put away the compass and steer by eye.

And for the record, it's not wider than a mile at all. Barely an eighth of a mile, in fact, and scarcely four miles long. My cruising guide says it was the same Moon River as in the song and that guide was endorsed by none other than Walter Cronkite, so it must be true. I took a picture anyway and then set off under sail for the wonderfully named little town of Thunderbolt on the Wilmington River, from where I could take a bus into Savannah. After a day and two nights immobile in the rain it was good to be moving and even better to be heading towards a city. In mid-afternoon the sun finally broke through and just as I came past Dutch Island, a fleet of sleek Lightning two-man racing dinghies came out of the yacht club and unfurled their spinnakers. I sailed through the middle, discreetly undressing in the sudden heat. By the time I sailed up to the dock of the flash Palmer Johnson Marina I was once again in shorts and T-shirt. I only stopped there to buy a Skipper Bob guidebook, but after I got talking to the weekend manager, Leon, he said that since I was just a tiny boat and since they mainly catered to luxury yachts of 60-odd feet or larger, I could just stay right where I was for free. I wouldn't be in anyone's way as it was a quiet time of year. I offered to pay for at least one night of my intended two nights' stay, but Leon refused and so I tucked in behind a big boat. *Wanderer* looked like an accessory instead of an interstate traveller.

~~~

SAVANNAH WAS LIKE Brunswick but better. Bigger, of course, but also thriving on tourism and industry including a busy river port that accessed the sea by way of the Savannah River. The city is surrounded by plenty of suburbia, but the centre is old, charming, full of polite people and built on a solid base of racial oppression that to the casual observer was utterly absent now. The businessman who gave me a lift to town the next day, while I waited hopefully for a bus on a Sunday morning, was middle-aged, black and, judging by the Mercedes he drove, pretty successful. All he did by way of explanation or conversation was to offer me his business card with 'Jesus Saves' and the address of a church printed on the back. He asked where I was going, said he could drop me off a couple of miles nearer to it and then ended up taking me all the way to town with not a word more said.

The black lady and her daughter who stepped back from the ATM to let me go first while the mother rummaged for her credit card did so with a smile and a 'Oh Lord, this'll take a while'. When she found her card, her daughter said, 'Gosh, Momma, you sure look nice today.' I caught the daughter's eye and said, 'That's a good time to say it – when she's standing in front of a cash machine.' They laughed and then the daughter said, 'Well, since you in front of one, then yo' lookin fine too.'

The young girl at the information centre took time to explain how the bus timetable worked on weekends, the lady in the curio shop on the waterfront stopped chatting to her friend and took me next door to her shop and opened it up early so I could buy camera film. The assistant at Waldenbooks spent 15 minutes searching for Homer Hickam books while everyone behind me waited patiently. The couple at the bus stop on my way home asked me for the time and said 'thank you, sir' when I answered. When I got back to the marina, Leon brought me a complimentary box of doughnuts, explaining that he handed boxes out each day to the other boats that were tied up.

'But I haven't paid for dockage,' I protested.

'But you like doughnuts, right?' he said and handed me a box.

Savannah, it seemed, was just a city of extraordinarily polite and helpful people. And they weren't doing it just because I was a novelty item in my cute little boat. To all but one of these people I was just another anonymous tourist, but they couldn't have been nicer. I like Savannah just because of that, never mind that it's a great place to stroll around.

I did plenty of that, too. I walked through all the old city squares and along the refurbished cobblestone waterfront. I took dozens of photographs – especially of the huge oaks in the squares and of anything that bloomed. I noticed that I was delighted to see tall trees and flowering plants, as well as to smell things like mown grass and woodsmoke. Even though I was only sailing on the ICW and was coming ashore about every second day on average, I still felt a little

Savannah had the scents of spring at last.

separated from the sight and smell of land vegetation. Perhaps it was because so much of what I'd sailed through to date was flat, lightly forested and still in mid-winter hibernation. Now, I was coming into early spring and I was seeing hills and proper mature hardwood forests for the first time in three months. Even walking down a suburban street and seeing bougainvillea flowering gave me a thrill. For the first time on this journey I caught the wild luscious smell of spring. That was a promising sign. If spring was here, then summer couldn't be far away.

That night I looked at my diary and calculated how far I had left to travel. I'd sailed 940 miles and had about 1500 to go. No time to waste. The next day I sailed north again.

Rain and occasional tigers

ON MONDAY MORNING I dashed down to a sail loft half a mile away and as soon as they opened at 7.00 am I had them sewing a new Velcro strip on the front of my wet-weather jacket. In the hailstorm the previous week I'd had to hold it closed at the top with my teeth. If I let go, the neck opened and my hood flew back and cold water poured down my neck. But now, five minutes' work fixed for good something that had bugged me intermittently for weeks. I dashed back to the boat, left a thank-you note for Leon and cast off. I was looking forward to leaving Savannah, not because I hadn't enjoyed my visit, which was great, but just because I was keen to do some sailing. It was a bright, cool day with light winds but I managed to raise the genoa to help the motor along. As I puttered down the Wilmington River the long morning shadows were shortening. It's a wonderful time to be on the water – but even better when you can visualise the remainder of humanity off to another week of work by car, train, rickshaw or whatever. For me it was just another lovely day with the prospect of many more like it.

I made good time on flat calm waters – across the Savannah River and over the Georgia line into South Carolina. Then up Fields Cut, across the Wright River, into yet another unoriginally named New River, up Ramshorn Creek and down the Cooper River to the junction with long, narrow Calibogue Sound. It was kind to me except for the gentle headwind that made me lower the genoa. I continued to motor up the five-mile sound towards the passage behind ritzy Hilton Head Island. This was home to a major marina where rich people moored their party boats as they cruised up and down the coast. All I saw was a brief section of waterfront with some tall, narrow, expensive new houses crowded together. They were built in what I consider to be one of only two architectural styles that suit a waterfront. One style is the white mud houses of the Greek Isles and the other is the wooden clapboard, gabled Cape Cod style. Everything else built anywhere in the world just looks horrid. (For more expert opinions on architecture contact the author at www.wot-a-bleedin-knowitall.com.)

Beyond Hilton Head Island was Port Royal Sound, which promised to be a little more active than the sheltered Calibogue. It sprang from the aptly named Broad River and was joined near the ocean by the Chechessee River and the Beaufort River. Each of these rivers was larger than average – about a mile across for the smaller ones and twice that for the Broad. All this volume of water entered the Atlantic through heads only a mile wide. The tidal pull was strong but at the point where I had to cross the sound, all three came together and created a crossing of four miles at its narrowest point followed by a long haul up the Beaufort River. That didn't surprise me since Port Royal Sound is a broad, deep water that forms one of the best and biggest natural harbours on the southeast coast. In the 17th and 18th centuries it was widely used by privateers, traders, slavers and exporters of cotton, indigo dye and rice. Now, though it is less trafficked than before, it has left a legacy which I planned to visit, in the shape of the delightful town of Beaufort (pronounced Bew-ford, to distinguish it from its North Carolina twin, Beaufort, pronounced Bow-fit). One bank of the Beaufort River is formed by Parris Island, the huge Marine Corps training base. Back in the 1950s half a dozen marine recruits were drowned by the speedy incoming tide when they were crossing some marshes and I doubt they were the only ones to experience a Port Royal tide that way. Nowadays the base is a major industry for the community and the prosperity of the whole state is closely attached to the fortunes of the military.

By the time I exited the protection of the passage behind Hilton Head, the wind was a stout northwesterly at about 15 mph. The tide seemed to be running into Port Royal Sound, against the river flows, and this threw up mean two-foot waves that smashed into and over the bow. They were short and steep and *Wanderer* actually crashed off the edge of a lot of them with a heavy thump into the trough behind. I could barely see forwards for the spray that was thrown into my face, but when I turned and looked behind I could see a distant shoreline that was still bathed in sunshine. On we sailed, out of sight of a family on the beach who watched mystified as this tiny dinghy set off into the cold, green, pounding waves. Visibility for a man standing is about three miles due to the curvature of the earth, but since I could only sit, I could see about half that distance at this time and so the banks on either side of me were out of sight. But because of the sunshine and the lack of any unfavourable weather forecast I had no hesitation in crossing the sound under motor alone. I knew if I had engine troubles I would have plenty of time and plenty of directions to sail to safety quickly. Mainly, it was the absence of grey foreboding skies that made this crossing so much easier than the one I abandoned on St Andrews Sound. Though the waves were actually nastier and the distance to cross was much further I was never concerned about not making it. Morale is all in the head and nothing raises morale like sunshine. My little engine overcame the opposition and I was pretty sure that *Wanderer*'s hull would take the heavy pounding.

After about an hour of this and three turns at the pump, I started to come within the protection of the northern shore of the Beaufort River. The waves gradually died down and although I was battling the river current, my progress was a good deal faster. The wind backed some more until it was once again in my face as I made the turn westwards up the river. By now, masses of small powerboats that had been upriver were making the run home to Beaufort. I'd been the only vessel that I'd seen crossing the sound that day so it was nice to have some company. When I made the turn north for Beaufort, I cut the motor, raised the main and genoa and pretty soon I was making six to seven mph. The tide had turned, I think, and with the boost from that I was almost able to keep ahead of the powerboats. They had a speed restriction to reduce the wake they threw up as they headed into the narrows of the river near the town and adjacent marina. Now, nearly at dusk, the sun sent a cool golden light over the trees on the shore and they sent shadows out to meet me on the water. I anchored just off the old stone town as the last of the sun sank behind the treeline and the first of the mosquitoes came out. I'd made a whopping 46 miles, but only the last six were solely under sail. On the plus side, I'd done those in less than an hour and covered the previous 40 miles in eight hours, which was a fine average speed given the conditions. I'd pushed on through another small barrier, gained some more experience, and another tiny chip of fear had broken off and blown away in the wind. All in all, it was a pretty good day.

~~~

I MENTION THIS day in detail because it was somewhat typical of the next month. All the way up the Carolina coast I had days like this. Fine, clear and warm weather alternating occasionally with cold, rainy days when I'd button up in all my clobber and stare at the shores, wondering why I was still doing this. But every time I started to wonder when summer would arrive, I reminded myself that this was why I'd come here. To get out on the water on days when I didn't want to be there. That was the only way to overcome an irrational fear. After a thousand miles, I could see it was working. A month before, I'd never have tried to cross Port Royal. Now it was all in a day's work. It also heightened my appreciation of the good days in between. And there were plenty of those, too. Ashore in Beaufort I had a blissful day of sunshine and heat. I shopped for camera film and books in shorts and T-shirt and wandered the streets of old Beaufort in a serene, peaceful mood. All I was missing was the sound of cicadas in the macrocarpa trees. Instead I got the first of the clouds of pine pollen, which left yellow dust across every surface. Even on the water it formed a bright yellow, almost oily slick. Not at all unpleasant or troublesome, just novel.

Occasionally a tiny puff of wind on a calm day would strike a tree and it would seem to explode in a smoky cloud of pollen. A month later, as I followed the spring north to the Chesapeake, it was still happening and in Annapolis harbour I took a picture of a corner where the waves had accumulated a heavy layer of pollen. It formed swirling post-modern patterns that changed constantly and strained my eyes to look at. It reminded me of abstract art – Jackson Pollen maybe . . . My fondest memory of this time is the pollen drifting down and settling on the water as I lazily sailed past miles and miles of marsh-grass and pine forest. It was a Tom Sawyer sort of experience.

The next two weeks saw steady progress. With practice I was now able to pack up quickly and sail faster. It wasn't unusual to make over 25 miles by mid-afternoon. At the start of the trip, it took me almost 12 hours to do what I could now do in six or seven. With that and the end of daylight saving I had plenty of extra time available to me and I was far more relaxed now than in Florida. I stopped losing weight. I was still well-tanned, stronger, fitter and slimmer than usual, so I was happy with my physical condition, but I was starting to notice a few things about my personality.

I was becoming willing to talk to anyone about anything. Normally I don't suffer fools for long and certainly don't feel the need to talk much to strangers, foolish or not, but lately I was feeling the need for more conversation with anybody. I had few opportunities. I called Adrienne about once a month, which was all my budget allowed, but aside from that, my longest conversations were with people who invited me aboard their boats. That happened about once every three weeks on average. For the rest of the time my ration of conversation was con-fined to 'Morning', 'How much is that, please?', 'Thank you' and 'Is there a library within walking distance?' And even this only happened about every second day. Since I'm pretty comfortable with my own company it had taken several months for the lack of human inter-action to take its toll.

What made this isolation a little different was that now I had so much I wanted to talk about that was new and exciting, but no one to tell.

There was another factor, though. I wanted someone to talk to when

I was afraid of sailing. I would have liked to have someone experienced to call on for advice before I sailed on bad-weather days. But all I had was myself and my fears. I couldn't even talk to anybody at the start of the day about whatever challenge I was facing. If I had been able to do that, I would inevitably have made light of the problems and in doing so I'd have raised my own morale as well as set myself a public goal. Once someone is watching me, I hate to fail. That was the worst part about the trip. I needed someone to look on and threaten to laugh if I chickened out. Instead, all I had to spur me on was the knowledge that if I gave up too easily, I might hate myself when I was old and grey. That isn't an obvious motivating force and making use of it requires good self-discipline. An old sergeant major of mine defined self-discipline accurately as 'Doing what needs to be done, when it needs to be done'. The killer word in that phrase is 'when'. It means you can't procrastinate.

What that meant was that every morning when I woke up and tried to decide whether I should sail or not, I simply listened to the forecast, looked at the weather and sea conditions, and said to myself, 'If I had a crew of sailors greener than me, would I make them do it?' The weather was always the hinge that swung the door open or shut each day. With perfect weather, anything is possible in a boat. If I got a guarantee of 10-mph tailwinds every day, then I'd sail across the Atlantic in *Wanderer*, but of course on a bad-weather day it might be silly to sail on a creek let alone an ocean. I was held hostage to the weather every day and eventually I grew to hate the weather forecast with a passion.

Nearly every day, I answered yes to my question and decided I should sail. On the really bad days I didn't even have to ask the question. It was only on the marginal days I had to ponder. That meant I had to do it right then, all by myself, because anything less would be a denial of my own judgement or a failure of self-discipline. And what would my sah-major say then?

In situations where I still really didn't want to do it, I would use a trick I'd learned long ago. I would continue to make preparations, while promising myself that if I still didn't want to do it after I had completed them, then I would allow myself to bail out with no recriminations. On *Wanderer*, the preparations for sailing first meant dressing. Once I was in my foul-weather gear I always felt better protected, so that helped bolster my confidence. Then I'd pack away the bed and tent. Once they were gone I might eat or wash, but once that was done I had nowhere to spend the day unless I unpacked everything. I'd just spent an hour getting ready, and the prospect of another hour's work unpacking everything just so I could get back into bed and play host to a day of regrets and feelings of failure was too awful to contemplate. So off I'd sail.

Sometimes, when the fearful feelings were still strong, I'd allow myself another 'bail-out-free' card. I would decide to sail out into the open water, with the proviso that if the conditions were too bad, I could turn around and sail back to the anchorage with no loss of self-respect. That was a better trick, since the act of sailing anywhere in foul weather invariably got me and the boat wet, and if the open water was some distance away, then it might take an hour or so just to get to the point where I could choose to play my bail-out-free card. By then, it was perhaps two and a half hours since I'd first asked myself if it was wise to sail and I knew that it would take at least as long to sail back and anchor, and dry out again and set up camp. So, if I sailed back, that would take me up to lunchtime, and half a day would have been wasted. I'd have sailed maybe 10 miles forth and back and gained nothing. If I had really struggled just getting to the bail-out point, then I'd invariably look at the situation and decide that it actually wasn't that bad – and certainly not so bad that I should give up five hard-earned miles of sailing. I hate giving up ground that I've won.

Invariably, I'd push on, allowing myself yet another bail-out card – if things got worse, I'd stop early. But they often got better, and if they didn't, then like the day on St Andrews Sound, I still wouldn't give up any miles I'd gained. I'd beach the bastard first, but I'd never turn back.

On the whole trip, this system worked so successfully that on those days when I sailed, I never once turned back to the anchorage and only once did I decide to finish early. But even on that day, I battled forwards into a sheltered spot, waited four hours until the wind dropped and then went out and sailed until dark. I only made 15 miles in total but goddammit, I still had my bail-out-free card.

I've still got it. Unused.

~~~

I HAD EXACTLY such a day soon after leaving Charleston. I crossed the harbour under sail as the remains of two days of bad weather blew through. The sun came out later in the day, the wind dropped and I found myself sailing on calm narrow rivers and canals as I made my way to the Bull River campground. I tied up illegally to the short dock by the boat ramp and even snuck ashore for a shower in the campground. I also did the maintenance on my engine – changing the sparkplug, lubing the joints and replacing the gearbox oil. The next day I sailed in marginal weather and spent the whole time tossing up whether to bail out or not. The wind came up, there were medium-sized standing waves at the junctions with the South and North Santee Rivers and on connecting canals and creeks. Early on, the rain started again with fog and mist opening and closing as the wind rose and fell. What stopped me from quitting was the fact that I was sailing all day in narrow waters where I couldn't really wreck myself even if I capsized. I took a little spray over the bow and had to pump rainwater out, but it was never threatening, just inconvenient and uncomfortable. Another reason why I plugged on was that there was nowhere to stop that would offer a good place to ride out the next two days of foul weather that were predicted. So I pushed on, a little nervously, towards Georgetown. I finally motored up the wide Winyah River, past floating logs and other debris washed down in the floods that had soaked the whole Carolina coast for the previous month. I turned into the little port of Georgetown on the Sampit River at the end of the day, motoring on flat calm waters under steady rain. At least I was in a small town with a free dock for day use and the prospect of being able to go ashore and use the local library. Much better than a day spent at anchor surrounded by wet marsh-grass and no-see-ums, kicking myself for having stopped too early.

Georgetown was a lovely place to spend three days and four nights of fairly constant rain with occasional torrential cloudbursts. It was built on a bend in the river 300 years ago by English settlers and was a popular trading port for a long time, using the Winyah River to gain access to the sea. It is still an active small port that can somehow shoehorn full-size freighters into the tiny dock in front of the steel mill just a quarter-mile from the centre of the old town. The old waterfront has been revitalised with bars, restaurants, a promenade and a history walking trail that includes a museum, many historic houses and some of the original port buildings. This is very impressive for a town of perhaps 10,000 people. It was still too early in the season for other tourists so I had the waterfront almost to myself. A few hardy souls lived aboard their boats in the anchorage and a couple of others visited briefly, but overall it was pretty quiet and that meant I could make full use of their free dock by day.

That night it poured down and I nervously waited for my tent to leak. This time I had attacked it with seam sealer on a dry day and for once it held the water out. The forecast yet again was for heavy rain and thunderstorms with hail and high winds for two days, so I planned to sit it all out where I was. Opposite me was the free day dock that allowed me to go ashore. Because it was so close I just pulled up the anchor and paddled *Wanderer* in to the dock with the tent still up and my bed unrolled. Then I tied up, closed the tent securely and went ashore to explore. It was a major luxury to know that I was legally tied up to the dock, it wasn't costing me any money and I could return at any time to drop off things and relax on my bed if I wanted.

Over the following two days it intermittently rained and almost shone, and on two occasions it blew a mighty wind. I was tied to the dock one morning when a wind of perhaps 40 miles an hour blasted the rain all across the town. I listened to the radio reports of flooding and falling trees and so on. The rain was heavy but the wind just blew it to pieces and turned it to spray that was so thick it blotted out the island in the middle of the harbour, just 50 yards away. *Wanderer* leaped and rocked beside the dock as small waves raced around the anchorage and my tent bulged and hollowed as the wind hit it. The

The storm that blotted out the island 50 yards away and left ankle-deep hail in 30 minutes!

hail came next and made so much noise that I practised shouting at the top of my voice just for the hell of it. As with most thunderstorms it passed quickly, but when I went ashore soon afterwards I could see car crashes, flooded streets and drifts of hail at the corners of buildings. Pretty impressive results for a 30-minute downpour.

In the end, I spent four nights there and enjoyed them enough to recommend the town as a port of call to anyone. Georgetown was quoted in my cruising guide as one of the ten best small towns in America and I agree. It did very well indeed and yet it could easily have gone the way of so many other coastal towns of its size and just withered away.

~~~

I SAILED NORTH again on the fourth day, up the big Waccamaw River in bright sunlight and lazy heat. The water was up and still rising, flooding over some docks and leaving cypress trees apparently growing in lakes instead of swamps. The pine pollen came back, and the wind died away in the afternoon. High overhead, hawks and ospreys circled lazily on the updraughts. I sailed and then motored very quietly into a pool off the main river just south of Enterprise Landing. I settled into the middle of it and dropped the anchor and for the first time I put a trip line and buoy on it in case it fouled on any sunken logs. Later, I heated water and had a nice wash in the afternoon sun. When I finished I decided to dust off the pollen from my tent before the evening dew stuck it down. While teetering on the edge of the boat I overbalanced and fell into the water. It wasn't cold enough to take my breath away and luckily I was only wearing shorts. For some reason I was surprised to find it was fresh. God knows why it wouldn't be – I was 25 miles upriver from the Winyah and a further 10 miles from the Atlantic. I slapped my head as I thought how much effort I could have saved by taking a swim instead of a sponge bath on the boat.

That anchorage was one of the finest I had on the trip. Quiet, private, calm, safe and with a beautiful view in all directions. Better yet, the weather stayed fine the next day and I left in early morning sunshine for another gorgeous day of sailing in mild and steady breezes. I quit just after lunchtime when I got to Barefoot Landing having made in just one and a half days a healthy 48 miles, all but three of them under sail. I would have liked to continue but it was a long time since I'd seen a tiger in a shopping mall and I felt that I shouldn't pass up the opportunity to see one now that I had it.

Barefoot Landing is not far inland from the enormously popular Myrtle Beach on the Atlantic coast. This strip of white surf beaches has attracted legions of holidaymakers for generations. Naturally they want things to do aside from sunbathing so there are plenty of entertainments for them. Barefoot Landing was such a place. It was basically a tourist shopping mall with a main highway on one side and the ICW on the other. It had several hundred feet of free dock, which was enough for me to stop there even without the attraction of free tigers.

The shopping mall contained an unusual number of unusual attractions. I passed a Bible Factory outlet shop selling Bibles, a John Deere outlet shop and the Peace Frog outlet shop. This store sold T-shirts and handbags and pretty much anything on which could be printed or embroidered the logo of a frog on a lily-pad making the peace sign.

Same frog on every product. Nothing else in the shop. Who the hell invented it, who bought it and how did they sell such numbers that they could have a whole store devoted to it? A little further on were the usual ice-cream stands, T-shirt and sunglasses shops and the inevitable fudge and saltwater taffy makers. In between you had to traipse across a wooden walkway over a large pond – maybe an acre in size – that was home to a fair-sized collection of fair-sized alligators. There were a number of obvious escape routes for the alligators if they chose to leave, but since they are prolific in the wild, what would it matter if they did? Plenty of alligators turn up in the backyards of Floridians and Georgians with suspiciously contented expressions on their well-fed faces at about the same time as Rover or Fluffy disappears. Alligators are just another part of the scenery for Southerners. Scattered amongst the big lizards were dozens of medium-sized turtles. They seemed to have some sort of agreement with the alligators not to be eaten by them. Children could buy 25c-bags of turtle food from gumball machines and feed the critters. Occasionally one would be spotted wandering along the sidewalk in front of a shop and people would considerately step aside. No one seemed to need to be told to be nice to the animals – the alligators obviously could take care of themselves, though the turtles seemed a little vulnerable to me. But they thrived.

The whole Barefoot Landing complex was a village of open-air walkways with dozens of nice-enough little shops. It was large enough for a family to take the kids for half a day or longer. While it could be considered too fake and touristy and too close to kitsch, it was saved from being hideous by a lot of nice small touches. The turtle food thing was one, the mist shower that you could walk under to cool off without getting wet was another, the house of horrors for kids, the rocking chairs outside all the shops for elderly RV nomads to rest in – it all helped. Mostly, the sitters were weatherbeaten older men who would formerly have been farmers or welders or some other profession that wore bib overalls. Now they sat in them while their wives combed the shops inside with the smooth efficiency of a combine harvester. I sat down next to one gentleman with a healthy collection of shopping bags at his feet. They looked to be filled with things for grandchildren.

'Yepp,' I said as I sat down and looked at the bags.

'Yepppp,' he agreed and with no more than that exchange and a knowing look, we both understood that when he wasn't driving the RV, he would most likely spend his declining years performing the same duty as those little tartan shopping trolleys that are towed around by English housewives.

Now I understood the significance of the three strange factory outlet shops. The Peace Frog shop was to supply gifts for the grand-children, the Bible Factory shop was for the elderly wife and the John Deere shop was the sweetener that got the husband to park the RV there in the first place.

'Look, honey, it's Barefoot Landing – they have a tractor outlet shop. Let's stop a minute.'

And he would have enjoyed it more than most malls. There was an abundance of good food at cheap prices in the many restaurants and a wide range of specialty shops that you didn't normally find in the regular malls. One of these was home to the tigers.

I lied earlier when I said that I wanted to see the tigers. I had no idea there were any until I walked around a corner and Wham! There was a normal shop window chock-full of tigers. One sat up and yawned, the other two were napping. As far as I could see, the window was nothing more than thin Plexiglas without any reinforcing. I got quite a shock to see 2000 pounds of carnivores and so did the small dog that trotted around the corner on a leash in front of its owner. Nose down, the Jack Russell terrier was hurrying past when it must have caught a whiff of something. It looked up straight into the wide open jaws of a 700-pound cat. Jaws that could swallow a Halloween pumpkin, and teeth that could open the crate it came in. The terrier let out a yip, jumped sideways and then froze. Inside the window, the tiger stopped yawning and looked directly at the dog. A very large tongue licked its lips and suddenly the tiger that was stretched out on the straw lurched onto its paws and sat up. This was too much for the dog and it bounded forwards on its leash, almost dragging the lady owner along with it.

I walked around to the main entrance of the shop and discovered that people could go inside and pay to see a whole tiger attraction and even have their photos taken with the tigers. And I mean, *right* alongside them, human heads touching feline heads. Yowza! I have no idea how they got the licence to do this but I was astounded. Examples of the photos were on display and in one I saw the classic red-eye effect from a flash. These tigers must be extraordinarily mellow to tolerate flash photography. I read the information posters a little more and discovered that this was a way of raising money for a tiger conservation project. The tigers actually lived on some kind of tiger ranch not too far away and three or four of them came in each day for a five-hour shift in the window. Two shifts of tigers per day. Seemed fair to me. It was indoor work with no heavy lifting and if they felt abused or under-rewarded, then that Plexiglas window wouldn't contain any kind of major tiger grievance for long. Clearly they were either pretty happy with their berth or else they were over-medicated. They didn't look drugged to me, though. They looked to be very contented cats.

Since I was berthed in a fairly public place I decided not to cook up aboard *Wanderer* and spend the evening reading in bed. Instead, I shouted myself a roast pork dinner and watched TV in a bar. On my way home I walked past the tiger shop and, sure enough, there was a truck backed up to the rear entrance, loading up three tigers for the trip home. Soon after that, I was back in my home too, well fed, a little footsore and oddly charmed by Barefoot Landing.

Pamlico and Albemarle

IT TOOK ME another five days to make it the 150 miles to Beaufort, North Carolina. This small town had a well-deserved reputation for hospitality to boaters and I was keen to get there. It was also the last stop before the week it would take me to cross Pamlico and Albemarle Sounds. Pamlico and Albemarle. They sounded like Shakespearean characters but they preyed on my mind a good deal. Once I got to Beaufort, I would have to confront them.

Beaufort was at the end of a long stretch of predominantly narrow waters. Mostly I sailed on canals and rivers that were separated from the ocean only by a narrow sand foreshore. These rivers and sounds ran north–south, unlike the rivers and sounds in Georgia which crossed my path, but occasionally they widened out in places like Bogue Sound, which had islands and bays and was large enough to have fair-sized waves. I was able to sail the narrower canals quite successfully as they were easily wide enough for tacking as long as there wasn't an absolute headwind. If that happened, I motored. The weather was still changeable but I had two beautiful days near Wrightsville Beach. I walked from the harbour to the beach and stretched myself out on the sand. I didn't get many chances to do that, strangely enough. When the weather was good enough for sunbathing I always wanted to sail. The next day I sailed happily north, well provisioned and rested.

Beaufort was the older but smaller cousin to its relation across the river – Morehead City. I planned to put in to the small yacht anchorage in front of Beaufort town on Taylor Creek. It had a fast current and some strong tidal action. Like Georgetown, you could anchor just 30 yards from the main street and tie up your dinghy to a free dock by day. A week's worth of bad weather was forecast and on the last good day I raced under sail and motor to make it all the way up Bogue Sound and across the inlet and into shelter. The radio said there would be heavy rain, hail, high winds and big seas for the next few days. I made it to Beaufort just before dark and anchored safely. The next morning I went ashore, paid my fee, cleaned up, and visited the local maritime museum, which took the prize for the best small museum of the trip. The displays were exceptional, admission was free and they even had a lavishly appointed library that provided me with the perfect antidote to cabin fever over the next four days. But best of all, they had free cars. My guidebook told me that I could borrow a car from the museum, free of charge, to go shopping for two hours. I didn't believe it, but it was true. I just signed at the museum desk for a little Chevy van, hopped in it and drove off for a tour of the area. I went to Morehead City and visited the Wal-Mart, West Marine, the Food Lion, and I stocked up on second-hand books. When I returned the car to the museum I asked what they did about gas money for it and the lady said that some people donated money but others didn't. I popped $5 in the jar and thanked the lady at the desk. I have no idea how the museum and people of Beaufort fund this scheme, but I stayed as long as I could in the town and spent as much money as I could afford. I felt I owed it to them.

Three days passed quickly like this, and one morning I listened to a forecast that didn't predict any storms, though it did say that winds would get up in the afternoon. I studied the charts. One day's sail up the Newport River and down Adams Creek and across the Neuse River to Oriental. Then one day's sail down the Neuse River, up the Bay River, through the Goose Creek Canal, across the Pamlico River mouth and up the Pungo River to Bellhaven. Then a day's sail further up the Pungo River, into the Pungo–Alligator Canal and out into the open Alligator River. Another day's sail down the Alligator and halfway across Albemarle Sound. There I had the choice of turning left and going further up the sound and then into the Pasquotank River to Elizabeth City; or I could push on straight ahead and into the North River towards the tiny town of Coinjock. Four days if all went well. It was all doable if I timed it right. If I missed a day though, I'd be stuck in Oriental (OK), Bellhaven (also OK), or the middle of nowhere on the Alligator River (bad) for a few days while another front passed through. I listened to the weather again and reconsidered my plans. There was no way out. I had to set off immediately and then sail flat out each morning for the next four days to get safely across Albemarle Sound before more bad weather closed me down for several days.

I packed up and untied *Wanderer* in a tearing hurry and motored out of the anchorage into the Newport River. Ten minutes later I was sailing flat out upriver for the entrance to the Adams Creek Canal which would take me 10 miles through farms and fields and then downstream to the point where the creek mouth joined the Neuse River. Under a grey sky and fast-moving clouds I got through it all by noon and looked nervously at the wide Neuse River and the rising wind. Short, steep waves were powering down the river, rank upon rank of them, three miles wide. My course was directly across them, with the possibility of a capsize looming up in front of me. I didn't fancy returning to Beaufort for another week, though, so I tacked out into the river and immediately got soaked by a wave. All I could do was steer a good course and hang on. I had to pump twice in 40 minutes because of the spray that was blown into the cockpit, though overhead the sky was grey and dry. The wind was cold and very strong but not too gusty. I was as nervous as the last lobster in the tank all the way across, but I made it over the river in about 25 minutes and came within the slight shelter of Windmill Point at the entrance to the tiny haven of Oriental. I turned to starboard once I got behind the breakwater and prepared to sail up to the free dock at the end of the little harbour. No sooner had I turned downwind than the wind came up to a gale and sent me surging towards the wharf. To the left was a fishing boat tied to a factory pier that was built on pilings over the water. To the right a very expensive launch was tied up. In front was a concrete wall and a busy road. I had no room to turn and no way to let out any sail. I hadn't freed the anchor because I was planning to tie up, so I couldn't even chuck it overboard. All I could do was try and fend off the land by running up to the bow at the last second and sitting down with my legs outstretched to take the shock. I was ready to do this when I saw a bend in the channel that led around to the left between the factory and the road. Good, good, good. Perhaps it widened out and gave me room to slow down.

Or perhaps it ended in a small wooden footbridge that connected the factory to the land. It was only 20 feet in front of me. Bad, bad, bad.

I hit it so hard that the bow punched a plank up and the forestay split it in half. *Wanderer* bounced off it and got slapped sideways by her own bow wave as it ricocheted back off the factory foundations. Gusts of wind caught the main and sent it banging and crashing. Well, I knew how to handle that. Once again I dashed forward, slackened the vang and sent the boom and mainsail crashing into the bottom of the boat. It seemed I would never have a month when I wasn't forced to do this ugly manoeuvre. After that it was all routine.

Half an hour later I was neatly tied up to the concrete wall, sheltered

I hit the footbridge so hard I split a plank with the forestay!

from the wind by the factory. The mainsail was flaked and everything was looking good. I stepped ashore for a look around and saw a coffee shop on the other side of the road. The wind was now really blowing, with surprisingly large waves crashing into the concrete wall, dispersing sideways under *Wanderer* and causing her to bounce up and down vigorously. I watched her from inside the café as I drank my coffee and ate a cookie. After a little while, the owner, Susan, came over to talk to me and when she heard what I was doing, she called a friend of hers. Keith appeared a few minutes later and interviewed me. He was a computer consultant who ran the Oriental website that recorded stories from people who visited the town on their way up or down the ICW. It was called 'The Shipping News' and it was very professionally done. They even had a webcam that was mounted on a corner of Keith's verandah, pointing directly at the tiny harbour. Keith was happy to show me how it worked and he invited me to have dinner with him that night. He said I could use his email connection to let Ady know where I was, and I said I'd bring the beer. I spent the rest of the after-noon exploring Oriental. There isn't much there. A convenience store, an excellent chandlery, the café, a fish factory, a knick-knack shop, a large motel and a gas station.

Wanderer was bouncing wildly so I moved her further back into the sheltered corner and put another fender out to cushion her. It didn't look good for the next day but the forecast said the winds should die overnight. Just before dusk I walked across to Keith's house with a bag of beer and he showed me the web camera and the website. I emailed Ady to let her know that she could see me standing on a dock in North Carolina in half an hour's time. Keith aimed the camera so it would see me standing next to the café holding my New Zealand flag. I stood there just as dusk fell and Keith saved the picture for the website overnight. Then it was back inside for a pizza and beer dinner and a natter about Oriental, sailing, computing, women and the state of the world, before heading back to bed, to get another four hours of sleep in anticipation of the biggest day of the whole journey.

~~~

MY PLAN FOR getting across Pamlico and Albemarle Sounds demanded that I sail as far as I could in one day when I left Oriental. As soon as I got out into the channel and let out the sail, the wind grabbed me and blasted me down the river on a wild run. For two hours I whistled along at better than seven mph, chewing tobacco nervously and watching another yacht, with a ketch rig, ever so slowly coming up behind me. I constantly checked my safety line that attached me to the boat and I kept my lifejacket tightly fitted. Several times I felt like I was broaching and I contemplated trailing a loop of line to slow me down a little, but each time I thought about going forward and digging in the bow locker for the line I decided I'd be more likely to wreck myself doing that. I managed to cut a few corners and shorten the route down the river, and in doing so I may have made it worse for myself. I suspect that the centre of the river had the calmest water but I couldn't tell from my seat on *Wanderer*, so I opted to take the shortest route instead. That meant passing near headlands and these probably generated rougher water. Eventually, as the wind started to drop, I was able to turn off the Neuse and head into the Bay River. Despite my tiny amount of sail, it took until I had sailed off the Bay River and into the Goose Creek Canal before the trailing yacht finally passed me. By then, the wind had dropped right away and he was motoring but I was still sailing. I was terribly pleased that I'd stayed ahead of him for so long and I tried to keep up with him by cutting corners. I sailed past a forest fire on the banks of the canal with a fire extinguisher at the ready and managed to keep pace with him. On shore, fire crews sweated away in their heavy coats.

When I checked my progress I could see that by sailing so fast at the start, I'd made a lot more ground than I ever expected. I found myself up on the Pamlico River by 1.00 pm. That was 33 miles in only seven hours. The wind had now died away to nothing and I was almost becalmed. I decided that it couldn't get any better for a crossing of the Pamlico than that, started the motor and followed the ketch into the big water. For an hour I intermittently motored and sailed and eventually made it across the Pamlico River and into the equally wide Pungo River. Then the wind came back up and I was able to sail properly. By cutting in behind channel markers I was able to get ahead of the ketch, which continued to slowly motor along. All the way up the broad Pungo River to Bellhaven I waited for the wind to turn ugly but I was lucky, and at 5.00 pm when I finally turned off the Pungo River into the harbour at Bellhaven, I had covered an astounding 51 miles, and all but perhaps three of them under sail in conditions ranging from wild to lazy to brisk. That was the most I ever made on one day and I'm still pleased that I went for it. I felt I deserved a bit of luck after all the agonising I'd done to plan the attack on the sounds. One down, and one to go. I hoped my luck would hold.

It certainly held that night. Bellhaven is located at the junction of Pantego Creek and a bend in the Pungo River. I found the neatest little hole in the bank of the creek just past the town. It was like a pond about 30 yards across and 10 feet deep, almost totally surrounded by tall pine trees, accessed by a very shallow disused channel. Once inside, a hurricane could hit and I'd be fine. First, though, I had to shop for food. I tied up to the free dinghy dock and asked directions to a supermarket – 'half a mile to the lights and turn left, you'll see it a coupla hundred yards away'.

Bollocks it was. It took me 30 minutes just to walk to the lights, then, to the left was the creek and a bridge leading into forest. To the *right*, another half-mile away was something that looked like a supermarket. Left, right – why can't people tell the difference between the two directions? I mean, they never get confused with up and down or forwards and backwards, so why is left and right so hard to master? I turned right and marched off.

Ten minutes later I got there, bought my food and was setting out across the car park for the one-hour walk back to my boat, carrying my grocery bags and grumbling to myself that I wouldn't have set out if I knew it would take me two hours to do the shopping. Mumble, mumble, cuss, bitch, whine.

'Looks like you could use a lift.'

I turned and looked at a middle-aged man in a convertible Chrysler who had pulled up behind me.

'Off a boat?' he asked.

'Uhh, yeah I am actually. Tied up at the town dock if you're headed that way.'

'Hop in.'

Turned out he was a lawyer, and like so many people I had met, he was just keen for visitors to think well of his town. He took me right to the dock and wished me well. Ten minutes later I was dropping my anchor in the hurricane hole and 30 minutes after that I was scoffing down a giant bag of Frito-Lays while I relaxed in the warm dusk. Pollen blew off the pine trees in thick clouds, and through a few gaps in the trees I could look across neatly mown lush green lawns and see the lights of houses flick on as folks came home from work. It was quiet and I could hear crickets. I was well fed and watered. Fifty-odd miles done, and a lift back from the market. Someone was looking after me.

The next morning I was up and sailing by 7.00 am in ideal 10-mph winds. I felt safe all day as I trotted along at a reasonable pace. Sailing up 20 miles of canal with only one bend in it was tedious, and surprisingly, only one other vessel passed me all day. But it was warm and sunny, the wind over the stern stayed steady and by about 4.00 pm I was within three miles of my intended anchorage when I exited the canal and joined the Alligator River. The wind then dropped away to almost nothing and I was on the verge of lowering the sail and motoring to my stopping point for the night, but I'd sailed so well and the afternoon was so peaceful that I didn't want to spoil it by motoring. As I came up on the first channel marker outside the canal, the water was so calm that I could see the reflection of it clearly. To do that, the water has to be smooth and you have to be fairly close to the marker, so I know I cannot be exaggerating when I say that the wind came out of nowhere and hit me in an instant.

Before I covered the 30 yards to the marker, I was letting go of everything in a frantic attempt to avoid a capsize. I managed to turn into the wind, and while everything crashed and banged I considered whether or not to perform my standard emergency drill – drop the boom and everything into the bottom of the boat like an idiot. This time though, because I was facing into the wind, and well away from a lee shore, I was able to study the situation at leisure. The wind was perhaps 40 mph and I could barely stand up in it, but it hadn't been blowing long enough across the water to create dangerous waves. Further up the river I could see whitecaps, but I intended to anchor before then, so I carefully lowered the main, flaked it and then motored the remaining two miles to the doubtful shelter of a finger of land. I anchored close to the bank where an old pine tree was submerged, even at the risk of fouling the line. The only good thing about a fouled anchor is that you won't drag in the middle of the night. I expected the wind to continue all night and so I put a second hook down to keep me off the shore and then began sponging out. As I did so, a catamaran motored past and anchored about a mile away, right out in the middle of the river. Once I had my tent up, I surveyed the area. The wind was much calmer now – just a steady 15 mph. I felt very lonely, though, and a little worried at what that sudden blast of wind would have meant if I'd caught it out in the middle of the sound or even the river. I decided to call the cat on VHF and see if there was a reason for the sudden absence of traffic. Maybe they all knew something about the weather that I didn't.

'We didn't see another boat north of Oriental until you, and we came from Beaufort. We'll be in Connecticut in three days. Going up the outside from Virginia.'

That was depressing. It had taken me three days to do what they'd done since breakfast and it would take me the best part of two months to get to Connecticut via the inside route of Chesapeake and Delaware Bays.

'What's the weather like for tomorrow?' I asked.

'Not great for us crossing the sound, but that shouldn't trouble you.'

'Well, that's where I'm headed if I can make it – might try for Elizabeth City or might go for Coinjock, depending on the winds,' I said.

'Crossing Albemarle, huh? We'll keep an eye out for you.'

'OK, thanks. I'll be away early tomorrow and if the sound looks bad, I might stay at that marina at the mouth of the river, but I don't want to get stuck there for three days and I'm afraid that's what'll happen if I don't get across tomorrow.'

'Good luck, then, and we'll be monitoring channel 16 tonight if you need us.'

And on that somewhat dispiriting note I switched back to the weather channel and tried to read something positive into the predictions of 20 to 25-knot winds for Albemarle Sound tomorrow. Normally I wouldn't sail in that much wind, but the alternative would be a horrendous day at anchor here or a wet lumpy run down the river to a marina that was supposed to be located near the mouth and which, judging by the absence of any nearby town, would surely be almost as dire a place to spend a few days. Especially at $20 a day in fees. I listened to the weather three more times before turning in, but it didn't get any better. Tomorrow looked like being a rotten day no matter what I did.

~~~

I WOKE AT 3.00 am and couldn't get back to sleep. Albemarle Sound had me completely rattled. I would have been scared of it anyway just because it was a 20-mile haul across open water, but with its nasty reputation and the prospect of bad weather, I was thoroughly worried. I turned on the radio and for once I wanted only good weather. The 4.00 am forecast gave me a real surprise. The predicted winds dropped from 20–25 knots down to 15–20 knots from the southwest. Wooohooo!

I rolled out of bed faster than a cheating husband and packed up the boat in only 20 minutes. By 5.00 I was sailing down the Alligator River as fast as I could. I wanted to make it safely to the marina before the weather gods realised what I was up to. The wind was brisk and steady over the stern and I made the 17 miles to the marina by 9.00 am. As I got closer, the wind seemed to grow a bit. I decided I should gas up in case I needed to motor across the sound. By now it was blowing strongly and the waves were coming up to three feet in height on their long run down the river. There is a three-mile-long road and rail bridge across the mouth of the Alligator and the marina is on the far side of it. There's a swing bridge in the centre for boat traffic and a bridge tender on it at all times. As I approached I could see an anemometer on the roof so I called the tender up and asked for the wind speed. I hoped it would be reading about 15–20 knots as that was what I based my estimates of the sea conditions on. If this was what I got at 10–15 knots, then I'd not be able to cross the sound. She said it was steady at 18, gusting to 25. That was a relief, as it meant it shouldn't get too much worse.

Once through the bridge I turned towards the marina and immediately I got soaked. Beating into the weather was hard work but I made the mile into the small artificial basin and tied up. Before gassing up I was ready to quit as I watched the whitecaps racing down the river and breaking on the bridge abutments. Further out in the sound itself I could see the waves were bigger and I expected the centre of the sound to be horrid. Glumly I looked around the marina as I walked in to pay for my gas. There were few other boats and no one living aboard. There was nothing wrong with it – modern, tidy and clean, but nevertheless it was about as appealing as spending three days sleeping in the back seat of your car in a factory car park on a wet holiday weekend.

I came back to the boat and decided to pump out before I made a decision. Once everything was tidy I walked up and looked out again at the water on both sides of the bridge. Was it just a little less wild than before? Perhaps a bail-out card might work here. I could always come back to the marina. I cast off and cautiously sailed out under the genoa alone. It wasn't easy and I turned back to the marina twice, but each time it was hard going and I made so little ground that I wasn't sure it was worth the effort. Going downwind was much easier than beating back to the marina. I spent about 30 minutes sailing in circles, weighing up whether to play the bail-out card when the swing bridge opened and a handful of boats came through. Launches, yachts, a converted tug, they all came through the bridge and followed me out into the sound. That changed things completely. Suddenly the sea wasn't half as threatening and unsafe – it was the same sea, of course, but with a fleet of other boats it was just like a regatta. Lumpy and grey but exciting. I pushed the tiller over and took off ahead of them. They all gradually overhauled me, but that didn't matter. Others came up behind me and soon some boats from the other side were bearing down on me. Now that I had the company of a steady line of presumably competent sailors who could perhaps rescue me if I needed it, I was much more comfortable.

As the northbound boats passed me I could see them reach the point in the middle of the sound where about two-thirds of them would change course and head left, up the sound towards the Pasquotank River and Elizabeth City. That was what I wanted to do, too. The ICW has two routes that are of almost equal appeal. Route 2 was via the Pasquotank River, Elizabeth City and then 50-odd miles of the Dismal Swamp Canal to Norfolk, Virginia, on the Chesapeake Bay. Despite the unappealing name, the Dismal Swamp is actually a beautiful old canal surveyed in part by George Washington and built about 200 years ago. It takes sailors a long way inland for a two- or three-day sail on a very narrow canal before returning them to the Elizabeth River where the main section of the ICW starts at Norfolk. Aaron Clarke had recommended that I see the Dismal Swamp.

'You've gotta do it, man. Do the swamp. Seriously.'

'It's called the Dismal Swamp after Mr Dismal then?' I said.

'Yeah, yeah. I know what you're thinking, but it's a good swamp.'

'Oh. A *good* swamp. Well, OK then, that changes everything . . .'

So I wanted to do the swamp.

Route 1 also took me to Norfolk, Virginia, but did it by a slightly more direct route, being about 13 miles shorter in total. It takes boats almost straight across Albemarle Sound and around Camden Heads and up the North River. Then it meanders through marsh-grass islands for a few miles before entering the North Carolina Cut – a short canal

The beautiful Dismal Swamp, very poorly named.

with the little town of Coinjock in the middle. After that it runs up the narrow Currituck Sound and then enters a long canal, which also terminates on the Elizabeth River near Norfolk a day or two later.

I listened to the forecast again and it confirmed that thunderstorms were due in the afternoon. I thought about the power of the wind and hail that had hit me in Georgia the afternoon before I was rained in for 36 hours alone on Queen Bess Creek. Rain and wind like that hitting me on Route 2 when I was still several hours away from Elizabeth City would be no fun at all and it might be quite dangerous if the wind blew for any length of time. I kept thinking all the way out into the middle of the sound. Finally, when I came up to the point where I had to decide, I opted for the immediate safety of Coinjock over the distant attractions of the Dismal Swamp. Aaron would not be pleased, but maybe he'd never know.

Four hours later, when I was safely inside the narrow channels of the marsh-grass islands a few miles from Coinjock, the thunderstorms hit and the winds rose to 30 mph or more. They passed over within an hour, but I felt relieved that I hadn't been out of sight of land on Albemarle or Pasquotank, alone in a dinghy, as dusk approached. I docked at Coinjock and happily paid $1.25 per foot for the chance to take a shower, eat a meal I hadn't cooked and drink a beer in celebration. I had crossed Albemarle in moderately unpleasant weather and I'd managed to do it by being a good sailor. Cautious in general but bold when I needed to be. I was pretty proud of myself.

I'd crossed what I felt was the worst water on the trip and I'd done it with careful planning, good judgement and hard work. Albemarle was my Everest. I'd built it up into more than it truly was, but for that reason, when I got over it and looked back at what I'd done, I was even more pleased. In four days I'd made 159 miles or more, a large portion of it in conditions that would have had me gibbering with fear a few weeks before. I'd pushed myself to accomplish what I'd set out to do and now I felt I'd done the hardest part of the trip. Summer was coming, the sparkling waters of the Chesapeake were just ahead and then there was the excitement of New York and Boston. From here on in, until I got to Maine, it should all be plain sailing.

The Dismal Swamp

THE PLAIN SAILING lasted just 90 minutes. I had planned to spend a whole day in Coinjock just relaxing in the warm glow of accomplishment, but after a pleasant lie-in, I saw most of the other boats that had tied up for the night leaving and eventually I decided to join them. I came out of the shelter of the islands on Currituck Sound and caught a strong westerly wind. After an hour it veered round to the northwest and I found it difficult to tack across the rising chop. Twice I turned around to see what it was like sailing downwind, but for once the sea state made this just about as uncomfortable. When I found myself unable to make progress on one tack and running out of sea room I decided to flake the sail and motor out of trouble. I dropped the sail but accidentally let go of the halyard when I disconnected it from the top of the mainsail. Before I could snatch it back and attach it to the tip of the boom it flew out almost horizontally and stayed obstinately out of reach. I set the boom in the crutch and cinched it down and then started to motor around in circles, trying to get the wind to blow the halyard into the reach of my extendable boathook. To anyone watching from a distance on shore I must have looked utterly demented as I drove around in random patterns, flailing with a pole at invisible flying critters. Eventually a lucky swing of the halyard snagged the brass clip to my boathook and I was able to haul it in.

The rest of the transit of Currituck Sound passed roughly, but routinely enough. By mid-afternoon the wind had died away completely and so I flaked the sail and motored. This time I was wary of what might be coming and I wanted all the sails down in case I caught a repeat dose of the sudden wind that nearly toppled me two days before on the Alligator River. What I got instead was even more vicious.

At about 3.00 pm, just after I crossed from North Carolina into Virginia, a thunderstorm blew in and the most powerful wind I ever experienced hit *Wanderer* side-on. By then I was in shallow, winding passages amongst marsh-grass islands, and all around me fizz-boats with fishermen were darting in and out of channels looking for the perfect fishing spot. When the wind struck, the channel was so narrow that no real waves could form and the rain that came with it was heavy enough to batter the surface as flat as a pancake. Despite that, the wind kept rising and *Wanderer*, with no sails up at all, kept lifting out of the water so sharply that I hastily dropped the boom into the bottom of the boat so that there was less for the wind to act on. Incredibly, with nothing aloft but a naked mast, the wind still lifted her hull up. I grabbed the tiller extension and stacked out on the port side as far as I could, my boots tucked under the toe strap. My body from the hips up was parallel over the water as I leaned out to add weight to the windward side. Even so, *Wanderer* lifted up onto what would normally be considered a racing trim. Just at the point when I thought she might go over and leave me to try to stand on the centreboard, the worst of the wind passed over and I was able to sit up normally again. Around me, the fizz-boat drivers had put their bows into the wind and ducked down behind the steering wheels to keep their faces out of the hail and rain. The boats looked to be steering themselves as they weaved in and out of the channels.

I wasn't scared at this time since I could probably have walked ashore, just amazed at the power of the wind. I motored into the marina on a canal at Pungo Ferry to dry out. I could have kept on motoring to any one of dozens of pleasant anchorages, or even anchored in a nook just beside the marina, but before I could do either, the marina owner came over to talk to me and soon I found myself signed up for the night. When he left, I was faintly angry at myself for such an extravagance. It was partly the cost (though it was a reasonable fee) but mainly because I felt that paying for dockage was something I shouldn't do more than once a month unless there was something to celebrate. It seemed to devalue the achievement. Apart from Coinjock, the last place I'd paid for dockage was Brunswick, three states back down the trail.

I had just finished sponging out and setting up my tent when two guys walked up and asked me what type of boat I had. Since I was set up for the night, I was happy to offer them a beer from the bilge and chat away. Jeff and Bob were two friends who were kayaking together nearby and had seen me come in. Bob was looking for a small boat and he asked lots of questions about Wayfarers.

Just before dark they returned and invited me to dinner with them. Boy, was I happy with that idea. I got changed into my best going-to-church clothes and then we headed off to Bob's house to meet his family and collect Jeff's wife. The ladies weren't the least bit surprised at the extra guest, and while Bob's four-year-old daughter showed me her kindergarten artwork, Donna and Mary questioned me about my trip. Soon we were seated in a nice restaurant. When the waitress heard that I was a New Zealander she went out the back and came up with a nice bottle of Kiwi white for the second course. I wanted to pay for the wine at least, but they wouldn't let me and so I buckled down and enjoyed the meal and the conversation. Around ten o'clock, Bob and Jeff delivered me back to the boat and I put myself to bed in a happy glow. I guess it was lucky I'd paid for a dock after all.

Over the next two days I made my way along the upper reaches of the North Landing River and entered the Albemarle and Chesapeake Canal, which would take me to the Elizabeth River near Norfolk. First, though, I had to go through the 300-foot-long lock at Great Bridge. It was all pretty straightforward — I just motored in, tied up to the side and waited until the gates closed and the lock water rose about a yard. I untied myself when the other gates opened. The change in levels was very small and the lock was so big (because it handles large barges) that it wasn't much of an event. I remember it more for the hot banana bread that Maureen Flaherty gave me just before I went in. She and her partner were sailing a gorgeously maintained 45-foot yacht and had tied up to a boatyard dock just before the lock. I put in behind them to buy gas and she came on deck and gave me the bread. I asked why and she said she'd seen me at the Coinjock dock two days before and thought that anyone who sailed a dinghy over Albemarle deserved hot banana bread. We chatted away for a few minutes and ended up swapping some books. It was a good trade too, since I got Tom Wolfe's *A Man in Full* which is not only a good read but also a nice fat book to have in reserve in case of prolonged bad (i.e. bed) weather. I also visited the supermarket and bought a case of beer, but an unexpected thing happened when I got back to the boat.

As I was stowing the cans under the floor, one of them started leaking a high-pressure jet of beer through a pinhole puncture. Keen to avert a tragedy, I quickly opened it and relieved the pressure. Manufacturing error, I thought; no worries. I stowed the rest as usual in the bilge. Then they were free to roll around until I reached down and groped for one. They were handy, cool and only a little bit frayed from their travels around.

That taken care of, I resumed cruising up the canal toward the mighty naval base at Norfolk and the start of the Chesapeake Bay. In broad sunlight, and wafted along by zephyrs weighted with the scent of blooms and the colour of pollen clouds, it was hard to believe the weather forecaster when he predicted a week of high winds, high seas, rain and cold nights. Aha! I thought, just what I wanted. I might get to see the Dismal Swamp after all.

I was now nearing the point where the two routes of the ICW reconnected after parting in the middle of Albemarle Sound. Just ahead was the turn-off to the Dismal Swamp Canal. If I chose not to go to Norfolk and then out on the Chesapeake for a week, that would leave me just the right amount of time for a leisurely sail 50 miles or so down the canal and the upper Pasquotank River to Elizabeth City, North Carolina, and back again. That town was boater-friendly and had a free dock so I could stay there while the ugly weather blew through. The Dismal Swamp would be the most protected place I could be while the rain and 45-mph winds passed over.

I turned off the main ICW and sailed up Deep Creek towards the first of two locks on the canal. A road runs alongside most of it but it's screened by the tall trees on the bank. The other side of the canal is of course swamp, but as the canal is fully enclosed by its banks you don't notice that you're in a swamp at all. For me it was a delight, not just because of the change of scenery, but also because for a week I knew the weather couldn't hurt me. As the weather closed in on *Wanderer* I rugged myself up in full waterproofs and waited for the gates to open. Once I was inside, the lock-keeper leaned over the lock and looked down at *Wanderer*.

'That the whole boat?' he joked.

'Yep, I'm buying her on the instalment plan.'

'Well, come on up for a coffee. It's a raw kinda day for sailing and you've got half an hour till she fills.'

He was right. The spring feeling of the previous day had vanished. It was grey, damp and windless and a good 20 degrees colder. As I climbed up the 15-foot ladder from *Wanderer* to the side of the lock I noticed near the top the words '*Cushnoc 11/21/02*'. Well it's a small world all right. Here I was, tied up to the same spot as Aaron Clarke had been when he came through the canal six months earlier. He would be pleased to know I'd made it after all. I decided to write my own name on the wall when I came back up the canal at the end of the week.

I followed the keeper into the little lock-tender's office. In the back room there was a potbelly stove and whistling hot coffee. The keeper poured me a mug of gritty black coffee, no sugar or milk. I took a cookie for sweetening and sat down to talk. He was about 65, probably retired and he had the big solid look of a man who had worked all his life in bib overalls. A few minutes later he was joined by a friend, also in bibs and check shirt. Every man in a bib overall has at least three remarkable stories and I figured if I shut my trap and drank my coffee I'd hear something interesting now. Sure enough I did.

'Now, Frank was a bit like you,' the lock-keeper began, and his friend chipped in to agree and add details from time to time.

'He was Vietnamese. Couldn't speak much English. Sailed himself down to Florida on a raft. Not a Tom Sawyer raft or nothin'. Just a raft made outa what looked like a deck. You know, a wooden deck like you'd have in your garden.'

'Patio type a thing,' his friend confirmed. 'Water slopping over it all the time.'

'How'd he get along?' I enquired.

'Well, he had some kind of mast – just a pole, barely stepped. A coupla ropes to haul it upright. I doubt it coulda held a sail and I never saw any sign of that, but he had a 10-HP outboard on the back and a five-gallon can of gas.'

'Going to Florida?' I asked with raised eyebrows.

'Uh huh. He hadda five-gallon bucket too. That was his seat. He sat on that bucket and he ran that engine and he got himself and that raft all the way down to here from up in Maine somewhere.'

'Holy shit. He must've been touched in the head,' I said.

'Maybe,' said his friend.

'Well, I asked him where he slept and he said he had a canvas to pull over himself at night and he sometimes slept on land. One time he said he fell asleep on his bucket in the middle of the day and drove up on a beach. Said he fell off the bucket and woulda drowned 'cept he was only in four inches of water.'

'Couldn't he swim?'

'Nope, but he had a lifejacket he wore all the time.'

'Mad. Must be mad,' I said.

'Old Frank was something else, wuddn't he?' said his friend.

'Uh huh. Well, I heard from another boat that came through here, that he'd made it to somewhere south of Jacksonville, so I guess he probably got to the Keys if he got that far.'

'Maine to Florida on a 10-horse patio. Man, those Vietnamese don't know when to quit, do they?' I observed.

Ten minutes later the lock was full of water, my tum was full of cookies and coffee and my head was full of the strange tale of the maddest solo transit of the US east coast. The gates opened and I motored quietly away, marvelling at the patience and determination of anyone who would sail 2000 miles on a collection of four-by-twos. If a man would do that for fun, then you can see why Vietnamese boat people would sail a suitcase to Australia to escape communism.

That night, when I tied up to a free dock at an information centre on the North Carolina border in the middle of the swamp, I calculated my mileage so far. I had sailed 1523 statute miles since I began. I was certainly over halfway, and now that I was sailing more efficiently, I was confident I could make it to Maine before my visa expired at the end of July. The more worrying question was whether the money would hold out. I had less than a thousand New Zealand dollars left on my credit card – enough for about a month.

As I was putting up the tent that night, a voice from behind said, 'What are you doing with Frank's boat?'

A middle-aged couple stood on the dock looking at *Wanderer*.

'Well, I'm doing what Frank would do if he owned it still – I'm sailing up to Maine.' Ed introduced himself and his wife Carolyn and explained that they had met Frank when he sailed the coast years before. They recognised the name and the boat and we chatted for a while. They cautioned me not to take too many chances on the Chesapeake and admitted that although they had sailed Wayfarers themselves, they were happier now on their 35-foot yacht *Moonshadow*. On the whole trip, they were the only people to recognise *Wanderer* as Frank's former boat so my fears about owning Elvis's Cadillac were unfounded.

Next morning, I passed through the South Mills lock at the end of the canal and dropped down 20 feet to the Pasquotank River. From there it was plain sailing down to Elizabeth City. Unfortunately, the free dock there was open to southerly winds and these were forecast to come in a day's time, so when I arrived in the city I motored to the dock intending to stay there just one night. The owner of a dockside bar saw me trying to tie up to the big docks that were suited only for much longer boats and offered me a berth at his little dinghy dock next door. It was tad more sheltered than the free dock so I tied up and made myself at home. I had a beer and a sandwich there for dinner and explored the town.

For the next three nights and two days I stayed docked there while it rained and blew. I went ashore and spent the days in the library catching up on emails and reading magazines. The last thing I did was to walk to a marina and buy a waterproof chartbook of the Chesapeake Bay. That last night was awful – the tent leaked, the boat leaped and rocked continuously and I hardly slept because of the noise of *Wanderer* straining at her groaning mooring lines. I got up and doubled them up to be sure, but I still worried that something would chafe or snap and I'd be adrift in the middle of the night. The next day the sea was even worse, but I cast off and motored back up the Pasquotank and into the Dismal Swamp Canal. I wrote *Wanderer*'s name on the South Mills lock and then motored under cold grey clouds back to the dock at the information centre by dusk.

The following day, the first sunny one in a week, I passed back through Deep Creek lock again and anchored in a cove near the entrance to the Elizabeth River, next to Ed and Carolyn's boat *Moonshadow*. They invited me aboard for a beer. I took a few cans and some potato chips and we nattered away in the evening sunshine while my sleeping bags dried out on the boom and more clouds of pine pollen floated out of the forest and settled on the water. It was blissful after all the rain.

~~~

NORFOLK WAS THE next port of call, just seven miles away, but the weather on the bay was still not quite ideal as the wind hadn't yet moved around to the south, so I was happy to tie up to the free dock in the middle of town and go ashore to watch a movie that evening. The big excitement for me though, was coming to the end of the main portion of the ICW. For three months I'd been sailing north, steadily ticking off the miles marked on the chartbook, beginning in Miami at mile 1095. Now, after first heading south to the Keys and then back north, here I was, passing mile 0. From here on, apart from a short 150-mile stretch of the New Jersey shore, I would be setting my own course on the wide Chesapeake and Delaware Bays and then, of course, the Atlantic. I celebrated by opening a beer.

It was half-empty. Damn. Another leaky can of Miller.

Three days later when I returned to the boat I could smell a rich hoppy odour. I searched the bilge and, sure enough, another beer can was half-empty. I sponged out the hull and poured away the damaged can in case any bilge water had got in through the pinhole. Odd I thought – three cans from one case. Last time I buy Miller.

A week later it happened again – this time to an old can of Budweiser that had evaded many previous attempts at capture. I was quite fond of that can. I'd see it whenever I pulled up the floorboards, but it never rolled down to the spot beneath the hatch to be drunk. It preferred to remain wild and free and clearly intended to hitch a ride all the way to Maine with me. This was a trifle worrying. Unrestrained leakage of critical supplies like this could become dangerous. A boat without beer can barely float according to my understanding – the handling is degraded, the stability is reduced, the wind doesn't blow and the fish don't bite. In short, the whole trip was in jeopardy. The Miller cans could be written off as a bad batch, and maybe even the loss of the Budweiser can could be explained due to old age and fair wear and tear, but there was no doubt that something was up when the Coors Silver Bullet came up half-empty as well. Something majorly evil and minorly tragic was happening in the bilge. It was time to send out an SOS.

I emailed for advice and was astounded to get actual factual answers back from three sources. Two of them explained how to avoid it in future (i.e. either set the cans so they stay dry and don't roll around or else drink them faster). But one email gave an excellent technical explanation of how cans are made and that apparently they have weak spots on the rim that can be attacked by chemical reactions between sea water and aluminium. Sorry, *aluminum*. Did you know the Yanks are actually correct to leave out the i? Apparently it used to be spelled that way and then the Brits changed their minds and wanted to make it consistent with words like calcium, radium, uranium and opprobrium (an element that is now discredited). But the Americans kept to the old traditional spelling and now they get roundly abused for being illiterate hicks that don't know their science, when in fact they do know their science and their history and their English too. So there. After considering all the advice, I settled on a programme of faster consumption of beer. Where previously I would have two cans per week or thereabouts, now I upped it to three and felt totally reckless.

Scared

I BURST OUT onto the bay the next morning with the highest spirits I'd had in several weeks. The bad weather was gone and the forecast was favourable for the next five days. I had completed more than half the trip, I'd crossed the tricky Carolina and Georgia sounds already and I felt that it was all downhill from here. Indeed it was, but not in the comfortable sense that I expected.

That day started marvellously well. I motored lazily through the port of Norfolk and the naval base. I loafed alongside a destroyer that was putting to sea at about four knots. As the sun heated the day I stripped down to T-shirt and shorts and soaked up the rays. Slowly the wind came up, and by 9.00 am I had crossed the Hampton Roads and was sailing merrily up the western shore of the bay. The wind was ideal, 10 mph and coming from just aft of the starboard side. I was able to fill both sails and still admire the scenery as I crawled up the coast.

Now stick with me while I explain a bit about the mighty Chesapeake Bay. You might not be familiar with it and you might think of it as being a classic, wide, half-moon-shaped bay, perhaps 50 miles across. It's not. The bay is 220 miles long and only about 20 miles across at the widest point. It lies roughly parallel with the Atlantic coast and is separated from the ocean by the Eastern Shore of the bay, a relatively low-lying, irregularly shaped peninsula that ranges from one mile wide at the southern tip at Cape Charles, to 60 miles wide in the centre. It is composed of parts of the states of Virginia, Delaware and Maryland.

The Chesapeake Bay is formed from the last 220 miles of the ancient Susquehanna River. This river once flowed to the Atlantic, but with the rising of the oceans, millennia ago, it now provides just the headwaters of the bay. The ancient riverbed is shallow and the whole bay is never deeper than 80 feet. Most of it is barely half that depth. At intervals on its western side the bay is fed by the four biggest of the many rivers that flood it – the James, the York, and the gorgeously named Rappahannock and Potomac Rivers. These four have a bloody history resulting from the Indian wars, the War of Independence and especially the Civil War, but today the Potomac is more famous as the river that flows through Washington DC. A small boat like *Wanderer* can anchor just a stone's throw from the Mall in the tourist heart of the city and within sight of the Capitol, the White House, the Washington Monument, the Lincoln Memorial and so on. Since Ady wasn't able to join me I intended to spend a month lazily sailing up the eastern or western shores as the weather and my inclinations determined, rather than visiting Washington DC – I'd been there before and it would be expensive.

The bay catchment area is home to about eight million people and features numerous military bases, some heavy industry and some farming, but originally it was famous for its watermen. These are the oyster fishermen, clam dredgers, waterfowl hunters and catchers of blue crabs. Sadly, pollution, overfishing and climate change have reduced the catches of marine food to a tiny fraction of the bounty that was reaped just a century ago, but some measures are in hand to reverse the course. Waterfowl have made a comeback and there is a rising abundance of geese, ducks and other migratory birds that feed off the remains of crops harvested just before they arrive for the winter. Land is set aside on their flyway to give rest and feeding areas for millions of birds as they make the trek down and up the east coast, crossing the Delaware and Chesapeake Bays. The best description of the bay in all its aspects is given in James Michener's *Chesapeake*, which I had read as a child and which was the chief reason I was so looking forward to visiting it.

Feeling thoroughly chuffed I bimbled along that first morning at a gentle clip, basking in the sunshine and unaccustomed feelings of competence, comfort and expectation. It was a delightful morning – one that easily lived up to my hopes that the Chesapeake would be the highlight of my trip. The water sparkled, the clouds were high and unthreatening and the waves were barely more than ripples. Aside from my thinning wallet, all was as well as it could be. I was undeniably proud of myself. My diary records that this was the most enjoyable day of sailing since Key West. In late afternoon, after making 39 miles, all but four under sail, I put into Horn Harbour, just north of Mobjack Bay and the entrance to the York River. Horn Harbour was peaceful and sheltered. Tall trees everywhere, deer on shore and ospreys solemnly watching from old pine and oak snags. Even the fact that I broke a shear pin on my prop when I was leaving the gas dock at a tiny marina soon after I put in to the harbour didn't bother me. I raised the genoa and sailed further up the winding creek.

In the late afternoon light I could see families barbecuing on the wide lawns of their large colonial-style houses. Unlike Florida, though, these were old houses and the families were strictly middle-class and the houses were widely spaced. There was nothing less than a hundred years old and each house was screened from its neighbours by forest and meadow. Each bend of the creek exposed tiny bays, ideal for a small boat to drop anchor in. I explored them all and worked my way farther and farther up the creek until I found a perfect spot.

On shore was a single house with a family throwing wood on a bonfire. The kids were racing around the newly mown grass, shouting and laughing. The adults were drinking beer and toasting sausages on sticks in the leaping flames. They'd just moved into their new home, they shouted out to me. It looked like a renovator's dream. If I hadn't felt so good myself I'd have been homesick, but instead I waved and smiled and held up my own beer can to show them that I was doing fine, too. As the trees cast their long shadows across the grass I cooked bacon and inhaled the once-familiar smell of woodsmoke on a spring evening. Bliss. Absolute bliss.

THE DOWNHILL PART of the trip took all day to arrive. I sailed in the early morning in much the same conditions as the day before. With a mild breeze of 10–15 mph I made good time for seven hours, sailing from Horn Harbour further up the western side of the bay. I passed the Piankatank River and the mouth of the Rappahannock without incident.

Around 3.00 pm I started edging closer to shore to begin my approach to Smith Point. This is a promontory that pokes out a short way into the bay on the southern side of the Potomac River mouth. The blunt finger of land is split down the middle by a natural channel that opens out into a small but perfectly protected harbour formed by the Little Wicomico River. The entrance to this channel is about 20 yards wide and it lies right next to the mouth of the Potomac – which is seven miles wide. The Potomac is a very big, powerful river and the Little Wicomico is not much more than a creek. I wanted to anchor in the protected waters of the Wicomico River harbour for the night. This was the point where things went south.

As I came within about three miles of the entrance to the harbour, I began to get pushed around by tall, fast-moving waves. The wind hadn't risen at all – it was the same steady, stiff breeze I'd had all day, but suddenly a large wave pushed *Wanderer* forward sharply and then lifted her up. She slid down the forward slope at a terrific speed and I lost control of her for a moment. She crabbed sideways and then straightened out as the rudder bit into the water again. It was a horrible feeling – the sudden push, the lifting and then the light floppy rudder. I glanced around to see if I had caught a residual wake from a freighter but there was no other wave and this one didn't seem to be a long bow wave – just a sudden short, steep, nasty, isolated bugger. I put *Wanderer* back on course and immediately it happened again. This time she hissed forward and lurched sloppily around to be almost side-on to the next wave, which tipped her up a little and sent her spinning further to port.

The waves came at me from astern, though not exactly in the same direction as the wind. I was on a run and travelling at a smart clip when the first one hit, but in spite of that, they moved under *Wanderer* even faster, or so it seemed. I could see the rough water getting wider around me and it seemed as though I was in the middle of something odd. Far beyond me the water seemed calmer but though I turned towards a calmer patch, it vanished when I got there.

When the third one hit I turned nearly side-on to the waves on the way down, and when I lurched into the trough *Wanderer*'s bow dug in deeply. She came up though, but that was another thing that scared me. I'd read about boats that carried too much sail in too heavy a sea and actually drove themselves under the water by pushing their bow into a wave. In a panic I let go the mainsheet to stop a capsize and crouched down in the boat as she came back onto an even keel. While I was trying to bring her around onto course again, another wave shoved her forwards. Now I knew that I was sailing too fast. Each sudden rush down the forward side of the wave deprived me of steering and almost caused a broach. I needed to either speed up radically and crash through the waves like a motorboat or else slow down a lot and let them surge past me without carrying me forward at the same speed. Because the waves were suddenly seeming to travel in the same direction as me and at the same speed, the rudder was having no effect and that was why I was sliding sideways down the wave faces. I'd read about this but had had no experience of it before. I knew I had to slow down and so the first thing I did was to reach for the boom vang and the halyard. My universal answer to every kind of problem, be it a broken rudder, broaching, hitting a dock or whatever, was to drop the mainsail pronto.

Crash! The boom and mainsail were in the bottom of the boat once more. I gave a tug on the genoa-furling line that reduced that sail to a handkerchief and now *Wanderer* was wallowing. I furled the genoa and let down the outboard. Once it was started, I gingerly motored off at a more easily controllable pace.

I still surfed dangerously down the waves but I could steer better on the way down into the trough, and once there, when the waves sheltered me from some of the wind, I still had engine power to maintain steerage before the next wave grabbed me. Since I wasn't battering into waves, I could run the engine at nearly full speed, and in this way I was just able to keep some sort of steerage. That was probably the less-safe option but I couldn't see any way out of the problem now except to make for the entrance to the Little Wicomico and the harbour. Staying where I was didn't look safe, sailing into the waves wasn't working, motoring into them would quickly fill me with spray, and though I was only a mile off shore, the chart showed beaches with no shelter from the waves. I knew if I touched the bottom, *Wanderer* would stop and the next wave would pour over her low stern and swamp her. I had a feeling that I should have trailed a bight of rope behind me that would have slowed *Wanderer* down and kept her under control. I had the rope, I had the nous and I could have done it, but instead, I raced for the channel entrance under power. The whole episode took only half an hour and in that time I covered the last three miles, so I was clearly moving at a fair speed. As I neared the channel, the waves got worse, but finally I broke through a sort of wall of waves and there I was, just a hundred yards from the entrance and the water was relatively calm. I motored into the Little Wicomico River mouth and easily overcame the speed of its current as I puttered up the channel and into the harbour.

I was very badly rattled by what had happened. Not because of the danger, but because for the first time I had a feeling that I didn't know what had happened to cause the problem. Because I wasn't sure of the cause, I also wasn't sure of the cure. That meant I might have done the wrong thing this time and escaped disaster only by a lucky chance. If I did it again, I might wreck. On the other hand, if I had correctly understood what was happening, I might have been doing everything perfectly, and the sea conditions may simply have been too much for *Wanderer*. That was more alarming.

If I could only sail in winds of less speed than that, then the Chesapeake had me whipped. This was the first time in weeks that the winds had been slight enough to sail comfortably on the bay, and here I was, being slapped about by waves that ought to be no more than a third the size they actually were. It wasn't an idle fear either – plenty of better boats and sailors now rested on the bottom of the bay because they hadn't got it right when the weather hit. I didn't want to join them.

All evening long, I pondered the possible causes and listened carefully to the weather forecast for clues as to what had happened and what might be expected when I set off the next day into the same waters on my way across the bay to the Eastern Shore. Late that evening I dived into the warm water and washed *Wanderer*'s hull. I looked around me at the quiet forest and listened to the birds as they came home to roost. It was all so peaceful and pleasant and safe. I wanted to stay there for a long long time. I wasn't sure that I had the gumption to keep on sailing if the rest of the bay was going to be a battle like the one I'd just had.

Next morning I hauled up the anchor and motored down to the tiny river entrance. In the calm morning I could see the waves were up again just beyond the channel. I gave myself a bail-out card and set off into the rough stuff. Within five minutes I was facing the same sorts of waves. Once again *Wanderer* surfed and lurched and wallowed with the same lack of control as the day before.

This time I motored for 10 minutes out into the bay trying to see if I could drive clear of trouble. Beyond me, where the wind was coming from, the sea looked calmer, but behind me were a few nasty clouds and the wind was picking up as well. I was concerned that I might find myself out on the bay in worsening weather with no way of making it back in to safety. Once again, I turned and ran back with the wind towards the channel.

As soon as I turned, the change from beating into the weather and waves was remarkable. The sea seemed calmer, the apparent wind speed dropped and I felt far more comfortable. Clearly then, it wasn't that bad a day and all that was lacking was nerve on my part. For perhaps 20 minutes I dithered, sailing into the wind and then away from it. Finally, I decided that unless I wanted to motor back to the harbour and go ashore and hitch a ride to town and advertise *Wanderer* for sale and catch a plane home to New Zealand, I'd just have to suck it up and sail forwards. For the last time I turned into the wind and began tacking out into the bay. Twenty minutes later, as the wind dropped away to a brisk breeze off the port side, I found myself in normal seas with no more than a light chop. Astern I could see the same maelstrom of water, but now it was behind me and I was committed to crossing the bay.

TWO HOURS LATER I sailed through the shallow channel between Smith Island and the Martin Island wildlife reserve, asked a waterman for directions down the shallow winding channel, and then set course east for the blue crab capital of the world: Crisfield, Maryland. I made it into the harbour by late afternoon, and to reward myself for not quitting that morning, I tied up to the dock and paid for three nights. It was time to take stock of where I was and how much further I was willing to go. Aside from the worries I had about whether it was safe to sail the bay if I encountered more waves like those of the previous day, there was the question of money too.

Over the next two days, I did some heavy thinking and some emailing as well. I asked my bank for an extension to my credit limit but for the first time in 20 years they said no. Now that I was down to just a few hundred dollars, I felt it was time to see if the publishers of my two previous books would now contract me for a story about the trip. If not, I'd have to finish soon and head home. I emailed my agent in New Zealand to let him know what I was thinking and he said he'd handle it all for me if I sent him an outline of the book. I set about drafting a proper book proposal, but I had only just got started on that when the library closed. It wasn't going to reopen for three days due to the Easter break.

At a loose end and feeling a bit depressed by the freezing cold wind, I sought some central heating in the little local museum. Before long I was chatting to the lady at the desk. Margaret was interested in my trip and she even called her husband up to come down and take a look at *Wanderer*. After I finished showing him around, he asked if there was anywhere I needed to go. I said no, I was just waiting till the library opened in two days' time so I could finish writing my book proposal and send it to New Zealand.

'Oh look, you can use my PC here at the front desk,' offered Margaret. 'No one else is in here this weekend and if they object, well they can just fire me.'

'Oh, I don't want to get you in any trouble,' I said.

'I'm a volunteer, dear, they can hardly fire me,' she replied with a smile. 'And you can use the printer and make a copy on a floppy disc —

and it's a lot warmer here than on your boat.'

With that, she pulled up a chair for herself and indicated that I should take her place behind the PC. It was all very convenient so I sat down and started work on a book proposal. Four hours later it was done and on its way to New Zealand. Now all I had to do was wait and see if the fish were biting. I took the opportunity to write another Hughes Nughes bulletin. In it I described what I had experienced off Smith Point and asked for advice.

Many people replied, and with the aid of Frank's email I worked out what had happened and how to avoid it in future.

Dear Lee

I have just been reading Hughes Nughes 21. It brought back memories – I remember the area well for much the same reasons!

Regarding the technical stuff: Running is the only point of sailing when it is possible to overpower a sailing boat without realising it, and by the time this is realised, it is almost too late. We have all done it, so you are in good company – but it is quite frightening!

The trouble arises when travelling downwind at near wave speed but reduction of sail is still possible. At the same speed as the waves it's exhilarating with long surges on the front faces. But overtaking the waves quickly becomes damn dangerous and often it is too late. Reasons: As the stern rises, the rudder loses grip because it is immersed less; the waves are tending to crest and the water is aerated; the boat's own stern wave causes the wave to break at the rudder thus losing grip; also, as the hull rises (as the wave passes under) the mainsail gets more wind and the press of the sail also pushes the bow down into the back of the preceding wave. By this time it is almost too late to avoid a broach and often impossible to get the mainsail down as it jams on the shrouds and in the mast track. Answer: Reef or get the mainsail down in good time – before the boat approaches wave speed.

Never overtake waves downwind unless racing and there is a
safety boat. I always found it much easier to reduce speed early
after I scared myself the first time and I knew the different 'feel'
of the boat.

Glad you survived. There is only one worse experience —
running down to a lee shore in bad conditions when not sure of
your position . . . .

Regards *to* Wanderer

Frank

So there it was. I'd sailed into a place where the incoming tide met the outgoing river and piled up into nasty waves. Then I tried to sail flat out on a run through these waves and overtake them. That put me in danger of a broach. The way to stop this is to slow down the boat, or better yet, don't sail into that type of water.

More kindness of strangers

I WAS STILL rather rattled by my experience with waves off the Potomac and I now sailed very cautiously. I listened to the weather forecasts on days with tailwinds, charted courses well away from the river mouths, and kept a close eye on following waves, ready to reef the main or drop it altogether. Sailing out of Crisfield I took a route up a creek and through a canal to avoid the worst of Tangier Sound, but in the end the sea was calm and a fog stayed with me up the sound and all the way to the river entrance.

Sailing up the Wicomico to Salisbury was interesting. Sudden blasts of wind kept hitting me from odd angles and I spent a lot of the time trimming sheets, tacking and, once or twice, motoring when I found myself in a headwind on a narrow part of the river. I spotted a Canada goose unusually occupying a deserted osprey nest on top of a channel marker. On shore, geese and ducks strolled across roads, through backyards, and acted like lords of the manor. There were a lot of little tiny milestones like this that kept me occupied at this time, which was good because the ordinary business of sailing on the bay was becoming repetitive. Sleeping on board at night was all right, even after 130 days, but the thing I missed most was conversation with friends and freedom from the worry about the weather and the state of the sea. Every day I found my plans dictated by the weatherman. That was starting to chap my buns, as the saying goes.

Salisbury was a neat little city, but the wind blew, the temperature fell, and though I found a lovely little café to have coffee in while I read the paper and waited for the library to open, it was too cold for very much sightseeing. I did visit the free zoo in the middle of the lovely river-walk park − and very good it was too, but the big highlight was the Ward Museum of Wildlife Art. It had a section of sculpture that was absolutely astounding − gorgeously realistic sculptures of birds in all media as well as more abstract work. I took photos of pieces I would love to own and then walked through to read about the two brothers whom the museum was named after. They were carvers of wooden decoy birds for wildfowl hunters and had almost single-handedly established an art form. Over 80 years of their life in the 1900s in the little town of Crisfield they carved decoy birds that became progressively more accurate and perfect. In the early days, hunters used anything that floated and looked approximately birdlike. Some of the early decoys were a bit retarded − they looked like flowerpots with beaks. On the Chesapeake Bay, the style of hunting demanded whole rafts of decoys to attract geese and ducks to alight on the water near the guns. The hunters would anchor up to 200 decoy ducks around their camouflaged shallow skiff, then they would lie motionless, flat on their backs in a floating box perhaps four inches deep, covered with a canvas sheet, painted and dressed with grasses and dirt to look like a small island. Attached to the outer edges of the 'boat' was a skirt of canvas that also floated and looked like marsh-grass. On freezing winter days with the choppy sea slopping over the box and soaking the hunter, this must have been less than thrilling. Ducks have better eyesight than people and very few humans would be fooled by a store window mannequin at more than 50 yards, so duck decoys had to be even better. If they were good enough and the hunter used a duck call that sounded more like a quack than a bull moose, then the target ducks would see a flock of happy fellow ducks clustered near a small island. They'd swoop down to take a closer look and get blasted out of the sky for their trouble.

Since hunters needed so many decoys or 'stools' as they are known here (from the original stool-pigeons, used as lures in medieval times), the hunters had little time to pay attention to the finer details of carving or painting. But eventually, as flock sizes decreased and hunting became less commercial, the styles changed and the decoys became more realistic. By the end of their lives, instead of simply carving somnolent, rather spastic-looking ducks and geese, the Ward brothers, and others, were making perfect representations of birds preening, sleeping, diving and having a riotous time fluffing their feathers. Now the museum and a decoy carver's society hosted an annual competition for the best works in dozens of different categories, and many past winners were on display. Heavy sculptures of birds were somehow kept aloft in their display cases even though only a single-feather wingtip touched part of the case. The engineering of the displays was impressive, aside from the accuracy of the art and the beauty of the forms.

The other display I enjoyed was the long guns. These were one- to two-inch-bore muzzle-loaders, seven feet long and weighing far too much to be lifted and fired. Instead, they were mounted on the bow of a flat skiff that was paddled silently in the dead of a winter night by a hunter, as close to a raft of sleeping ducks in the middle of the bay as possible. Wildfowl hunters used their long guns like cannons to slaughter ducks in their hundreds until they were made illegal.

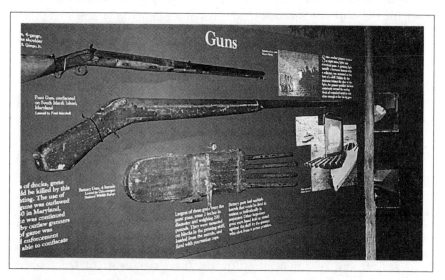

Long guns and a battery – a duck's worst nightmare.

With the gun tied to the boat and a sack at the stock to absorb the recoil, the hunter lay next to it and triggered the monster. A double fistful of shot propelled by about a pound or more of gunpowder scythed out into the ranks of sleeping birds and mowed them down. Then Labrador and Chesapeake Bay retrievers leaped into the water and gathered the booty. The museum had one of these guns on the wall, and except for the flintlock firing mechanism it looked just like a two-pounder anti-tank gun on the wall of the army museum in Waiouru that was used to smite small, unwary Panzers in the Second World War. No wonder the duck population suffered so much until they were banned. But the pièce de résistance was the battery next to it. Cunning hunters created a fan-shaped multi-barrel weapon that fired shot in an arc into the flocks. Six or seven ordinary shotgun barrels pointing outwards in a rising fan from a common firing mechanism were loaded and aimed into the flock from another boat. Anything that survived the opening blast from the long gun would rise into the air in black panic and fly directly into a thunderous hail of shot from this Heath Robinson duck-whacker.

The inevitable result of using this artillery, night after night, year after year, was that hunters almost wiped out the population of geese and ducks until laws regulated the taking of birds and game wardens finally confiscated the weapons. Now the populations are increasing again and ducks, geese and all sorts of bird life are as common as spring lambs in Canterbury.

As pleasant as Salisbury was, I had to pay dock fees and I wasn't getting any nearer to Maine or Christchurch, so on the fifth day I slipped down the river and headed cautiously back to the bay.

~~~

AS HAPPENED SO often on this trip, just when things started to look bad, all of a sudden they got good. My publishers decided they liked my book proposal and the royalty advance they gave me was enough to get me out of financial strife. On the strength of that, I dashed 90 miles back across and up the bay to Annapolis. I anchored in Spa

Creek a mile from the town dock. I spent five days in Annapolis, and they were some of the best days ashore of the whole trip. The anchorage in Spa Creek, a mile from the town dock, was perfect. It was secluded and scenic and yet it was handy to everything. The big old Victorian houses had backyards that came down to the water, and each street that ended at the water had room to tie up at a bulkhead. It was posh suburban – like being moored in a street in Mount Eden, except that instead of tarmac you had water. Plenty of boats were anchored there but not so many as to spoil it. The big attraction though was the company.

Chuck Rutkowski, anchored about 50 yards away, was *great* company. He had an easygoing personality but was practical at heart and he knew plenty about sailing too. We bumped into each other in town a few times but mainly I got to know him by having coffee on his boat each day. We nattered away for an hour over a cup of Java and a cigarette before I would row to shore and then head off on one of his minibikes to see the sights. I'd whizz around on the bike, and have another coffee in the dockside café opposite the wharves where slaves were once landed from Africa and where expensive launches and yachts now tied up their tenders. Twice I sailed *Wanderer* into the dock and tied up next to the other dinghies – most of which were about half the size of her. I'd also use the free Internet connection at the café and then I'd set off to explore the town some more. The weather was very nice – warm, settled spring weather with blossom on all the trees and tourists in short pants and T-shirts.

Annapolis has good chandlers and the chief reason I'd gone there was to buy charts of Delaware Bay. Other towns didn't have as much of a selection and there was nowhere to buy charts once I entered the Chesapeake–Delaware Canal. Chuck steered me to the best places to buy things and in return I helped him drink coffee that would otherwise just have taken up galley space on his boat. He really had run away to sea one day on a tall ship. He saw it in port in Massachusetts, walked down to talk to the mate, and next morning he was part of the crew, sailing on the Atlantic. Now he was master of the boat he'd always dreamed of owning – a sturdy, roomy Bristol 24 that

Chuck sailing his tender backwards on Spa Creek.

he'd bought for a song from an old couple who just wanted to be sure it would be sailed and not left to rot on a mooring. Behind it, Chuck towed a tiny plastic sailing dinghy that he climbed into to show me how to sail backwards.

'Nothing to it as long as you've got a little wind,' he said and came to a dead halt in the middle of the creek.

'What do you do when there's no wind?' I asked.

'Send up a smoke signal and ask for more,' he answered as he lit a cigarette. When it was puffing away nicely, he trimmed the sail to catch just enough of the breeze to meander forwards amongst the other boats.

'Where'd you learn to sail?' I asked.

'From the greatest old guy in the world. I was about seven years old, down at the beach with my dad, and this old guy saw me looking at his little boat and he took me out for a sail. I swear, if I hadn't learned to sail I'd have turned out no good.'

'When's your girlfriend coming out to see you next?'

'July.'

'Only two months away.'

'Fifty-eight and a half days.'

'But you're not counting them or anything.'

'Hell no. I just happen to know it's 58 and a half days.'

'Right.'

'OK, I got some wind. I'm coming back now,' he said and neatly sailed his tender stern first up to the side of his boat and climbed back on board.

'I told Adrienne about you. She says you should come and visit her in Christchurch if you come to New Zealand.'

'Any good sailing in Christchurch?'

'Nope. For that you want to be in Auckland.'

'That's where you live, right?'

'Uh huh.'

'And she's a thousand miles away in Christchurch, huh?'

'Yep.'

'And you're OK with this?'

'I used to be.'

'Yeah. I know that feeling.'

'Your Kirin is in Scotland?'

'Only for 58 and a half more days.'

~~~

TALKING TO ANASTASIA was great fun too. She walked up to the dock where I was tied up one day and said, 'I've got a Wayfarer too.' Hers was sail number 2639, and she was refitting it, along with a Bullseye. Aside from her interest in Wayfarers generally, she had a lot of good tales about her life in Africa as a Peace Corps volunteer. Like Laurent in Georgetown, she had also travelled in the Sahara and had lived in sub-Saharan villages for months at a time. It was quite a remarkable thing to do – a young single Western female travelling and living in the remoter parts of Africa. But I looked at how she had restored the derelict Bullseye boat despite never having owned a boat before, and I saw how she had decided to become a Wayfarer sailor despite never having sailed before, and I noted how she had taken photos of everything on *Wanderer* so she could modify her own Wayfarer if she wanted to, and I decided that if any woman could learn to sail by herself, she could. She was so interested in the finer detail of *Wanderer*'s design that I invited her to sail with me the next afternoon and see how *Wanderer* handled compared to her own Wayfarer. Clearly she was methodical, sensible, and ambitious enough to want to learn an entirely new skill and to do it perfectly the first time. I saw that when I took her sailing on *Wanderer*.

'You better do something or we'll stall,' I said, as she debated whether to tack through or steer away from the wind. But she stubbornly held course while she weighed up the choices and consequences. She wanted to make an informed decision and select the best course.

'What will happen if I go that way?' she asked.

'Try it and see,' I said.

'What will happen if I go the other way?'

'Try that too if you like, but do something fast 'cause we're losing speed and you've gotta be moving to have control. No control means no options. Then you're at the mercy of the sea.'

Later, when we were on a fast reach, the wind started to heel us over.

'Better do something fast or we'll be in the drink,' I warned.

Anastasia checked out Wanderer *thoroughly.*

'What's best – to let out the main or to turn?'

'Beats me, but you better pick one in a hurry.'

'But if I turn then I'll fall off our course and have to turn back.'

'Uh huh,' I said, as I leaned out further to keep us from tipping.

'And if I let out the main it'll be hard to trim it in again as tight as I want it.'

'True,' I said, as I arched my back to lower the centre of gravity and dramatise the need for action rather than discussion.

'So what would you recommend?'

'I'd recommend doing one or the other immediately.'

She turned the tiller and we flattened out.

'I'm not an impulsive decision-maker,' she explained.

'That's OK, soon it'll all be instinctive so you don't have to think much, but one thing is for sure – it's better to make a wrong decision early, than a right one too late.'

'So you think I ought to have let out the sail?'

'In this amount of wind it doesn't really matter what you do. Either one will work, but in stronger winds you need to be decisive and you need to have a sense of urgency when you act. It's not panic, though it might look like it. It's just definite action, taken speedily. You do it fast to minimise the risks and resume a good sailing trim. And if you've taken the wrong decision, you'll notice right away and you can correct it.'

'Just do something and do it quick.'

'Pretty much.'

'Got it.'

The next night, Anastasia invited Chuck and I to dinner. The meal was fantastic – salad, steak, vegetables, apple pie and two types of wine. All under candlelight. With napkins and more than one fork each. Chuck and I looked at each other and thought: 'What did two slobs like us do to deserve this?'

Even better than the food, was the conversation. I thought I was well travelled but so far I haven't lived in Timbuktu (yes, that's the desert city in Africa) like Anastasia, and I haven't literally run away to sea one day to join the crew of a 170-foot tall ship like Chuck. The whole evening was just so civilised. Anastasia chauffeured us back to the dock and we rowed out to our boats and went to bed like royalty — all wined and dined and babbled out. Both of us with a big wedge of apple pie in a baggie for breakfast, too.

~~~

I CALLED ADRIENNE in New Zealand soon after that and she asked me about Anastasia and our dinner together.

'So who is she?'

'Oh, just another Wayfarer sailor.'

'Mmm. What's she like?'

'Oh, she's lovely. Smart, capable, interesting to talk to. Reminds me of you in many ways. Pretty fair cook too.'

'So you had dinner at her place. With wine?'

'Yep, she'd bought some Banrock Shiraz. I like a bit of Banrock. And candlelight, too.'

'Candlelight?' she queried.

'Yep. And napkins. And silverware. Whole thing was flasher than a speed camera.'

'So what did you talk about?'

'Oh, sailing and stuff. Travelling, food, footie.'

'Footie?'

'Well, not much, but she's an Auckland supporter now. I admitted her to the brethren.'

'Sistren, surely?'

'No, she's an Auckland supporter not a Canterbury supporter. We're all brethren up here.'

'I see. So she hasn't actually seen Auckland play, then?'

'Now, now, don't be like that.'

'OK, then what?'

'Had a great old time and then she took us back to the boats.'

'*Us*?'

'Yep, me and Chuck.'

'Oh, I see. So Chuck was there, too.'

'Of course. Did I not mention him?'

'No, you didn't. He's the one with the Scottish girlfriend, isn't he?'

'English, but she lives in Scotland. Really nice guy. I wish you could meet him.'

'Well, I hope he had a lovely time, too. Say hello to him for me.'

'I will.'

'And thank Anastasia for feeding you.'

'I did already. Took her some fudge.'

'Good boy.'

'Wish you were here.'

'Me too.'

~~~

THAT WEEKEND, ANNAPOLIS also hosted a boating festival and all sorts of historic vessels visited the port, including Ted Turner's old America's Cup yacht *Courageous*. After taking dozens of pictures of replicas of 18th- and 19th-century American ships including a Royal Navy frigate (the US was defended by the RN then), I rode home on one of Chuck's minibikes and then rowed myself out to *Wanderer*. Chuck called me

My inflatable tender and a minibike lent to me by Chuck — all very petite.

over to his boat for a taco dinner so I took a couple of cans of beer and we discussed my plans to sail north the next day. A week in Annapolis was just what I'd needed after the quiet times in Crisfield and Salisbury. Now, with money arriving any day soon, all I wanted was some fair weather to take me to New York and on to Maine. After dinner, I smoked a cigarette sitting in the cockpit of Chuck's boat while the sun dropped behind the oaks and elms in the gardens on shore. Tree shadows crept out across the still water to brush the hull. Blackbirds flew to the highest branch they could find and sang their evening songs across the creek. A little blue cloud of smoke drifted off the boat and mingled with the steam from our coffee cups.

'We've got it pretty good,' said Chuck.

'Yeah, no doubt about that,' I agreed.

And he looked at me, and I looked at him, and we both wished we were looking at our girlfriends instead.

Fog

IN KEEPING WITH my newly rediscovered confidence and optimism, I set off from Annapolis in brisk breezes under a grey sky. I motored down the Severn River and into the bay. An hour later I was sailing flat out under the tall highway bridge that crosses the bay to Kent Island and the Eastern Shore. It towered 200 feet above *Wanderer*'s mast as we plunged along on a reach. The waves didn't trouble her at all, and with everything up the mast I was almost able to keep pace with *Courageous* as she was towed back to her home port of Baltimore. I'd dearly have loved to beat an America's Cup yacht, but it wasn't to be. I planned to just sail 20 miles to Rock Hall on the opposite shore at first, but I made such good time that I pushed on further and further up the bay, past Tolchester and along the smooth shore towards the head of the bay. In late afternoon, the wind died away and a fog descended. By the time I turned into Churn Creek and anchored in Codjus Cove, it was raining steadily. I didn't know it then but that was the last time I'd be free of fog for the next 10 days. Still, I'd made 34 miles and that was pretty good.

I didn't start too early the next day since I only planned to sail about 20 miles to the start of the canal. According to my calculations I'd get there when the tide was flowing against me and I'd have trouble motoring against it, so I planned to stay the night in Chesapeake City at the entrance to the canal. The 'city' was actually a town of only a few hundred people, but when they dug the canal 150 years earlier, it was a major metropolis. I bought some gas since I wanted to be fully fuelled before heading down the Delaware, then motored to the basin on the other side of the canal and tied up to a free dock for the evening. I walked all around the little town and visited the museum that told the story of how the canal was built. Over the years it had been widened until now it could take the largest ocean-going freighters passing between the two bays. It saved them a 250-mile haul down one bay, around Cape Charles and up the other bay.

As usual, the plan for the next couple of days hinged on the weather. I needed favourable winds to make it through the canal and down the bay at least half of its 100-mile length. There were few stopping places on the way down on either shore and the Delaware had a reputation for rough water when the winds ran contrary to the tides or current of the river. The forecast sounded unlucky at first, with a southeasterly headwind predicted for the next day. It wouldn't affect me in the canal, where the current was much stronger, so I decided to get through the canal if I could and then anchor behind a small island not far away if the headwind was a problem.

I sailed as early as possible and oozed along at a comfortable five mph on what seemed to be an ebb tide. The fog was so thick I couldn't see either bank of the canal unless I crept along the shore, well out of the path of larger traffic.

Once I got out of the canal and turned southeast down the river to head into the bay I found myself in dense fog and with no wind at all. I decided to motor on and see how far I could get before the wind kicked up. I had to set courses between channel markers, and since the fog reduced visibility to 30 feet or so, I used GPS to verify when I was nearing them. I got a shock when I saw I was now doing eight mph. The river was whisking me along at twice my predicted speed. With a yell of delight I revved the engine up a little and immediately decided to go like hell for the little town of Fortescue, 30 miles further down the bay. If I made it in before the winds came up, I'd save a whole day.

All morning and into the early afternoon I motored down the bay, sliding past giant nun buoys and other markers as freighters towered out of the mist on the way upstream. I saw absolutely nothing of the Delaware shore and only set eyes on the New Jersey shore when the fog burned off a little around 3.00 pm. The wind finally arrived and I was able to sail a little, past fishing boats dredging for clams. By 4.30 I was approaching the entrance to tiny Fortescue, where I planned to anchor on a fast-flowing creek.

I made a hash of that. I scouted out a spot carefully, motoring up and down the creek and even going ashore to ask about the holding and the current. I didn't want to drag an anchor and find myself abroad on the Delaware in the middle of the night. There were ample marina docks along the creek, but they were operated by the state of New Jersey and they cost a little more than I could afford. Eventually I anchored near the bank and set up my tent and bed. After an hour I could see the outgoing tide was going to drop me on the sloping bank and leave me lying on an angle. I didn't like that, so I decided to move. I didn't pack away the tent or roll up the bed. I figured I could start the motor, whip up the two anchors and move further out into the channel.

Everything went wrong. The little stern anchor came up easily, but the big forward anchor fouled itself. Before I could get it up, *Wanderer* was swung around onto the bank. I went forward and stood on the bow and heaved as hard as I could. It was caught on a log and I wrestled with it for 10 minutes, almost pulling *Wanderer*'s bow under water. Finally I felt it start to slip. A piece of the log moved and then it came free in a rush. I dashed back, started the motor and put it into gear just in time to catch the prop on the bank. The shear pin snapped and there I was, wedged on the shore with no engine power. I threw out an anchor to keep me there and then went below to dig into the dirty locker for my tools and spare shear pin. I was down to my last pin, and though I could make more out of brass screws I had a feeling I might need another pin before I could get out of this. There was no way I could row or paddle against the current, I needed power to get off the bank, and if I didn't do it soon, I'd be there until the tide returned in the middle of the night.

After five minutes' work on the engine, I had the prop off, the pin replaced, the prop on and the engine back on its mount in the water.

Now all I had to do was work myself off the shore, push out into the channel, start the motor and get control before I drifted into something else. Poling myself off the shore was the hardest. I couldn't do that until I'd pulled up the anchor, and as soon as I did that the bow whipped around and nosed itself into the remains of an old dock, so I had to push off backwards against the current. I managed to do that, but before I could get back and start the motor the current pushed me back into the bank. I did it several more times before I twigged that I'd have to push myself further out into the channel. The problem was that the oar wasn't long enough to reach the bottom at that point and I couldn't row anywhere with the tent still up. Eventually I bumped my way down the shore past snags, old docks, mud banks and marsh-grass until I found a pool where I lingered just long enough to run to the back, fire the engine, and whip *Wanderer* around to face into the current. In doing so I caught the prop on the bottom again but luckily this time the pin didn't break. After nearly an hour, I was finally under control. I motored back up the creek and looked for an anchorage, but with the light starting to fail I finally decided to tie up to a dock and sort out the chaos in the boat. I dashed ashore to pay at the dock office but it was now empty and there was no after-hours number to ring. I nipped back to the boat, spent an hour tidying up the mess and then bedded down in darkness. I planned to leave first thing the next morning so I figured no one would know I'd even been there.

Sure enough, early the next morning I was able to steal away to sea under cover of yet more fog. The sea was calm again and there was no wind, though a headwind was predicted. I motored steadily towards Cape May on the tip of the New Jersey shore. At this northern entrance to Delaware Bay, there was a three-mile canal that took boats into the short section of the New Jersey ICW that ran 150 miles north towards New York City. If I could make it in there, I'd have safe sailing for a few days, regardless of the weather. The ICW there was well protected and had dozens of spots to anchor for a small boat. It also had regular openings to the Atlantic every 20 or 30 miles. Some of these weren't recommended for small boats since they had strong currents and sand bars, but others were all right. That meant if the weather was nice I could sail fast up the ocean side instead of meandering along the ICW.

The wind was just rising as I motored into the Cape May canal. I ran all the way through it to a marina at the other end where I was able to buy four replacement shear pins. That would see me through to the end of the trip, I hoped. The staff there let me tie up to the dock long enough to walk a couple of miles to the old Victorian seaside resort town of Cape May, where I was able to check my email at the library. I also made it to an ATM and found that my money had come through, so I withdrew $200. Half would replenish my cash stash hidden in the bow and the other half would buy some grocery treats.

The old town of Cape May has a blanket protection order on its architecture. A dozen blocks of Victorian houses are a major tourist attraction. To me they look a bit too much like overly ornamented gingerbread houses, but seen en masse they have a definite charm. If you like frills and flounces then you'll like Cape May houses. The streets were covered with gorgeous spring blossom from overhanging trees, though with the cold wind and mist it was hard to decide what season it really was. That afternoon I sailed across the Cape May inlet harbour and up towards the town of Wildwood where I planned to anchor.

Here on the Jersey shore, the 'Garden State' has done its bit for nature by keeping the thousands of low-lying grass islands on the ICW open for birds migrating on the great East Coast Flyway. Small birds pause at Cape May to eat and rest before tackling the 25-mile crossing of the bay. From that came wildlife refuges all around Cape May, and then a steady supply of tourists and birdwatchers. Quite a neat symbiosis. And for me, an abundance of quiet sheltered anchorages. I dropped a hook in a shallow bay and set up my tent for the night. Despite the cold wind and grey sky I felt so good that I heated water and had a good bath before settling down to eat potato chips and read about Frank McCourt's life as an immigrant in New York. He also complained about the lack of bathroom facilities, but for him it was a fact of life and for me it was a choice. Tom Sawyer had it right – work is whatever a body is compelled to do and fun is whatever it's not. I didn't have to be here, so that made washing with a tin cup and sponge enjoyable. Sort of.

The fog never lifted the next day either. The weather was cold and grey and occasionally it rained a little, but I didn't mind. I was warm and dry, I could sail a little and I was safe from rogue waves and killer whales as I slipped along the channels that took me towards Ocean City. I made only 29 miles that day and I tied up to an abandoned dock for the night. Atlantic City was 15 miles ahead and I was prepared to celebrate my arrival there with a small bet if I could find a cheap place to dock. Atlantic City is the East Coast's Las Vegas and I hoped there might be cheap accommodation or dockage in the way that Vegas has cheap motels and cheap meals to encourage gamblers. The weather forecast was for more fog and rain and I was getting pretty weary of it. I wanted to see some bright lights.

I sailed slowly the next day in light winds under yet more fog, though the sun came out briefly and weakly in the late afternoon. At one point as I was sailing close to the city, I was going under bridges and alongside freeway on-ramps. Now it felt like I was sailing through 'Spaghetti Junction' in Auckland. People stood on the bank and fished, a few little powerboats buzzed past and waved, and on shore a little boy about six years old actually started jumping up and down with delight when he saw me sailing past.

'Come here, come here,' he yelled, and when I changed course towards him he turned to his father who was fishing and yelled, 'He's coming, he's coming.' I sailed to within a few feet of him and then turned around in circles, tacking and gybing while he actually clapped and stamped his feet.

'Where you going?' asked the dad.

'Maine,' I yelled back. 'Came from Florida.' He didn't look like he was familiar with either place.

'What kinda boat is that?' he asked.

'A little one.'

'Well, all right,' he said with a grin. When I sailed off, the boy waved until I was out of sight. I have no idea why he was so happy to see all this, but he was absolutely thrilled by it. As for me, he made my day, and now when I think of the Jersey shore I don't think of *The Sopranos* or industrial waste or brick tenements. I think of a little city boy who saw a tiny boat with all its sails up and thought it was neater than the Cartoon Channel and a Happy Meal combined.

~~~

A COUPLE OF hours later I was cruising into the yacht harbour at Atlantic City, the big casinos standing tall behind the acres of boats. I called up a couple of the marinas but now that the state of New Jersey owned most of the dock space, the prices weren't as low as the casinos had set them. I decided to save my money for New York. It was late, the fog was back and the temperature was dropping again, so I turned and motored across Absecon Inlet to a quiet basin on the other side and dropped anchor. As the fog got heavier and the light dimmed I decided that I had just about had a gutsful of this weather. It was mid-May and spring was overdue. I listened to the forecast glumly that night. More goddamn fog, some rain maybe and then probably high winds for a day or two. Temperatures would stay in the low forties. Bugger. As the fog thickened and the shore, just 50 yards away, vanished, I felt quite lonely. Once again, I turned on the radio, dug into a book and read the evening away in the cosy warmth and bright light of my pressure lamp. Once in a while I'd peek out into the dusk to see if anything had changed, but it was the same pale grey wool as the day before and the day before and the day before . . .

~~~

I MOTORED THE next morning, in fog, just 18 miles north to the little town of Beachhaven. All the way, I puttered past little powerboats with families out fishing in the channels that wound through the wide but shallow waters. The route was shown with channel markers in the water, but frequently the visibility dropped and I needed to sail by compass. I wondered as I passed the little boats whether they all had compasses and charts or GPS. In the fog, the channel markers weren't visible. I found out later that one boat did get lost and stayed lost for over a day. The ICW here passes several outlets to the Atlantic but they are dangerous for small boats, and even on the ICW, well inside the barrier islands, the incoming tide can throw up odd waves and strong currents that can slow or speed your passage. It's an interesting place to cruise and I wished I could sail it instead of motoring. I was also thoroughly fed up with seeing nothing of the land I was sailing past, so I decided to spend the day ashore and wait for the predicted wind to blow the clouds away. I docked at the Beachhaven Yacht Club marina and paid $1.25 per foot. There were several other places nearby but I liked the look of the shelter at this one, and it had good showers and a laundry and was handy to the centre of town.

Almost the whole length of the Jersey shore from New York down to Cape May consists of resort towns strung out along the Atlantic coast road that runs down the barrier islands. Some inlets, like that at Ocean City, have bridges across them, but others, like Atlantic City, require big detours inland and back out to the ocean road. The houses on the shore range from large expensive Victorian mansions to modern condos and tiny mid-century baches. The crossroads between the main roads are sometimes just sand tracks. Whole villages of little cabins that remind me of my childhood are inhabited by New Yorkers during the summer weekends and holidays and the rest of the time they are empty. Like most beach resorts, the towns are heavy on food and entertainment and light on other services.

I pulled on an extra layer of clothes to counteract the cold wind blasting off the Atlantic and set out to visit the town while my laundry dried. It didn't take long to find that the library was closed but would open the next day. I bought a remaindered book for $5 and settled down in a bar with a beer to read about the battle of El Alamein. The heat and sand of the desert seemed a hell of a long way away. I bought some French fries for dinner and watched out the window as the wind wound itself up to a steady 20 mph and inexplicably blew in even more fog and cloud to obscure the view.

I pulled out my diary and added up the mileage I'd made. I had sailed 2018 statute miles since leaving Fort Lauderdale five months ago. Two thousand miles was about 3200 kilometres. That seemed like a long way to me, though to real sailors, it's barely a single trip across the Tasman to Australia. As I drank my beer I wondered how much further I would have to sail before I was over my fear of the sea.

~~~

FEELING GUILTY THE next morning at having done so little sailing in the past two days, I resolved to get something up the mast no matter what. The forecast wasn't great – 15 to 25-knot winds – but I didn't mind that too much. Soon I would be sailing along a windward shore and there were dozens of places to pull in and shelter. I would get occasional help from low–lying islands in the ICW that would stop the waves from building up too high, so I waited for the fog to clear, and finally, at 10.00 am, it lifted. I cast off and sailed out of the marina under cold blue skies. For the first time I could see across to the inland shore a couple of miles away. The following wind seemed to be a good deal stronger than advertised so I just used the genoa. Almost immediately I was flying along at top speed. Within a few minutes, though, the wind blew in clouds that shut the blue window and lowered more grey blinds across the horizon. I furled the genoa a little, and though that worked well I was a bit nervous about what would happen when I turned across the wind and began sailing on a reach. It seemed to me that the wind was about 25 knots already and might have been gusting harder. Within a mile I was starting to look for places to pull in. There weren't many around that offered protection from the westerly.

Coming close around a point of land I caught a blast that heeled me over alarmingly. I let go the genoa and turned up into the wind and waited for the gust to pass, but it didn't. Instead, it stayed at the new higher speed. With everything whipping and banging about I decided to furl the genoa some more and keep sailing until I found a place to shelter. It was looking like this wind would be more than I could handle once I got out into the broader waters of Barnegat Bay. Further out I could see whitecaps on the waves as they raced a couple of miles across the shallow water. Once I was sailing again, I saw from my chart that there was another marina just ahead and I decided to put in there while I figured out what the day had in store. Just as I was coming around the entrance to it a violent blast of wind hit me, and though I was in a good position to handle it I was surprised at the power. I guessed it must be nearly 40 mph. By now I was quite adept at sailing into an anchorage or marina under the genoa alone, so despite the wind I sailed up to the nearest unoccupied dock at the Spray Beach Yacht Club, dropped the sail and tied up. Soon after, I had *Wanderer* secured, and just before I set off to find someone to ask where I could stop for a few hours, two elderly-looking chaps strolled up and introduced themselves to me.

'I'm Howard, club secretary here. This is Geoff. Saw you come in and catch that gust. Guess you're looking for somewhere to tie up, huh?'

'Well, I thought I might stop here for a bit until the wind drops and I can sail on. Seems to be blowing a bit harder than I expected.'

'Whatja expect?' said Geoff.

'Well, NOAA radio said about 15–25 knots and I figure it'll always gust a little more.'

'NOAA don't knowa shit. Weather channel says 25–35 knots for the next two days. Wind gauge in the club recorded the gust that got you at 45 miles an hour.'

'Really? Boy, I'm glad to hear that. I don't feel such a chickenshit now for tying up.'

'Where are you bound?' asked Howard.

'Maine, if this weather ever gives me a break. I've seen hardly anything except fog since Annapolis.'

'Annapolis? You sailed that up the ocean from there?' asked Geoff.

'No, I came up the bay, through the canal and down the Delaware to Cape May and then up the inside.'

'Well, that's quite a sail in a little boat. What is she – 20 feet?'

'No, just 15 feet 10 inches but I pay for 16 feet of dockage. She's a Wayfarer. English boat. Built for couples to go gunk hole cruising on weekends, but she's pretty seaworthy.'

'I can see that. You handled that gust well. We saw you sailing along and I said to Geoff, "he better know what he's doing today", added Howard. 'Listen, you don't have to pay for dockage here. I used to be club commodore and you can tie up anywhere you like. I doubt you'll want to sail in this stuff today.'

'You might be right about that. I'm over sailing in grotty weather. Done enough of that already,' I replied.

'Won't see good weather till maybe Memorial Day,' said Geoff.

'So this isn't unusual — all this fog?'

'Well, it depends. Some years you get it and some you don't, but it's not unusual, and if it's not fog, then you can still catch storms at this time of year. Summer's great, but you gotta wait till it gets here. This spring has been a poor one, though,' answered Geoff.

'Come on up to the club as soon as you're settled here,' said Howard. 'There's a lot of people would like to meet you.'

So once again, generous people came to my aid, and before long I was drinking a hot coffee in the clubhouse and telling a few of the members what I was doing. They invited me to come to dinner at the club that night. It was their regular pot-luck supper and the ladies would be cooking and I couldn't insult them by saying no. So I said yes. I had been keeping my eye on the anemometer scale that was mounted on the wall. It never dropped below 25 mph and regularly gusted to thirty-five. I looked out the glass doors at the grey sea and sky and watched *Wanderer* heaving on her mooring lines as she bounced up and down in the chop that slapped the docks. I actually felt that I would have been able to sail safely in these winds. With just a genoa up and with some common sense and constant attention to the job, I would have been able to sail until I got tired of it and then put in somewhere to find shelter. There was an abundance of marinas north of here. The problem wasn't that I was scared of sailing in this weather. The problem was that I wasn't scared any more. If I had been, I'd have felt the irresistible compulsion to go out there and face it. Instead, I knew I could do it if I had to, but doing it would get me cold, wet, and very tired, and despite the constant alertness and background tension, I'd also be very bored. Eight hours of that just didn't hold any attraction for me. Out there was a lot of work and discomfort. In here was hot coffee and chocolate cake. Down the road was a library with an email connection to my girl. It wasn't a hard decision.

Geoff said he'd talk to the commodore and let him know I was staying here and I could move my boat to whichever dock I thought would offer the most shelter from the wind.

'We have to go now, but we'll leave the back door open for you. The toilets are unlocked, you can use the shower and the kitchen and we'll see you tonight,' said Geoff.

'The weather channel's on the TV there, but I don't think it's going to get better for a day or two,' added Howard.

Five minutes later I was alone in the clubhouse, looking out at the waves bashing into the wooden sea wall. All around was the same grey sky and sea. It had been that way for a week and in that time I'd had real sailing fun for maybe two or three hours. That was no good. On the other hand, I hadn't been properly scared now for quite a while – since before the Potomac. Did that mean I was over my fear? And if it did, then just exactly what was I trying to prove by sailing on?

The Gimmee

I WALKED TWO miles back down to Beachhaven and spent the afternoon in the library. It was an unusual building. It looked like a converted house but it was purpose-built as a library in the 1920s using bricks and materials recovered from 18th-century buildings. Instead of a large central hall with rows of books, it had separate small parlours with books on the walls and comfortable armchairs — a bit like a home library. A cosy place on a cold day. Upstairs was a mezzanine floor with more books. In one corner was the sole PC and Internet connection and it was here that I did some steady thinking about my plan for the rest of the trip. I didn't reach any conclusions and at closing time I headed back to the yacht club for the pot-luck supper.

The members couldn't have been friendlier; they poured me a whiskey and helped me load up a plate. I was able to quiz them about the weather and the route to New York. Pete, another former club commodore, urged me to stay until the weather improved. All of them cautioned me about the dangers of crossing inlets with the wrong tide or wind. 'Don't be in a hurry' was the gist of their advice. Pete said I was welcome to sleep in the clubhouse if I didn't want to sleep on *Wanderer*. Around 8.00 pm they washed up in the kitchen, said their goodbyes, wished me well and told me to stay there as long as I wanted.

'The TV's got cable and it's warmer in here than out there,' said

Pete. He was right. It was still cold, still blowing a good 25–35 mph, and *Wanderer* was bouncing up and down like a cork. After they all left, I settled down in front of the TV. At midnight, I finally hauled myself off to bed on *Wanderer*.

Since this was a very late night for me I expected to drop off to sleep immediately, but I didn't. I tossed and turned and wriggled around, unable to sleep because of the motion of the boat, which was bordering on violent, and also because I was still mulling over the things I'd been thinking about in the library. I finally got two hours' sleep in the early morning.

The weather next day was more of the same. I stayed in bed till nearly 10.00 am, listening to the NOAA radio and studying charts. I updated my diary, ate a sandwich and occasionally peered out at the opposite shore. The fog had lifted, but the sky was the colour of school uniforms and the wind was as cold as a toilet seat. *Wanderer* still leaped and rocked incessantly. I walked around the entire marina, but there was no other dock that was better protected and all the other docks I'd seen in Beachhaven and Spray Beach were equally exposed to this miserable westerly. On the Weather Channel I saw the cause of all this unpleasantness. Hundreds of miles inland, a front was

They let me use anything the club had to offer.

generating the worst concentration of tornadoes in a hundred years. In the Midwest, town after town was blasted apart, with the pictures showing even more wrecked trailer houses than usual. God surely must hate white trash, judging by the way he blasts their trailers. All across the east coast the front was causing floods, but in just two weeks the Midwest got a whole year's supply of tornadoes.

I walked back to *Wanderer* and pulled out my diary and wrote down some notes to see if my thoughts made sense on paper:

I'm still scared most of the time but nowhere near as bad as I was. I could sail today in 20–25 knots with confidence and safety, but I just don't want the tedium and discomfort.

I'm bored. No remaining part of the trip holds any appeal in this weather. Aside from New York, I'm only looking forward to the end when I can walk into a bar at Eastport and ask for a beer.

Because I'm not finding it hard or frightening any more, just a bit ho-hum and uncomfortable, I think this means I have now conquered most of my fear.

If what I wrote was true, then the aim of the trip had been accomplished. I had no further business here.

~~~

I WALKED BACK down to the town and found a payphone where I could call Anastasia. The first thing was to find out if I could tidily end the trip by selling *Wanderer* conveniently. If she was no longer interested in buying my boat, then I'd be better off sailing north to somewhere in New England, near to New York, where I could advertise it for sale and also store it cheaply on land. Manhattan wasn't the right place for that. I called her at home that morning and said that if she wanted to come and get *Wanderer*, I was sure we could agree on a price that would suit her. Anastasia agreed in a flash.

'I'll meet you in New Jersey or New York and bring *Wanderer* and you back to Annapolis. You can catch a flight home from Baltimore-

Washington International. Can you stay a few days and sail her with me?'

'You bet. And thank you for that offer. I'd like to spend a day or two in New York first, though.'

'OK, I'll come up on the weekend and collect you.'

'Terrific. I'll see you in four days.'

That gave me time to sail to New York, do a couple of things and then meet Anastasia on the New Jersey shore, so that she wouldn't have to haul a boat trailer through Manhattan traffic.

~~~

THE NEXT CALL was tougher. I didn't know how Adrienne would take the news that I was finishing in New York and coming home two months early. I figured I'd be home in New Zealand in 10 days' time. That would come as a shock to her and I hoped it would be a pleasant one. I didn't want her to think her boyfriend was a quitter. A coward. A piker. All mouth and trousers.

I got Ady on her cellphone, and through the static and the crossed lines I had to shout out the news that I was coming home at the end of the next week. I couldn't tell what she thought as she kept saying 'Next week? Next week!' Then we were cut off and I was left wondering whether she was horrified or thrilled or disgusted. I decided to call her again when she was at home in a few hours' time.

Then it was back to the library to send my final Hughes Nughes letter to everyone who had been following the trip. I had to turn down invitations to call on a friend in Massachusetts and Aaron Clarke's family in Maine, to sail with a Wayfarer owner in New York, to return and visit Geoff Orr in Florida and to visit Brian McLeery at the end of the trip. In each case I felt like I was letting them down and being ungrateful for all their help and encouragement. Sitting in the warmth of the library I got quite morose, but as soon as I walked back out into the cold wind and saw the heaving boats at the yacht club, I knew I was making the right decision. This was thoroughly substandard spring weather and it might linger this way for another month.

I finally managed to call Adrienne from the yacht club phone that night using my calling card.

'What do you think about me coming home early, babe?' I asked nervously.

'Oh, oh, oh. I didn't know if I'd heard you right at first, but I've been flying around on a cloud ever since. It's wonderful. It's fantastic. You just get off that boat and come on home as fast as you can. I'll be waiting.'

So that was all right. And that night, despite the motion of the boat, I slept like a log.

~~~

I SAW PETE at the yacht club just after breakfast the next morning. The sun was trying to show through broken clouds and the wind had dropped to about 15–20 mph.

'Heading out, Lee?' he asked.

'Yep. Going to New York and then I think I'll be going home.'

'Back to Noo Zealand, huh?'

'Yeah. I miss my gal.'

'Well, come back and visit us if you can.'

'Thanks, Pete. I will.'

~~~

I CAST OFF and raised the genoa. In a couple of moments I was out of the yacht club marina and turning north for the last leg of the trip. Behind me a large Corps of Engineers workboat steamed slowly past the ICW markers. As I raised the mainsail and watched it fill, *Wanderer* stiffened and began to heel. I leaned out and looked back at the workboat. She was about 60 feet long. Not too big for me to race. I trimmed the sails, zipped up my jacket and leaned further out. She might not realise it, but as far as I was concerned, we were competing.

Seven hours later, I was still keeping pace with her. I'd drunk a small bottle of water, changed my tobacco chew twice and eaten a banana. Aside from that, I'd concentrated on sailing as fast as I knew how. I'd cut corners wherever I could, crossing shallow beds and ducking behind islands where the big boat couldn't follow. On the long straight stretches as we raced up Barnegat Bay she overtook me. After all, she was making at least 12 knots, but she had to stop twice to replace channel markers and I was able to get ahead of her then. I pulled out my GPS and checked my speed from time to time. The best I made was nine mph, but the average wasn't too bad. Over the whole day I covered 34 miles in just on seven hours. The wind stayed steady and stiff. I started on a run, tacked a bit and finished on a reach, stacked out as far as I could lean while I raced to cross the big boat's bow, to sail first through the bascule bridge at Toms River. She had called ahead to have it opened but I was trying to cross under one of the other spans. In the end I had to give way to her as I couldn't quite be sure I would avoid going under her bows like a dandelion under a lawnmower as I crossed on my final tack of the day. Being a military boat the skipper wouldn't acknowledge my presence, but the crew at the stern waved as I turned away from the channel and began to search for a place to tie up for the night.

It was a great day's sailing. I went far and fast on a small boat on a wide bay. The wind was up and the sea was choppy but I sailed with confidence and pleasure and not a hint of fear. And I had tied with the workboat for line honours. All those things combined to make it one of the best days' sailing I'd had in weeks. But mainly I remember it because it was the last time I ever sailed *Wanderer* alone. At the end of the day, tired and covered in salt spray, I motored the last half-mile up a canal to a marina on Chadwick Island and paid my fees.

~~~

THAT NIGHT, THE wind dropped, just as it was forecast to do. The next day it was supposed to rise to a gale, with heavy rain, but I couldn't face the idea of sitting on *Wanderer* for three days in a marina in the off season. Unfortunately, conventional sailing techniques just wouldn't get me any further north unless I waited until the weather improved.

Anastasia was coming to collect me in three days' time, so sailing to New York was out of the question. I was only 30 miles or so from Manhattan in a straight line, so I decided to employ an old sailors' trick.

I rented a car.

By mid-morning the next day I had driven to a Park'n'Ride near New York, and caught the subway to the Madison Square Garden stop on Eighth and East 34th. Ten minutes later I was walking south down Fifth Avenue towards the harbour. I was determined to sail on New York harbour, even if it was on a 500-ton ferry. But along the way I had another stop.

Manhattan is a small island. About the size of central Wellington, it is easy enough to walk around the busy downtown section that begins at the southern tip of the island where the old fort, The Battery, defended the harbour. From there it's only three miles north to Central Park, and in between lies almost all of what a tourist would think of as being New York: Wall Street, the Empire State Building, Fifth Avenue, Times Square, Broadway, Chinatown and all the rest.

But it was also home to a place, within sight of the harbour, that had fascinated me – the Twin Towers. It was a place that had been the end of a journey for so many New Yorkers, and I felt it would be right to end my little adventure here too. As I walked down the narrow streets of the oldest part of the city, I came upon subway station signs for the World Trade Center. They were still calling it that even though it was gone. The site itself was now a tidy construction site surrounded by a heavy semi-permanent mesh fence. The basement area was big enough and deep enough to drop Mount Eden inside, but now, far below, toy-sized diggers worked away. It was easy enough to see in and watch the men and machines – it was much harder to imagine the towers that once loomed above the city. To look at the buildings on the perimeter of the site and know that the towers were once five times taller is difficult to do. I'd been to New York before and had taken the elevators up to the observation deck at the World Trade Center. From there, I had looked out at New Jersey, just across the harbour. The buildings were so high, that if they had been standing now, with a telescope I could have seen my boat tied up at Chadwick Island, 35 miles away. But if I hadn't done it, and taken the pictures to prove it, looking at the site now I'd find it hard to believe that anyone had built such a thing. And even harder to imagine the kind of person who would think that knocking it down would help their cause.

And that's the thing about New York and Americans in general that draws me to them. I could have probably sailed more comfortably up the east coast of Australia or around the Mediterranean, but I deliberately chose the US. And the reason is that America is such a huge contrast to New Zealand. It isn't the size of the country or the wealth, or the breadth and depth of their culture. It's just their attitude. Collectively, Americans don't believe that anything is impossible. This is a country that in 10 or so years *simultaneously* fought an enormous war in Asia over nothing more than a dubious domino theory, fought itself in the streets of its cities over civil rights, doubled the size of its economy, and sent men to the moon to pop wheelies and play golf for no other reason than raw curiosity and to spite the Russians. Any one of those things would have been more than most countries could cope with, but in the US, the idea of doing them all at once was never even an issue. They wanted to do them, so they did them. And when they'd had enough of doing them, they stopped. That's the other side of American industriousness and determination. It can be redirected in an instant to something entirely new. One day the moon, the next day PlayStation 2. So standing there, looking down at Ground Zero, I did what so many other visitors were doing. I wondered what would come next. What would they build there? A memorial? Another tower? Even taller? Who knows. But one thing is for sure. It'll surprise us, it'll be nearly impossible to do, and as soon as it's done, we'll look at it in awe and wonder what they'll think of next.

And that's what I thought of too. What next for me?

~~~

I WAS STILL fairly young, fairly fit, and fairly single. It was a bright sunny day and I had the greatest city in the world laid out in front of

New York — 4000-odd kilometres of sailing behind me.

me. There was money in my pocket and I had nothing else to do but take a look around. For the first time in a year I wasn't obligated to do anything or go anywhere. I was completely free to sample anything the Big Apple had to offer.

So I walked down to The Battery, climbed aboard a tourist ferry and went sailing. It wasn't quite the way I'd hoped to see the harbour, but it would have to do. We cruised up and down the Hudson and East Rivers, went under the Brooklyn Bridge, sailed up to Ellis Island and the Statue of Liberty and past the South Street Seaport where I had planned to dock *Wanderer*. Overhead, the clouds began to drift over the Verrazano-Narrows Bridge and fill the waters of the bay with their grey reflections. The wind came up and sent a couple of large yachts crashing through the wakes left by ferries and freighters and barges. Fifty feet up on the top deck of the ferry, dry, warm and safe, I smiled at the sight, but quite a large part of me wished I was down there with them, six inches from the water in a boat that feels like a bathtub, butting my way through the waves to another safe harbour.

Epilogue

Happily ever after

FIVE DAYS LATER, I was sitting in the customs hall at Auckland International Airport while an inspector turned out the contents of my bag and searched it for God knows what. I wasn't too bothered. I knew I had nothing in there to interest him and my mind was on other things. The last week had gone slowly. After sailing on the harbour ferry I spent another 36 hours in New York, walking the streets, eating anything I liked, visiting Central Park and the Metropolitan Museum of Art and shopping slowly for a few things. That night I slept on land, between the clean sheets of a Manhattan hotel bed, for the first time since I left Geoff Orr's house in Florida in January. I did as much shopping as I could, but in the end all I bought was a pink New York baseball cap for Anastasia and a pink headband for Adrienne.

The next day, Anastasia picked me up at the marina and we loaded *Wanderer* onto her trailer and began the three-hour drive back to Annapolis. I stayed at her house for the next three days, emptying *Wanderer* of all the things I was taking with me and sorting into neat piles everything that would remain with the boat. She fed me, let me use her computer, and in between times, we took *Wanderer* out for some more sailing practice when the weather was good. When we had enough of that, she took me shopping in Annapolis. I was hunting for a laptop and a cup holder. I'd asked Adrienne if she wanted anything from the US and she'd said that her little car didn't have a beverage holder and would I please get her one. For myself, I took one look at the price of laptops and decided that at less than half the price of one in New Zealand, I'd be mad not to buy one. Anastasia, who is a computer whizz, found just the right one for me. She paid US$1200 for a top-of-the-line model, which was about half what I'd have paid in New

Zealand. Then she gave me cash for the balance of the price we'd agreed for *Wanderer*. Now I was all set to write a book when I got home, and Anastasia had a boat that was completely fitted with everything a single-handed cruiser could want. The boat and the gear were in excellent repair, and there was ample safety equipment, spare parts, tools and camping equipment. I looked at *Wanderer* sitting on the trailer in Anastasia's driveway, next to her other Wayfarer and the Bullseye she was restoring, and I thought to myself that this was about as perfect an ending as I could imagine. She would be a great owner for my little boat. Above all, *Wanderer* would get sailed.

On the way to the airport the next day Anastasia asked me if I had got everything done that I wanted to.

'You bet,' I said, patting the laptop.

'Have you got Adrienne's cup holder packed away?' she asked.

'Ahhh, no. I looked at a bunch of them but they wanted about twelve bucks apiece and that seemed a bit excessive for a hunk of plastic.'

'I see,' she said. 'But you got your laptop.'

'Yes.'

Pause.

'Anastasia, I wonder if you'd mind stopping at the next mall. There's something I've forgotten.'

Ten minutes later we were at the airport and I was clutching a cup holder in one hand and hugging Anastasia with the other.

~~~

I SENT A customs officer away to find Adrienne and explain the delay. While they searched I read a book until, finally, they repacked my bag and let me through the gate and there she was. It took me about 45 seconds to ask her to marry me, and right there in the arrivals hall she said yes. I gave her a big ring that I'd bought on Wilshire Boulevard in LA the day before. It would be about four carats if it was real but I'd be mad to buy her a ring that she hadn't chosen, so it was just a glass one in a nice box. We went out that weekend to jewellers all over town and finally found a real diamond ring that she thought was perfect. I paid for it with the last of the money from the sale of *Wanderer* and slipped it on her finger. It looked just right.

Two sayings sum up the adventure of that year gone by:

Even the mediocre can have adventures;
even the fearful can achieve.

and

Marriage is the only adventure
open to the cowardly.

It was all the redhead's fault.

My first adventure is complete; the second has just begun. It has no particular destination – it's just a journey undertaken for the pure pleasure of travelling. Luckily, it requires no great reserves of courage or determination – just a moderate degree of optimism and a wonderful partner, like the one standing behind me as I write this.

I think I'm done now, so in a little while I shall go for a walk with my girl in the last of the cold Canterbury sunlight and I'll look at the yachts on the estuary and I'll wonder how it was that such a little boat as mine could have attracted so many friends.